SHOPPING
FOR A
BETTER WORLD

**A Quick and Easy Guide to
Socially Responsible Shopping**

by
Richard Adams
Jane Carruthers
Charlie Fisher

with
Michelle Broome, Sean Hamil, Mandy Jetter,
Craig Mackenzie, Dot Toase and Phil Wells

NEW
CONSUMER

KOGAN
PAGE

New Consumer wishes to thank the many trusts and agencies whose support made possible the research work which created this guide. In particular our gratitude goes to the Joseph Rowntree Charitable Trust for their vision and generosity. Full credit and our grateful thanks is also due for the pioneering work done in this field by the Council on Economic Priorities, New York, USA.

Printed on recycled paper

All but three of the companies rated in this shopping guide are profiled in depth in the New Consumer book, *Changing Corporate Values* (Kogan Page, 637pp, April 1991). The material upon which the ratings and profiles are based was collected between March 1990 and June 1991. Every effort has been made to check the accuracy of the information with original sources and the companies concerned. Nevertheless, it is inevitable that some brand ownership changes will have taken place prior to publication. New Consumer claims no knowledge of company programmes not in the public domain or which have not been supplied to it by the company concerned.

· First published September 1991 by Kogan Page Ltd
120 Pentonville Road
London N1 9JN

A CIP record is available for this book from the British Library

ISBN 0 7494 0483 3

Edited, typeset and designed by John Button
Printed in England by Clays Ltd, St Ives plc

Contents

Does it Matter How I Shop?

In 1992 British shoppers are going to spend nearly £400 billion on personal goods and services. We all make some choices about how we spend; most of us look for good quality at a reasonable cost. But have you thought just how powerful your spending power really is? Nearly every penny that we spend goes into the tills of businesses. By choosing one product over another, because it is cheaper or of better quality, say, we send signals through the market, signals that support the companies who make the products we favour. This is consumer power. But it needn't stop here.

Some companies show a real commitment to building a sustainable future for our country and our planet. Others show a greater interest in building up their profits at the expense of the environment, their staff and their customers. Some place a high value on training, opportunities for women or ethnic minorities whilst others regard employees as a cost, not a valuable resource. Some have taken account of public concern about animal testing, community support and access to information while their competitors cloak their activities in secrecy. By encouraging companies whose *policies* we like we can also send signals through the market. This is new consumerism.

Shopping for A Better World provides you with the information you need to select goods made by companies whose policies and practices you will want to support. You can turn your shopping trolley into a vehicle for social change! We have covered more than sixty issues of social and environmental concern grouped into 13 convenient categories. You make the decisions from our ratings of 2,500 brands. You'll often find that better rated companies also offer better value-for-money products. Good social and environmental practice tends to carry through into all aspects of company policy. With minimal effort and expense your shopping power can be used to help build a better world.

How to Use This Guide

Products available in your supermarket, garage, chemist, department or DIY store are listed in this guide by product group. If you are uncertain as to which category a product will be in, disposable nappies for instance, use the comprehensive index at the back of the book to find out (baby products). In each product group brand names are in alphabetical order. We have also rated retailers, many of whom market own-brand products.

You can, of course, take this book with you when you go shopping to check on the brand name of any product you are about to purchase. New Consumer's rating always applies to the company making the product, so any item made by the same company, or its subsidiaries, will always have the same rating.

For practical reasons, such as time or crowded stores, you may not want to use the guide as you shop. This is why we have included a quick reference list on the inside back cover where you can fill in the names of your preferred products. Why not look up five or six grocery or household products before you go shopping each week and make a note of which brands get your social responsibility vote? You'll quickly build up your own personal selection in a way that makes them easy to remember.

This book is not a guide to value for money, quality of product or other factors that relate to the product or its manufacture. You need to make your own decision on those issues and publications like *Which?* from the Consumers Association will offer guidance. *Shopping for a Better World* rates the companies behind the products. Neither is New Consumer telling you what to think about various social and environmental issues, our job is to supply the information — you make the decisions.

For the first four categories we have used ✔✔ to indicate above average performance. A ✔ means a moderate performance or mixed record whilst a ✘ stands for below average or little evidence of a positive record. A ✘✘ indicates a poor performance on this issue. The categories that deal with the environment, animal testing, the third world, South Africa and political donations indicate the degree of involvement or support. In the Alert! column we note whether the company making the brand is responsible for products or services about which social concerns have been expressed; alcohol, tobacco, gambling or military sales. Please see the Ratings Key preceding the tables for detailed explanations.

A '?' means that, in spite of considerable efforts, we have been unable to obtain sufficient information to make a rating decision.

After the ratings tables we provide one-page summaries of key facts and notable points about every company whose products are rated. Because of space we can only include a small selection of background material in these profiles so we would encourage you to become a member of New Consumer to receive our regular updates, magazine and new publications. Please see page 287 for details.

What is New Consumer?

New Consumer is a charitable, membership-supported public interest research organisation. We produce publications that inform the public about the social, environmental and ethical policies of companies and also encourage companies to apply high standards in their activities. Our research is used by the press, by campaigning groups, and by companies themselves. New Consumer is supported by major charitable trusts and international development agencies in the UK and by the European Commission.

We subject ourselves to the same assessment as the companies we study. As a tightly run, low-budgeted organisation we scrutinise not only corporate spending but our own. Top salary for 1990/91 (our full-time Director) was £14,384 — with no perks.

In April 1991 New Consumer published *Changing Corporate Values* (Kogan Page, 637pp, £48), a widely acclaimed detailed reference book on business and social responsibility. October 1991 sees the launch of *The Global Consumer* (Gollancz, £5.99) which looks at how our everyday purchases help or hinder the third world. In February 1992 comes *The Good Employers Guide* (Kogan Page, £9.99), a book specially for job seekers in industry, the professions or public service but wondering how their personal values will fit in with the ethos of the organisation they are hoping to join.

You can make a difference!
Join New Consumer now.

You are helping to make Britain's companies more socially responsible every time you use this guide. You are sending a clear message by avoiding products from companies whose policies you feel pursue profit regardless of social or environmental cost. But New Consumer is mainly concerned with positive action and enables you to buy from those companies whose concern is shown by top ratings as responsible corporate citizens.

Help us continue this work and stay informed by joining New Consumer. Members receive a quarterly, fact-filled magazine and updates to this shopping guide. There's a free advisory service for ethical savings and investment and every member receives the next, updated, full edition of *Shopping for a Better World* at a special pre-publication discount of 30 per cent.

Join today. Simply fill in the card enclosed with this book, the tear-out sheet on page 287 or send your name and address, together with your cheque payment, to New Consumer, 52 Elswick Road Newcastle upon Tyne NE4 6JH. Alternatively you can pay by credit card by telephoning (091) 272 1148.

* £15 Regular Membership

* £55 Special Membership: receive a gift copy of *Changing Corporate Values*.

If you are not sure you want to join at this stage, but would like more information about what more you can do to shop for a better world send for a free copy of our leaflet, *Creative Consumerism,* from the same address.

New Consumer is a registered research and public information charity informing people on how they can use consumer power for positive economic, social and environmental change.

Disclosure of Information

We need information to make choices, and companies like to tell you the things they think you ought to know, particularly if they will encourage you to buy their product.

But what about the things that they don't tell you?

Shoppers today want to know much more than the price and how long the guarantee lasts. We put disclosure of information top of the list in assessing how socially responsible a company is. There are lots of different groups who have a stake in the way a business is run. The shareholders and the staff are obvious ones, but what about the customers, the suppliers and the community as a whole? We need to know many things about a company's social policies to form an opinion, but many corporations treat facts about pensions, labour turnover, training budgets, safety, equal opportunities, environmental impact and pay grades like state secrets.

The law doesn't help much. Companies have to inform their shareholders about their financial position yet this does not prevent unexpected bankruptcies by major corporations. On social issues the legal requirements to disclose information are minimal. Many annual reports contain just one sentence each on matters such as consulting employees, health, safety and welfare at work, and provision of equal opportunities for disabled people, details of which must be indicated. The salary of the highest-paid employee must be stated, together with a listing of the number of employees earning over £30,000 per annum. This, together with a note about directors' share interests and political and charitable gifts, is all the law demands. Our analysis of company literature shows that in too many cases only the absolute minimum is disclosed. In practice the way a company deals with social issues in its literature is one of the best guides as to how seriously that corporation treats social responsibility issues.

But the New Consumer analysis goes well beyond publicly available literature. Every company was presented with a detailed four-part questionnaire; to this we added facts from press and business reports and surveys from specialist business information organisations. The level and quality of response forms the basis of our rating.

Social disclosure is important. The 125 companies in this book have sales which exceed £1,000 billion worldwide. Their products are bought or used everyday by the majority of UK consumers. Of the companies covered, nearly 68 per cent responded in a way which cast fresh light on their corporate social responsibility policies. Nineteen per cent failed to respond at all, and 13 per cent argued that collecting social data or determining general social policy guidelines at corporate headquarters was not a priority or was too difficult. Any company which admitted that it was unable to collect financial information in the same way would see an immediate slump in share price. As consumers we should be pushing hard for much more detail about how company decisions are made and their impact on people, the community and the environment. Some companies rate well above the average — always a good sign that they take public opinion seriously.

As an individual you can make a difference:
- Rate your employer on what sort of information they disclose.
- Ask your MP and MEP to support legislation to make companies more socially accountable.
- Steer clear of companies who get a low rating for disclosure — you don't know what they might be hiding.
- Buy from those companies who treat your right to know as a priority.

♀

Women's Advancement

Fifty-two per cent of the world's population are women, yet in most societies they are subject to social and economic disadvantages. In Britain women continue to be grossly under-represented in senior management and on company boards, many firms take far fewer women than men at graduate training level, and pay discrimination remains widespread. We lag behind America, where many more initiatives to create upward mobility for women in the workplace have been introduced.

At board level women who do hold positions are usually non-executives, as such they are not a part of the senior management team, and even of these many have a family connection with the firm. A recent survey of 180 of the top 200 Confederation of British Industry (CBI) firms and ten of the leading building societies found that only 0.5 per cent of executive directors and 3.9 per cent of non-executive directors were women.

It is not good enough for companies to say, as some did, that the poor representation at senior levels in their companies of women reflected historical cultural bias in society as a whole, though it is true that more companies are now recruiting significant numbers of female graduates. It is impossible at this stage to assess whether these will find their way to the top of their organisations, or whether they will be side-tracked into middle-ranking staff positions which do not provide a route to the top.

Commitment to sex equality can be indirectly assessed by a company's benefit and employment package. Companies need to be willing to adapt existing terms and conditions to allow women to combine both a career and family responsibilities. Like it or not, it remains the case that childcare is seen primarily as a woman's responsibility. This places a dual burden on women who also wish to pursue a career. In this context crèche and childcare provision, leave for family reasons, job-sharing, flexitime, career break schemes, paid maternity leave and paid paternity leave are all important.

We found that there was considerable variation in the provision of these benefits. Paid maternity leave is virtually universal, varying from the statutory minimum to considerably more generous terms. An 'experimental' one-off work unit crèche has been recently introduced by one or two companies. Job-sharing and career break schemes are beginning to be introduced, particularly by major companies. However, where these benefits were on offer it was almost always only for salaried staff. This reflects the fact that it is this group who are in shortest supply, and who it is most expensive to lose.

There are a huge number of companies who unashamedly 'target' women as customers; shouldn't they also be targeting them as top class employees?

As an individual you can make a difference:
● Give preference to products from companies with a good rating on women's issues.
● Check your employer's policy on providing family benefits and career development for women.
● Avoid products from companies with a poor rating on women's issues; if they ignore half the human race do they deserve your support?

Equal Opportunities and Ethnic Minority Advancement

The existence of prejudice based on sex, race, religion, or disablement remains a serious problem for societies worldwide. As well as being morally wrong, it creates problems in economic and social terms, most graphically illustrated in Britain by inter-racial violence in inner cities. In almost all the main industrialised countries there are very significant ethnic minority communities. By denying such a huge proportion of the population the opportunity to realise their full potential, society denies itself. Official recognition of the need to tackle the problem is provided in Britain by a full battery of sex, race and disability equality legislation.

All the companies in the book were asked if they had a written equal opportunities policy. UK law obliges all companies to make an equal opportunities statement with reference to the disabled in their annual report, but there is no legal obligation to make a more wide-ranging equal opportunities statement. All the UK companies, and the UK subsidiaries of foreign companies, were asked whether they designated a specific department or individual to administrate their equal opportunities policies. The existence of an equal opportunities statement was taken as evidence that the company had at least acknowledged discrimination as an issue. The extent to which members of ethnic minority communities were represented at the higher reaches of the organisation and in graduate recruitment was also taken into account. The companies were also asked whether they operated any form of ethnic monitoring procedures which would enable them to monitor the effectiveness of their equal opportunities policy lower down the organisation, in particular with regard to recruitment.

Support for Fullemploy (a training and business development organisation dedicated to expanding the economic base of minority ethnic communities) was interpreted as evidence that a company acknowledges that there is a need for some form of concerted private sector involvement in tackling the disadvantaged economic position of ethnic minority communities. In the USA this kind of direct intervention by the private sector is much more advanced, and many companies actively seek to purchase supplies from minority-owned businesses. There is still much we must do to create a workplace free of hidden barriers based on our prejudice.

As an individual you can make a difference:

● Ask whether your employer has positive policies to encourage equal opportunities for members of ethnic minorities and disabled people.

● Find out whether the proportion of ethnic minority workers where you work or shop reflects the proportion in the local community.

● Select products from companies with a good rating on this issue.

Charitable Giving and Community Support

What role, if any, should a business have within the social arena? Are corporate social programmes genuinely socially motivated, or just an extension of marketing policy? Can what a company gives, who it gives it to, and its reasons for doing so provide a useful — if sometimes crude — indicator of that company's view of its social responsibility?

Corporate giving varies from country to country. In the USA it is much greater than in the UK, partly because of the lower level of public welfare. In the USA a company's charitable giving is seen as an important indicator of the health of its corporate citizenship. In Sweden, and throughout Scandinavia, there is a contrary and deeply held belief that employers should provide the financial resources for the state to use for the well-being of every citizen through public services. In Britain the consensus lies somewhere in between, but while companies are playing a greater role in community affairs it is clear that they see a continued need for public sector provision.

For this guide the community involvement of the company, or its main UK subsidiary where it is a foreign-owned company, has been assessed for the UK only. Each company was asked to indicate what it gave in cash and in kind, through the secondment of staff, free rental of property, or the donation of goods and services, in the UK. Membership of Business in the Community or the Per Cent Club was also taken as recognition of the company's role in the community.

Business in the Community, set up in 1981, aims to demonstrate the creative role that business can play in economic revitalisation and enterprise, and to encourage companies to do so. It is a partnership involving 250 leading companies and 30 other organisations, including central and local government, trades unions, and professional, educational and voluntary organisations. It acts as an umbrella organisation to promote community action by the private sector, and is the flagship of the private sector's community involvement in the UK.

The Per Cent Club was set up in the UK in 1986. Its aim is to promote increased levels of community charitable support by companies. Based on an American idea (where there are One, Two, and Five Per Cent Clubs), the qualification for membership is the contribution of no less than half a per cent of pre-tax UK profits to the community, which is considerably more than the average British company currently gives. Commercial sponsorship is not recognised as a contribution. The validity of Per Cent Club membership as a method of evaluating a company's community involvement is undermined by the fact that, as the Per Cent Club itself admits, 'many companies are reticent about calculating and reporting the full extent of their support for the community, particularly in terms of the financial cost of in-kind contributions'.

By far the most striking finding of New Consumer's survey work in this area is that corporate giving and community involvement remains on the margin in most companies, even those with established programmes.

As an individual you can make a difference:
- Start with yourself — plan to give a regular percentage of your income to charity.
- Check whether your workplace has a give-as-you-earn scheme, if not encourage them to start one.
- Find out what your employer's or favourite retailer's policy is on charity and the community — just asking the question often means that an answer will be thought through for the first time.

Environment

The last three years have seen us all being encouraged to do our bit to save the planet. Environmental campaigning organisations have helped us to recognise threats such as global warming and destruction of the ozone layer. A number of major environmental disasters such as *Exxon Valdez* and Chernobyl have highlighted the need for action. The impending imposition of a number of EC directives also mean that the British government and the business community can no longer ignore issues such as lead in petrol, CFCs in aerosols, marine pollution and acid rain.

In spite of the increased overall awareness of environmental issues, companies vary enormously in their recognition and response to 'green' concerns. Different businesses have widely differing environmental impacts, and have responded in varying ways.

New Consumer has assessed a company's environmental performance both on its potential environmental impact, and on any positive initiatives it has taken to minimise that impact. We have *not* taken account of environmental disasters or accidents because of the difficulty of making comparisons. Notable environmental incidents are mentioned in the short company profiles.

Companies were asked whether they had a written environmental policy, and whether there was any specific management responsibility for environmental issues.

Potential Environmental Impact

Those companies which we regarded as having very heavy potential impact are those involved in the extraction of non-renewable resources, which could result in a major pollution incident or disaster. These include oil companies, major chemical companies, companies directly involved in the nuclear industry, and those companies with operations that require registration or consents from the UK regulatory bodies. Our 'moderate impact' category includes those companies involved in transport, the manufacture of cosmetics, toiletries, household chemicals, pharmaceutical products, agrochemicals, electronics goods, electrical appliances, tobacco, paper and paper products, textiles, carpets, footwear, chemicals (small manufacturers), agriculture, forestry, fish farming, and suppliers to the nuclear industry. Sectors considered to have a potentially light impact on the environment are food manufacturers, soft drinks and confectionery manufacturers, brewers, fast food chains and DIY and furniture retailers.

Environmental Action

The answers to a large number of questions on environmental initiatives have been used to evaluate a company's environmental performance. Because of the varied operations of the companies in the survey, no one company was expected to fulfil all the criteria. Areas of action or initiative included production or retailing of organic produce; provision of environmental services such as oil spill response teams; use or development of alternative energy sources and new technology to improve environmental performance; the use of sustainably-produced materials; recycling; pollution control; planning and transport initiatives; and reduced consumption of materials in packaging and chemicals in manufacturing. We also asked companies whether they had undertaken an environmental audit, and whether they had received any environmental awards in the last two years. Membership of any corporate environmental associations, such as the Industry Council on Packaging and the Environment (INCPEN) and Business in the Environment, was taken as evidence that companies were at least aware of environmental issues.

As an individual you can make a difference:
● Reuse and recycle whenever you can; avoid disposables.
● Conserve energy, walk, cycle, use public transport or share cars.
● Support companies with a positive environmental rating.

Animal Testing

Pressure groups argue that animal testing is inhumane and unreliable. Companies know that it is costly and time-consuming, and imposes stress on staff. Governments and consumer groups understandably want to ensure that products are safe. Although not required by law to carry out animal testing on new non-medical or pharmaceutical products, companies are obliged to take adequate steps to ensure that their products are safe for human use. Testing on animals has come to be regarded by the law as one way of ensuring such provision.

The arguments for using animal testing to demonstrate a product's safety diminish when reliable alternatives are available. Increasingly such tests either reduce the numbers of animals used or replace animal testing entirely. Seventy five per cent of animal experiments are carried out for medical research purposes, with experiments involving the testing of cosmetics and toiletries accounting for less than one per cent — other areas of experimentation include drug research; household product tests; toxicity tests on environmental pollutants such as pesticides and industrial chemicals; agricultural experiments (breeding programmes); warfare and space research (mainly in the USA and USSR); and psychology experiments.

From the consumers' point of view a number of questions arise about the ethics and validity of animal testing. How relevant are tests carried out on other species to the human situation? Are there any suitable alternative tests which do not involve animals? Do manufacturers *need* to develop new products and ingredients rather than using tried and tested ones? A strong argument against testing consumer products such as cosmetics, toiletries and cleaning products on animals is that there are already a vast array of products and ingredients that have been tested. However, there is no guarantee that the active ingredients or colourings even in 'cruelty-free' cosmetics or toiletries have never been tested on animals — almost all have. Some cosmetics' companies cast doubt on the validity of competitors' claims not to have used ingredients which have been tested on animals in the last five years. Because of the length of time required to market a new product — between three and five years — companies could claim, quite legitimately, that a product has not been tested on animals within the last five years, when in fact its development did involve animal testing.

New Consumer found that many companies believe that animal testing for some products is no longer needed. Some companies, such as ICI and Unilever, carry out their own in-house research into alternatives to animal testing. Other companies support the development of alternative methods of testing by providing research funding for bodies such as FRAME, the Fund for the Replacement of Animals in Medical Experiments. As part of its 'Cruelty-Free' campaign the British Union Against Vivisection (BUAV) publishes an *Approved Product Guide* which lists those producers of cosmetics, toiletries and household products which meet its stringent non-animal testing criteria. It requires companies to meet two criteria:
a) neither the finished product or its ingredients have been tested on animals within the last five years.
b) the manufacturer has a strict policy not to undertake or commission animal tests either now or in the future.

Campaigns such as the BUAV's 'Choose Cruelty-Free' campaign 'to highlight the suffering of animals to test cosmetics, toiletries and household products' have contributed to the growing pressure on companies to end animal testing.

Companies have been rated depending on their level of involvement, the types of products they test on animals, and whether or not they are actively seeking alternative methods of testing.

As an individual you can make a difference:
- Ask companies we record as testing on animals to eliminate live animal testing from non-pharmaceutical products.
- Write to your MP/MEP asking for changes in legislation to discourage animal testing.
- Let companies know that you will do without non-essential products until they can be developed without testing on animals.
- Select products from companies that have stopped animal testing.

The Third World

Britain has long been a trading nation. In 1989 Britain's imports totalled £121 billion, 78 per cent of this being manufactured products and only 20 per cent primary commodities. The importance of former colonies has declined over time, mostly because of closer links with the European Community, which now provides over 50 per cent of the UK's imports. The third world accounts for just 12 per cent. In selecting those nations considered to be developing countries, we combined assessments from the World Bank list of lower and middle income countries, the Brandt Report, the United Nations Conference on Trade and Development, and the EC's list of developing countries.

Despite its declining importance in financial terms, trade with developing countries remains of great importance when considering social issues. World trade provided the UK with a significant engine of development at a crucial period in its history in the 18th and 19th centuries, and now it can and must do so for the so-called developing countries. Yet the UK still holds a position of considerable power, and an unequal relationship often does not operate to the mutual benefit of both partners.

At its best, the trading relationship between the UK and a poor country can be mutually beneficial. British industry has a wealth of expertise and technology that can assist local industry to make rapid progress towards the kind of economic development that benefits society at large. Many companies are investing in research to provide better yields of agricultural commodities, such as rubber or palm oil. Such research can lead to the improvement of rural wages and increased security. However, if such technology is not available to small farmers, the same innovations can accelerate the process of land monopolisation by agribusiness.

Large companies also have access to financial resources which poor countries cannot muster. Setting up industries from scratch is expensive in capital as well as technology, and provided the return is there large companies can afford the risk. The car industry is a case in point: few countries have built an integrated industry of their own, yet many have assembly or manufacturing plants, cutting the outflow of vital foreign exchange. While the UK market can be a lucrative source of the hard currency which poor countries need to pay for fuel and infrastructure developments, this is often obtained at the cost of exporting products and raw materials for which there might be pressing local requirements.

Evaluation of commercial impact on developing countries is a highly complex task, and there are few objective guidelines and measures. The key issue is clearly to assess the costs and benefits to the host community of the activities of the company in question. Our ratings for this complex issue concentrated on two factors; the extent of involvement of a company in the third world; and the existence, or not, of comprehensive and applicable policies relating to the developmental impact of that involvement. Involvement can take the form of subsidiaries and associate companies in developing countries, sourcing products and raw materials or marketing in the third world. The comprehensive and applicable nature of a policy has been assessed depending on whether it addresses the major issues related to the business; it is written, published and available to staff; it refers to some means of application and evaluation; and it is substantiated by example. We obtained information to compile these ratings from the answers to a questionnaire and the detailed information obtained for another New Consumer publication, *The Global Consumer* (Gollancz, October 1991). Particular examples of good and bad practice are mentioned in individual company profiles.

As an individual you can make a difference:
- No nation is an island, and we need trade; buy *The Global Consumer* for a product-by-product guide to which products offer the best value as far as the third world is concerned.
- Let companies know of your concern about the effects of trade on the third world; ask them what policies they have to address this problem.
- Avoiding third world products usually makes the problem worse; buy from companies who get good ratings.

South Africa

For those concerned about social responsibility in business, South Africa has long been a major concern. Most debate has centred around whether the implementation of full economic sanctions, the policy called for by the African National Congress, is appropriate and effective, and whether it should be continued until the apartheid system is abolished. Those companies who continue to do business in South Africa have consistently argued that this policy will only encourage economic collapse. They state that they provide jobs and opportunities for the advancement of black people, and act as a positive lobbying force for change within the country.

In contrast to many British companies, many US firms have withdrawn from South Africa, often in a creative manner, selling shares to black employees and setting up equal opportunities foundations. All firms operating in South Africa told us they were totally opposed to apartheid; the debate continues on whether those firms which have withdrawn hastened moves towards democracy and whether those who remain are playing their part in maintaining a stable society in which democracy can take root.

The ratings indicate which companies have significant involvement through ownership of subsidiaries employing more than 100 workers; and those companies with some involvement either employing fewer than 100 workers or with franchise or licensing agreements in South Africa.

As an individual you can make a difference:
- Make clear to companies with South African interests your own views about their involvement.
- Use the ratings to guide your purchasing decision and make sure retailers know the reason for your choice by writing to them.

Political Donations

Though companies can't vote, many of them make their political preferences very clear. Unlike most individuals, but in common with trades unions, they can bring substantial influence to bear on the political process. Since the birth of electoral politics, it has been recognised that being in hock to particular individuals or interest groups can lead to politicians becoming captives of their financiers rather than the servants of their voters. Another concern is the danger that some parties will end up with more money to promote themselves than others. In many countries this has led to laws which limit the level of private finance that political parties and candidates can accept, and to the provision of public finance for such activities.

In Britain there are few such limits. Companies in the UK can make political donations to political parties without requesting shareholder permission. Their only formal obligation is to publish details of any donation over £200 in their annual accounts. It is from this source that information on political donations in the UK can be derived. Many companies we talked to who did not make any political donations stated that this was a matter of policy on the part of the company, almost certainly from a desire to be seen as neutral within the political arena.

The suspicion that some British politicians may be unduly influenced by their corporate backers is fuelled by the contrasting legislative situation regarding trades unions' political donations, introduced in the *1984 Trades Union Act*. Up to this time a percentage of union membership fees went into their union's 'political fund', much of which was then used to support the Labour Party. The Conservative government felt that this was unfair, as it meant that any trades unionist who did not support the Labour Party was forced to contribute to its funding.

The Act ordered the unions to set up separate political funds, the existence of which must be balloted on every ten years. These were to be paid for by a special levy which union members could vote to abstain from, and the political fund was to be accounted for annually. Most co-operative societies make donations to the Labour Party via the Co-operative Party. Unlike company donations, all these societies must obtain the approval of their members before making political donations, although these donations can thereafter be made automatically unless overturned by a resolution at their annual members' meeting.

Unlike trades union members, shareholders have no right to contract out of their company's political donation, and the vast numbers of people whose money is invested in companies through pension funds and insurance policies are not even able to vote with their feet by selling their shares.

The Conservative government's apparent lack of concern about placing stricter controls on how companies make political donations has been related to the fact that almost all such donations go to the Conservative Party or organisations which are closely associated with it.

We found that of the 125 companies in this survey, 26 made political donations in the UK during the period 1987-91. All but Kellogg are British. Only the Co-operative Movement made donations to the Labour Party. Organisations associated with the Conservative Party, whose support is regarded by law as political include Aims of Industry, an organisation which promotes 'free enterprise' and which reputedly has close links with senior members of the Conservative Party; British United Industrialists, which a number of companies have described as an organisation concerned with the 'maintenance of free enterprise'; and the Centre for Policy Studies, the right-wing think tank established by Sir Keith Joseph and Margaret Thatcher in 1974.

As an individual you can make a difference:
- Ask your MP why shareholders can't make their voice heard about company political donations.
- If your employer makes political donations, ask who is consulted about the policy.

Alerts!

Alcohol, Tobacco, Gambling and Military Sales

Some companies provide products and services which raise a great deal of public controversy. We have selected four areas where there is widespread concern: alcohol, tobacco, gambling, and military sales. There are serious questions to be asked in each case about availability and control. The first three can all be destructively addictive and affect others; weapons are designed to be destructive, and the arguments centre around their use for defence in a world already oversupplied with methods of annihilation. There are many products which have also raised social concerns: fireworks, fast cars and pornography are just a few; however, our selections cover a range of issues where people ask 'Do their benefits outweigh their disadvantages?'

Alcohol

The social and personal effects of alcohol are a long-standing concern. A significant minority of people suffer from alcohol-related problems. Alcohol changes the mood and thinking of the drinker and has addictive properties, as the estimated two million alcoholics in Britain know only too well. Alcohol is associated with liver and pancreas diseases, high blood pressure, cancers, lung and blood disorders, and a litany of mental illnesses.

To compare the costs of alcohol abuse with the benefits of social drinking is difficult. The full cost of an accident, a crime or a tragedy related to drinking is incalculable. However, it has been estimated that the financial cost to society of alcohol abuse amounts to at least £1.6 billion a year.

Excise duties and VAT on alcohol bring in six per cent of all government income. In Britain there is one on-licensed premises for every 300 adults, over 200,000 licensed premises in all, including 52,000 off-licenses.

Companies in the survey that are involved in the manufacture or who are major retailers of alcohol are noted in the alert column.

As an individual you can make a difference:
- If you drink, drink moderately.
- Shop where alcoholic drinks are clearly segregated from other products.
- Give preference to brewers who generously support sensible drinking and alcohol abuse-support programmes.
- Encourage your workplace to recognise alcoholism as a widespread problem and provide counselling.

Tobacco

In 1990, 93 billion cigarettes were sold in Britain. About 14 million British adults smoke and, though public concern is clearly reflected in declining sales figures, the proportion of people under 25 who smoke remains high. Although still disputed by tobacco producers, the serious effects of smoking on health have been comprehensively documented in numerous national and international studies. Lung cancer, many types of respiratory problems and heart disease are just some of the illnesses which have been attributed to smoking.

Companies which manufacture or are major retailers of tobacco have been noted as such in the alert column.

As an individual you can make a difference:
- If you smoke, try to give up. It is bad for you and for others.
- Think seriously about buying any products from companies who also manufacture cigarettes
- Press for a complete no-smoking policy at work
- Urge a ban on all tobacco advertising and smoking in all public places; write to your MP/MEP.

Gambling

Like the consumption of alcohol, gambling comes in many forms, from purely social to a compulsive addiction. The 'industry' has a reputation, outside the mainstream operators such as those covered in this guide, for retaining links with organised crime. With gamblers estimated to have lost approximately £2.6 billion in various forms in the UK in 1989, the industry is a significant source of consumer expenditure. The involvement of any of the companies in gambling operations including through the operation of betting shops, casinos, football pools, bingo halls, amusement arcades and operation of fruit machines is noted in the alert column of the tables.

As an individual you can make a difference:
- Recognise gambling as a social entertainment with a potentially addictive aspect.
- Think seriously about buying any products from companies with major gambling interests.

Military Sales

Whether it is right to use force to achieve political and economic ends is a long-running ethical debate. Virtually all societies place strict controls on who can possess weapons, and in what circumstances they can use them. Iraq's invasion of Kuwait highlighted the need for effective security arrangements in order to contain unprovoked aggression. It also revealed the role of the arms trade in making it easy to go to war.

The world's annual military budget is greater than that for health. In 1989, at £600 billion, it was equal to the income of the 2.6 billion people in the world's 44 poorest nations. Does the world spend too much on arms? Is this expenditure a source of instability in the world? Is it right that anyone should profit from the trade in armaments? The core strategies of the major arms suppliers are clear. They intend to produce increasingly more complex, expensive and 'efficient' variants of existing armaments, contributing to a continued arms race, and compensating for falling sales in the developed world by selling to developing countries.

Sales or services as part of defence-related contracts which are not weapons-related or otherwise 'specially designed' for military purposes, such as the sale of bandages or shelving, or the provision of canteen facilities, are not included in the company ratings. Companies have been rated depending on their level of involvement, which is indicated in the alert column.

As an individual you can make a difference:

- Consider whether companies involved in military sales have marketed their military products responsibly. If you feel they haven't then think seriously about buying their products.
- Write to your MP to urge stricter controls on the export of arms.

Ratings Key

In general a ✔✔ rating indicates a high performance in the issue as defined by the rating key. A ✔ rating means that the company has an above average record. A ✘ indicates a below average performance, while ✘✘ indicates that the company showed little evidence of action or polices for that issue. For all categories a rating of ? means that there was insufficient information on which to base a rating. Each rating is made up by assessing and scoring several different factors.

Disclosure of Information

✔✔ The company provided substantial and substantive materials on their social and ethical policies, including completing New Consumer's questionnaire, providing publicly and non-publicly available literature and through direct dialogue.

✔ The company provided some specific information, either by partially completing New Consumer's questionnaire or by providing printed information or through direct dialogue. Certain key questions were left unanswered.

✘ The company provided a little information or made some reference to social issues in its publicly available literature. Most key questions were not answered.

✘✘ The company provided no information or simply sent its annual report which contained no reference to social or ethical policies or practices.

Women's Advancement

✔✔ Evidence that women are fairly represented in the company and that there are adequate benefits to encourage their advancement. Women represented at some level on the UK board of directors, 20 per cent or more managers women, 40 per cent or more graduate recruits women, evidence of monitoring and a high level of benefit provision.

✔ Evidence that steps are being taken to improve the opportunities for women. Either women are represented on the board or women make up 10-19 per cent of managers and 20-39 per cent of graduate recruits. Evidence of monitoring or provision of benefits.

✘ Some representation of women at managerial levels and above, and some provision of benefits. No women on the board or evidence of monitoring.

✘✘ Scant evidence of women's representation or of benefits to encourage their advancement. No women on the board, no monitoring, fewer than 10 per cent of managerial posts filled by women and fewer than 20 per cent of graduate recruits women. Provision of minimal benefits.

Ethnic Minorities Advancement

✔✔ Evidence of ethnic minority advancement within the company including three out of the following: at least one ethnic minority executive director on the UK board; more than five per cent of managers or graduate recruits are members of ethnic minorities; there is some form of monitoring; there is support for Fullemploy.

✔ Evidence that steps are being taken to improve opportunities for ethnic minorities within the company, including a combination of the following: an ethnic minority non-executive director; one to five per cent of management or graduate recruits from ethnic minorities; monitoring; and support for Fullemploy.

✘ The company may be aware that ethnic minorities are poorly represented and is taking some steps to improve opportunities, though the numbers in managerial positions are still low: fewer than one per cent of managers or graduate recruits are from ethnic minorities. The company have a monitoring scheme and support Fullemploy.

✗✗ Little evidence of steps to improve opportunities or actual figures for number of ethnic minority members in the company.

Community Involvement

✓✓ Either 0.8 per cent or more of pre-tax profit used for charitable purposes in the UK or donations were continued in spite of losses; and evidence of action including secondment of staff, gifts in kind, give-as-you-earn schemes and membership of the Per Cent Club or Business in the Community.

✓ 0.4-0.7 per cent of pre-tax profit donated to charity in the UK and evidence of non cash donations and membership of the Per Cent Club and/or Business in the Community.

✗ 0.2-0.3 per cent of pre-tax profit donated to charity in the UK and/or some evidence of other, non-cash, charitable initiatives.

✗✗ Less than 0.2 per cent of pre-tax profit donated to charity in the UK and little evidence of other, non-cash, charitable initiatives.

Environment

✓✓ Moderate, light or minimal impact. Evidence of an environment policy specific to a process, and management specifically responsible for environmental issues. Evidence of action across the majority of possible initiatives.

✓ Either very heavy or heavy impact with evidence of a process specific policy; management specifically responsible for the environment; and action across the majority of possible initiatives. Or moderate, light or minimal impact with evidence of a written environmental policy, management responsible for the environment and some positive initiatives.

✗ Either very heavy or heavy impact and either evidence of a written environment policy; management specifically responsible for the environment and a few positive actions or no policy but evidence of a number of positive actions. Or moderate or less impact with a policy and specific management responsibility and a few positive actions.

XX Either moderate or less impact and no evidence of any policies, managerial responsibility or positive action. Or heavy or above impact with no policy or specific managerial responsibility and few positive actions.

Animal Testing

✔✔ The company is not involved in any animal testing, either in-house or through outside contractors.

✔ The company tests only medical or pharmaceutical products on animals, either in-house or through outside contractors, and is funding or carrying out research into alternative tests.

✗ The company is involved in animal testing of non-medical or non-prescription products, either in-house or through outside contractors, and is funding or carrying out research into alternative tests.

XX The company is involved in animal testing of non-medical and/or non-prescription products, either in-house or through outside contractors and is not funding or carrying out research into alternative tests.

Third World

✔✔ A company with heavy involvement that has specific and significant positive policies for its activities in the third world.

✔ A company with light involvement that has specific and significant policies for its activities in the third world.

n A company with insignificant involvement in the third world.

✗ A company with light involvement and no significant policies for its activities in the third world.

✗✗ A company with heavy involvement and no significant policies for its activities in the third world.

South Africa

n No significant involvement with South Africa.

y Either owns subsidiaries in South Africa employing fewer than 100 staff, or has licensing or franchising agreements in South Africa.

Y Owns subsidiaries employing more than 100 staff in South Africa.

Political Donations

C Donations to the Conservative Party or free enterprise group.

L Donations to the Labour Party or other associated group.

n Makes no political donations.

Alerts!

Alcohol

A Manufactures alcoholic drinks.

a Retailed more than £1 million of alcoholic drinks in the last financial year.

Tobacco

T Manufactures tobacco products

t Retailed more than £1 million of tobacco products in the last financial year.

Gambling

G Heavily involved in the gambling industry: owns betting shops, football pools companies, bingo halls, etc.

g Owns, leases or manufacturers gaming machines.

Military Sales

M In the last financial year sales of military products and services amounted to more than £25 million.

m In the last financial year sales of military products and services were more than £5 million but less than £25 million.

Ratings by Product

For more information about how to use this section, read 'How to Use This Guide' on page 5. A detailed cross-referenced index to product categories will be found on pages 277-284, while the three-letter codes in column two — which refer to the company producing each product —are explained in the list on pages 273-276. An asterisk * after a product name indicates that it is owned jointly with another company.

		🌍	♀	⚔	🏭	🌳	🐰	🍲	💉	🎬	Alert!
AIRLINES											
Britannia Airways	TOC	✗✗	?	?	✓	?	✓✓	✗	n	n	
British Airways	BAW	✓	✓	✓	✗✗	✗	✓✓	✗	y	C	atM
Caledonian	BAW	✓	✓	✓	✗✗	✗	✓✓	✗	y	C	atM
Virgin Airways	VIR	✗✗	?	?	✗	?	✓✓	?	n	n	
AUDIO AND VIDEO EQUIPMENT											
Amstrad	AMS	✗	?	✗✗	✗✗	✗✗	✓✓	✗	n	n	
Amstrad/Fidelity	AMS	✗	?	✗✗	✗✗	✗✗	✓✓	✗	n	n	
Carlton	DIX	✗	?	✗	✗	?	✓✓	✗	n	n	
Hitachi	HIT	✗	?	?	✗✗	✗	✓✓	✓	n	n	m
JVC	MAT	✓✓	✗	✗	✗	✓	✓✓	✓	y	n	
Logik	DIX	✗	?	✗	✗	?	✓✓	✗	n	n	
Matsui	DIX	✗	?	✗	✗	?	✓✓	✗	n	n	
Miranda	DIX	✗	?	✗	✗	?	✓✓	✗	n	n	
National	MAT	✓✓	✗	✗	✗	✓	✓✓	✓	y	n	
Panasonic	MAT	✓✓	✗	✗	✗	✓	✓✓	✓	y	n	
Philips	PHI	✗	?	?	✓	✓	✓✓	✗	Y	n	M
Quasar	MAT	✓✓	✗	✗	✗	✓	✓✓	✓	y	n	
Saisho	DIX	✗	?	✗	✗	?	✓✓	✗	n	n	
Sharp	SHP	✗	?	?	✗✗	?	✓✓	✗	n	n	

											Alert!
Sony	SON	✔	✘	✘✘	✔	✔	✔✔	✔	n	n	
Technics	MAT	✔✔	✘	✘	✘	✔	✔✔	✔	y	n	
Toshiba	TOS	✔	✘	✘	✔	✔	✔✔	✔	y	n	M

BABY PRODUCTS

Ashton & Parsons	SKB	✘	?	?	✔	?	✔	?	Y	C	
Avon	AVN	✔	✘	✘✘	✔	✔	✔✔	?	n	n	
Baby Club	CAA	✘	?	?	?	✘	✔✔	✔	n	n	
Baby Fresh	SCT	✔	✘✘	✘✘	✘✘	✔	✔✔	?	n	n	
Baby Ribena	SKB	✘	?	?	✔	?	✔	?	Y	C	
Breakfast Timers	BOO	✘	?	?	✘	✘✘	✔	✘	Y	n	
Dinnefords	SKB	✘	?	?	✔	?	✔	?	Y	C	
Farex	BOO	✘	?	?	✘	✘✘	✔	✘	Y	n	
Farley's	BOO	✘	?	?	✘	✘✘	✔	✘	Y	n	
Heinz Baby Food	HEN	✔✔	✘	✘✘	✔	✔	✔✔	✔✔	n	n	
Huggies	KMB	✘✘	?	?	✘✘	✘	?	?	Y	n	
Infacare	PAG	✔✔	✔	✔✔	✘	✔	✘	✔	y	n	
Mamatoto	BOD	✔✔	✘	✘✘	✔✔	✔	✔✔	✔✔	n	n	
Milton	PAG	✔✔	✔	✔✔	✘	✔	✘	✔	y	n	
Napisan	PAG	✔✔	✔	✔✔	✘	✔	✘	✔	y	n	
Osterfeed	BOO	✘	?	?	✘	✘✘	✔	✘	Y	n	
Ostermilk	BOO	✘	?	?	✘	✘✘	✔	✘	Y	n	
Osterusks	BOO	✘	?	?	✘	✘✘	✔	✘	Y	n	
Robinsons	REC	✘	?	✘	✘✘	?	✘	?	Y	C	
Tea Timers	BOO	✘	?	?	✘	✘✘	✔	✘	Y	n	
Ultra Pampers	PAG	✔✔	✔	✔✔	✘	✔	✘	✔	y	n	

BAKING AIDS, CAKE MIXES AND FLOUR

Atora	RHM	✘	?	?	✘	?	?	✘	n	C	
Be-Ro	RHM	✘	?	?	✘	?	?	✘	n	C	

											Alert!
Brown & Polson	CPC	✗	?	?	✗✗	?	✓✓	✗	n	n	
Granny Smiths	DAL	✓✓	✓	✗	✗✗	✓✓	✗✗	n	n	n	
Greens	DAL	✓✓	✓	✗	✗✗	✓✓	✗✗	n	n	n	
Harvest Gold	DAL	✓✓	✓	✗	✗✗	✓✓	✗✗	n	n	n	
Homepride	DAL	✓✓	✓	✗	✗✗	✓✓	✗✗	n	n	n	
McDougalls	RHM	✗	?	?	✗	?	?	✗	n	C	
Pearce Duff	DAL	✓✓	✓	✗	✗✗	✓✓	✗✗	n	n	n	
Royal	DAL	✓✓	✓	✗	✗✗	✓✓	✗✗	n	n	n	
Viota	RHM	✗	?	?	✗	?	?	✗	n	C	
BATHROOM PRODUCTS											
Armitage Shanks	BCI	✓	✗	✗✗	✗	✓	✓✓	✗	Y	n	
Croydex	HAN	✗	?	?	✗	?	?	✗	Y	C	Tm
Qualcast	BCI	✓	✗	✗✗	✗	✓	✓✓	✗	Y	n	
BATTERIES											
Ever Ready	HAN	✗	?	?	✗	?	?	✗	Y	C	Tm
Gold Seal	HAN	✗	?	?	✗	?	?	✗	Y	C	Tm
Silver Seal	HAN	✗	?	?	✗	?	?	✗	Y	C	Tm
BEER											
Abbot Ale	WBR	✗	?	?	✗	?	✓✓	?	n	C	Atg
Allbright	BAS	✗	?	✗	✗✗	✓	✓✓	✗	y	n	AtG
Alloa's	ALL	✓	?	✗✗	✗	✓	✓✓	✗	n	C	Atg
Allsopps	ALL	✓	?	✗✗	✗	✓	✓✓	✗	n	C	Atg
Ansells	ALL	✓	?	✗✗	✗	✓	✓✓	✗	n	C	Atg
Arrol's	ALL	✓	?	✗✗	✗	✓	✓✓	✗	n	C	Atg
Aylesbury	ALL	✓	?	✗✗	✗	✓	✓✓	✗	n	C	Atg
Barbican	BAS	✗	?	✗	✗✗	✓	✓✓	✗	y	n	AtG
Bass	BAS	✗	?	✗	✗✗	✓	✓✓	✗	y	n	AtG
Beamish	FOS	✓✓	✗	✗	✓✓	✓	✓✓	?	n	n	Atg

											Aler...
Becks	SCN	✗	?	?	✗	?	✓✓	?	n	C	Atg
Benskins	ALL	✓	?	✗✗	✗	✓	✓✓	✗	n	C	Atg
Bentley's	WBR	✗	?	?	✗	?	✓✓	?	n	C	Atg
Best	WBR	✗	?	?	✗	?	✓✓	?	n	C	Atg
Boddingtons	WBR	✗	?	?	✗	?	✓✓	?	n	C	Atg
Breaker Malt	BAS	✗	?	✗	✗✗	✓	✓✓	✗	y	n	AtC
Brew XI	BAS	✗	?	✗	✗✗	✓	✓✓	✗	y	n	AtC
Brewhouse	FOS	✓✓	✗	✗	✓✓	✓	✓✓	?	n	n	Atg
Budweiser	FOS	✓✓	✗	✗	✓✓	✓	✓✓	?	n	n	Atg
Caffrys Ale	BAS	✗	?	✗	✗✗	✓	✓✓	✗	y	n	AtC
Camerons L.A.	BWG	✓	?	?	✗	✗✗	✓✓	n	n	C	AtC
Carling Black Label	BAS	✗	?	✗	✗✗	✓	✓✓	✗	y	n	AtC
Carlsberg Export	FOS	✓✓	✗	✗	✓✓	✓	✓✓	?	n	n	Atg
Carlsberg Pilsner	FOS	✓✓	✗	✗	✓✓	✓	✓✓	?	n	n	Atg
Carlsberg Sp. Brew	FOS	✓✓	✗	✗	✓✓	✓	✓✓	?	n	n	Atg
Castle Eden	WBR	✗	?	?	✗	?	✓✓	?	n	C	Atg
Charger	BAS	✗	?	✗	✗✗	✓	✓✓	✗	y	n	AtC
Charrington IPA	BAS	✗	?	✗	✗✗	✓	✓✓	✗	y	n	AtC
Chestnut Mild	FOS	✓✓	✗	✗	✓✓	✓	✓✓	?	n	n	Atg
Coates Somerset	ALL	✓	?	✗✗	✗	✓	✓✓	✗	n	C	Atg
Colt 45	FOS	✓✓	✗	✗	✓✓	✓	✓✓	?	n	n	Atg
Copperhead	ALL	✓	?	✗✗	✗	✓	✓✓	✗	n	C	Atg
Courage Best	FOS	✓✓	✗	✗	✓✓	✓	✓✓	?	n	n	Atg
Courage Dark Mild	FOS	✓✓	✗	✗	✓✓	✓	✓✓	?	n	n	Atg
Directors	FOS	✓✓	✗	✗	✓✓	✓	✓✓	?	n	n	Atg
Double Diamond	ALL	✓	?	✗✗	✗	✓	✓✓	✗	n	C	Atg
Drybroughs	ALL	✓	?	✗✗	✗	✓	✓✓	✗	n	C	Atg
Falcon	ALL	✓	?	✗✗	✗	✓	✓✓	✗	n	C	Atg

		🔧	♀	〈	🏭	🌳	🐰	🥛	🍷	⚙	Alert!
Flower's Bitter	WBR	✗	?	?	✗	?	✓✓	?	n	C	Atg
Foster's Draught	FOS	✓✓	✗	✗	✓✓	✓	✓✓	?	n	n	Atg
Friary Meux	ALL	✓	?	✗✗	✗	✓	✓✓	✗	n	C	Atg
Gaymer's	ALL	✓	?	✗✗	✗	✓	✓✓	✗	n	C	Atg
Green Label	FOS	✓✓	✗	✗	✓✓	✓	✓✓	?	n	n	Atg
Guinness	GUI	✓	✗✗	✗✗	✓✓	?	?	?	y	n	A
Hammonds	BAS	✗	?	✗	✗✗	✓	✓✓	✗	y	n	AtG
Hancocks HB	BAS	✗	?	✗	✗✗	✓	✓✓	✗	y	n	AtG
Harp	GUI	✓	✗✗	✗✗	✓✓	?	?	?	y	n	A
Heineken	WBR	✗	?	?	✗	?	✓✓	?	n	C	Atg
Helden Brau	WBR	✗	?	?	✗	?	✓✓	?	n	C	Atg
Hemeling	BAS	✗	?	✗	✗✗	✓	✓✓	✗	y	n	AtG
Highgate Mild	BAS	✗	?	✗	✗✗	✓	✓✓	✗	y	n	AtG
Hobec	ALL	✓	?	✗✗	✗	✓	✓✓	✗	n	C	Atg
Hofmeister	FOS	✓✓	✗	✗	✓✓	✓	✓✓	?	n	n	Atg
Holsten Export	FOS	✓✓	✗	✗	✓✓	✓	✓✓	?	n	n	Atg
Holts	ALL	✓	?	✗✗	✗	✓	✓✓	✗	n	C	Atg
Hosten Pils	FOS	✓✓	✗	✗	✓✓	✓	✓✓	?	n	n	Atg
Ice Gold	BWG	✓	?	?	✗	✗✗	✓✓	n	n	C	AtG
Ind Coope Burton Ale	ALL	✓	?	✗✗	✗	✓	✓✓	✗	n	C	Atg
John Bull Bitter	ALL	✓	?	✗✗	✗	✓	✓✓	✗	n	C	Atg
John Courage	FOS	✓✓	✗	✗	✓✓	✓	✓✓	?	n	n	Atg
John Smith's	FOS	✓✓	✗	✗	✓✓	✓	✓✓	?	n	n	Atg
John Smith's LA	FOS	✓✓	✗	✗	✓✓	✓	✓✓	?	n	n	Atg
Jubilee	BAS	✗	?	✗	✗✗	✓	✓✓	✗	y	n	AtG
Kaliber	GUI	✓	✗✗	✗✗	✓✓	?	?	?	y	n	A
Kestrel	SCN	✗	?	?	✗	?	✓✓	?	n	C	Atg
Klassiek	ALL	✓	?	✗✗	✗	✓	✓✓	✗	n	C	Atg

		⚥	🏭	🌳		🛢				Alert
Kronenbourg 1664	FOS	✓✓	✗	✗	✓✓	✓	✓✓	?	n	n	Atg
Lamot	BAS	✗	?	✗	✗✗	✓	✓✓	✗	y	n	AtG
Long Life	ALL	✓	?	✗✗	✗	✓	✓✓	✗	n	C	Atg
Lowenbrau	PHM	✗	?	?	✗✗	?	✗✗	✗	y	n	AT
M&B	BAS	✗	?	✗	✗✗	✓	✓✓	✗	y	n	AtG
Magnet	FOS	✓✓	✗	✗	✓✓	✓	✓✓	?	n	n	Atg
Marston's Pedigree	WBR	✗	?	?	✗	?	✓✓	?	n	C	Atg
Matthew Brown	SCN	✗	?	?	✗	?	✓✓	?	n	C	Atg
McEwans	SCN	✗	?	?	✗	?	✓✓	?	n	C	Atg
Miller Lite	FOS	✓✓	✗	✗	✓✓	✓	✓✓	?	n	n	Atg
Moosehead	WBR	✗	?	?	✗	?	✓✓	?	n	C	Atg
Murphy's Stout	WBR	✗	?	?	✗	?	✓✓	?	n	C	Atg
Newcastle Brown Ale	SCN	✗	?	?	✗	?	✓✓	?	n	C	Atg
Newcastle Exhibition	SCN	✗	?	?	✗	?	✓✓	?	n	C	Atg
North Eastern	BAS	✗	?	✗	✗✗	✓	✓✓	✗	y	n	AtG
Norwich	FOS	✓✓	✗	✗	✓✓	✓	✓✓	?	n	n	Atg
Oranjeboom	ALL	✓	?	✗✗	✗	✓	✓✓	✗	n	C	Atg
Piper Export	BAS	✗	?	✗	✗✗	✓	✓✓	✗	y	n	AtG
Ploughmans	FOS	✓✓	✗	✗	✓✓	✓	✓✓	?	n	n	Atg
Prize Medal	BAS	✗	?	✗	✗✗	✓	✓✓	✗	y	n	AtG
Royal Dutch	ALL	✓	?	✗✗	✗	✓	✓✓	✗	n	C	Atg
Ruddles Best	FOS	✓✓	✗	✗	✓✓	✓	✓✓	?	n	n	Atg
Ruddles County	FOS	✓✓	✗	✗	✓✓	✓	✓✓	?	n	n	Atg
Sam Brown	BAS	✗	?	✗	✗✗	✓	✓✓	✗	y	n	AtG
Satzenbrau	GUI	✓	✗✗	✗✗	✓✓	?	?	?	y	n	A
Simonds	FOS	✓✓	✗	✗	✓✓	✓	✓✓	?	n	n	Atg
Skol	ALL	✓	?	✗✗	✗	✓	✓✓	✗	n	C	Atg
Smithwicks AFB	GUI	✓	✗✗	✗✗	✓✓	?	?	?	y	n	A

		🍺	♀	🔍	🏭	🐖	🐑	🧀	🍷	🎡	Alert!
Springfield	BAS	✗	?	✗	✗✗	✓	✓✓	✗	y	n	AtG
St Christopher	ALL	✓	?	✗✗	✗	✓	✓✓	✗	n	C	Atg
Stella Artois	WBR	✗	?	?	✗	?	✓✓	?	n	C	Atg
Stones	BAS	✗	?	✗	✗✗	✓	✓✓	✗	y	n	AtG
Stud Lite	BWG	✓	?	?	✗	✗✗	✓✓	n	n	C	AtG
Sweetheart	BAS	✗	?	✗	✗✗	✓	✓✓	✗	y	n	AtG
Tartan Special	SCN	✗	?	?	✗	?	✓✓	?	n	C	Atg
Taylor Walker	ALL	✓	?	✗✗	✗	✓	✓✓	✗	n	C	Atg
Tennent's	BAS	✗	?	✗	✗✗	✓	✓✓	✗	y	n	AtG
Tetley	ALL	✓	?	✗✗	✗	✓	✓✓	✗	n	C	Atg
Theakston	SCN	✗	?	?	✗	?	✓✓	?	n	C	Atg
Three Horses Export	ALL	✓	?	✗✗	✗	✓	✓✓	✗	n	C	Atg
Toby	BAS	✗	?	✗	✗✗	✓	✓✓	✗	y	n	AtG
Top Brass	FOS	✓✓	✗	✗	✓✓	✓	✓✓	?	n	n	Atg
Trent	ALL	✓	?	✗✗	✗	✓	✓✓	✗	n	C	Atg
Triple Crown	FOS	✓✓	✗	✗	✓✓	✓	✓✓	?	n	n	Atg
Ushers	FOS	✓✓	✗	✗	✓✓	✓	✓✓	?	n	n	Atg
Wadworth 6X	FOS	✓✓	✗	✗	✓✓	✓	✓✓	?	n	n	Atg
Walker Bitter	ALL	✓	?	✗✗	✗	✓	✓✓	✗	n	C	Atg
Watneys	FOS	✓✓	✗	✗	✓✓	✓	✓✓	?	n	n	Atg
Webster's	FOS	✓✓	✗	✗	✓✓	✓	✓✓	?	n	n	Atg
Webster's XL	FOS	✓✓	✗	✗	✓✓	✓	✓✓	?	n	n	Atg
Whitbread	WBR	✗	?	?	✗	?	✓✓	?	n	C	Atg
White Label	WBR	✗	?	?	✗	?	✓✓	?	n	C	Atg
Wilsons	FOS	✓✓	✗	✗	✓✓	✓	✓✓	?	n	n	Atg
Worthington	BAS	✗	?	✗	✗✗	✓	✓✓	✗	y	n	AtG
Wrexham Lager	ALL	✓	?	✗✗	✗	✓	✓✓	✗	n	C	Atg
Yorkshire Bitter	WBR	✗	?	?	✗	?	✓✓	?	n	C	Atg

		🔍	♀		🏠	🌳					Alert
Youngers	SCN	✗	?	?	✗	?	✓✓	?	n	C	Atg
BISCUITS											
Abbey Crunch	UNB	✓✓	✗✗	✗✗	✓	✓	✗✗	✓	n	C	
Allinson Cookies	HIL	✗✗	?	?	✗✗	?	?	✗	n	n	
Applefords Cluster	WTB	✗✗	?	?	✗✗	?	?	?	n	n	
Blue Riband	NES	✓	?	✗	✓✓	?	✗	✗	Y	n	a
Breakaway	NES	✓	?	✗	✓✓	?	✗	✗	Y	n	a
Burton's	ABF	✗✗	?	?	✗✗	?	?	✗	Y	n	a
Cadbury	HIL	✗✗	?	?	✗✗	?	?	✗	n	n	
Caramel Wafer	NES	✓	?	✗	✓✓	?	✗	✗	Y	n	a
Caramel Wafers	ABF	✗✗	?	?	✗✗	?	?	✗	Y	n	a
Carr's	UNB	✓✓	✗✗	✗✗	✓	✓	✗✗	✓	n	C	
Cheddars	UNB	✓✓	✗✗	✗✗	✓	✓	✗✗	✓	n	C	
Club	BSN	✗	?	?	✓	?	?	✗	n	n	A
Clublets	BSN	✗	?	?	✓	?	?	✗	n	n	A
Crawford's	UNB	✓✓	✗✗	✗✗	✓	✓	✗✗	✓	n	C	
Edinburgh Shortbread	ABF	✗✗	?	?	✗✗	?	?	✗	Y	n	a
Elkes	NOR	✓	?	✗	✗✗	✗✗	✓✓	?	n	n	
Family Circle	BSN	✗	?	?	✓	?	?	✗	n	n	A
Fortt's Bath Oliver	BSN	✗	?	?	✓	?	?	✗	n	n	A
Fox's	NOR	✓	?	✗	✗✗	✗✗	✓✓	?	n	n	
Fruit Jaspers	UNB	✓✓	✗✗	✗✗	✓	✓	✗✗	✓	n	C	
Gold Bar	UNB	✓✓	✗✗	✗✗	✓	✓	✗✗	✓	n	C	
Harvest Chewy	QOC	✗	?	?	✗✗	?	?	?	n	n	
Hob Nobs	UNB	✓✓	✗✗	✗✗	✓	✓	✗✗	✓	n	C	
Hovis	BSN	✗	?	?	✓	?	?	✗	n	n	A
Huntley & Palmers	BSN	✗	?	?	✓	?	?	✗	n	n	A
Iced Gems	BSN	✗	?	?	✓	?	?	✗	n	n	A

											Alert!
Jacob's	BSN	✗	?	?	✔	?	?	✗	n	n	A
Jaffa Cakes	UNB	✔✔	✗✗	✗✗	✔	✔	✗✗	✔	n	C	
Jammie Dodgers	ABF	✗✗	?	?	✗✗	?	?	✗	Y	n	a
Kit Kat	NES	✔	?	✗	✔✔	?	✗	✗	Y	n	a
Krackawheat	UNB	✔✔	✗✗	✗✗	✔	✔	✗✗	✔	n	C	
Lyons	ALL	✔	?	✗✗	✗	✔	✔✔	✗	n	C	Atg
Maryland	ALL	✔	?	✗✗	✗	✔	✔✔	✗	n	C	Atg
McVitie's	UNB	✔✔	✗✗	✗✗	✔	✔	✗✗	✔	n	C	
Mini Cookies	UNB	✔✔	✗✗	✗✗	✔	✔	✗✗	✔	n	C	
Ostlers	ALL	✔	?	✗✗	✗	✔	✔✔	✗	n	C	Atg
Peek Freans	BSN	✗	?	?	✔	?	?	✗	n	n	A
Penguin	UNB	✔✔	✗✗	✗✗	✔	✔	✗✗	✔	n	C	
Pennywise	UNB	✔✔	✗✗	✗✗	✔	✔	✗✗	✔	n	C	
Ritz	BSN	✗	?	?	✔	?	?	✗	n	n	A
Romany	BSN	✗	?	?	✔	?	?	✗	n	n	A
Rover	UNB	✔✔	✗✗	✗✗	✔	✔	✗✗	✔	n	C	
Simmers	UNB	✔✔	✗✗	✗✗	✔	✔	✗✗	✔	n	C	
Snowballs	ABF	✗✗	?	?	✗✗	?	?	✗	Y	n	a
Solar	UNB	✔✔	✗✗	✗✗	✔	✔	✗✗	✔	n	C	
Sports	UNB	✔✔	✗✗	✗✗	✔	✔	✗✗	✔	n	C	
Striker	ABF	✗✗	?	?	✗✗	?	?	✗	Y	n	a
Symbol	ALL	✔	?	✗✗	✗	✔	✔✔	✗	n	C	Atg
Taxi	UNB	✔✔	✗✗	✗✗	✔	✔	✗✗	✔	n	C	
Toffypops	ABF	✗✗	?	?	✗✗	?	?	✗	Y	n	a
Trio	BSN	✗	?	?	✔	?	?	✗	n	n	A
Tuc	UNB	✔✔	✗✗	✗✗	✔	✔	✗✗	✔	n	C	
United Golden Crunch	UNB	✔✔	✗✗	✗✗	✔	✔	✗✗	✔	n	C	
Valupak	ABF	✗✗	?	?	✗✗	?	?	✗	Y	n	a

		♂♀	👤	🏭	🐄	🌳	🐰	🍶	🍴	🎞	Alert!
Victoria	UNB	✔✔	✗✗	✗✗	✔	✔	✗✗	✔	n	C	
Viscount	ABF	✗✗	?	?	✗✗	?	?	✗	Y	n	a
Wagon Wheels	ABF	✗✗	?	?	✗✗	?	?	✗	Y	n	a
Yo Yo	UNB	✔✔	✗✗	✗✗	✔	✔	✗✗	✔	n	C	
BREAD											
Allinson	ABF	✗✗	?	?	✗✗	?	?	✗	Y	n	a
Betabake	ABF	✗✗	?	?	✗✗	?	?	✗	Y	n	a
Champion	RHM	✗	?	?	✗	?	?	✗	n	C	
Countryman	DAL	✔✔	✔	✗	✗✗	✔✔	✗✗	n	n	n	
Crackerbread	ABF	✗✗	?	?	✗✗	?	?	✗	Y	n	a
Delba	BOK	✗✗	?	?	✗✗	?	?	?	n	n	
Energen	RHM	✗	?	?	✗	?	?	✗	n	C	
Family Loaf	DAL	✔✔	✔	✗	✗✗	✔✔	✗✗	n	n	n	
Granary	RHM	✗	?	?	✗	?	?	✗	n	C	
Grissini	BSN	✗	?	?	✔	?	?	✗	n	n	A
High Bran	ABF	✗✗	?	?	✗✗	?	?	✗	Y	n	a
Hovis	RHM	✗	?	?	✗	?	?	✗	n	C	
Kingsmill	ABF	✗✗	?	?	✗✗	?	?	✗	Y	n	a
Mighty White	ABF	✗✗	?	?	✗✗	?	?	✗	Y	n	a
Mothers Pride	RHM	✗	?	?	✗	?	?	✗	n	C	
Nimble	RHM	✗	?	?	✗	?	?	✗	n	C	
Oatbake	RHM	✗	?	?	✗	?	?	✗	n	C	
Procea	DAL	✔✔	✔	✗	✗✗	✔✔	✗✗	n	n	n	
Ryvita	ABF	✗✗	?	?	✗✗	?	?	✗	Y	n	a
Sunblest	ABF	✗✗	?	?	✗✗	?	?	✗	Y	n	a
Sweda Wheat	BOK	✗✗	?	?	✗✗	?	?	?	n	n	
Turkestan	DAL	✔✔	✔	✗	✗✗	✔✔	✗✗	n	n	n	
Weight Watchers	HEN	✔✔	✗	✗✗	✔	✔	✔✔	✔✔	n	n	

		⚷	♀	〈	🏭	🌳	🐁	👶	🐟	🐇	Alert!
White Hall	DAL	✔✔	✔	✗	✗✗	✔✔	✗✗	n	n	n	
Windmill	RHM	✗	?	?	✗	?	?	✗	n	C	
BREAKFAST CEREALS											
All-Bran	KEL	✔✔	✔	✔✔	✔	✔	✗	✗	Y	C	
Allinson Wholeflakes	HIL	✗✗	?	?	✗✗	?	?	✗	n	n	
Alpen	WTB	✗✗	?	?	✗✗	?	?	?	n	n	
Alpen Tropical	WTB	✗✗	?	?	✗✗	?	?	?	n	n	
Bran Buds	KEL	✔✔	✔	✔✔	✔	✔	✗	✗	Y	C	
Bran Fare	WTB	✗✗	?	?	✗✗	?	?	?	n	n	
Bran Flakes	KEL	✔✔	✔	✔✔	✔	✔	✗	✗	Y	C	
Cmn.Sense Oat Bran	KEL	✔✔	✔	✔✔	✔	✔	✗	✗	Y	C	
Coco Brek	WTB	✗✗	?	?	✗✗	?	?	?	n	n	
Coco Pops	KEL	✔✔	✔	✔✔	✔	✔	✗	✗	Y	C	
Corn Flakes	KEL	✔✔	✔	✔✔	✔	✔	✗	✗	Y	C	
Country Brek	WTB	✗✗	?	?	✗✗	?	?	?	n	n	
Country Mills	WTB	✗✗	?	?	✗✗	?	?	?	n	n	
Country Store	KEL	✔✔	✔	✔✔	✔	✔	✗	✗	Y	C	
Cruesli	WTB	✗✗	?	?	✗✗	?	?	?	n	n	
Crunchy Nut Crn Flks	KEL	✔✔	✔	✔✔	✔	✔	✗	✗	Y	C	
Farmhouse Bran	WTB	✗✗	?	?	✗✗	?	?	?	n	n	
Force *	NES	✔	?	✗	✔✔	?	✗	✗	Y	n	a
Frosties	KEL	✔✔	✔	✔✔	✔	✔	✗	✗	Y	C	
Fruit & Fibre	WTB	✗✗	?	?	✗✗	?	?	?	n	n	
Fruit 'n Fibre	KEL	✔✔	✔	✔✔	✔	✔	✗	✗	Y	C	
Fruit 'n' Nut Bran	WTB	✗✗	?	?	✗✗	?	?	?	n	n	
Golden Oaties	QOC	✗	?	?	✗✗	?	?	?	n	n	
Grape Nuts	PHM	✗	?	?	✗✗	?	✗✗	✗	y	n	AT
Harvest Crunch	QOC	✗	?	?	✗✗	?	?	?	n	n	

											Alert!
Honey & Nut Cnflks	WTB	✗✗	?	?	✗✗	?	?	?	n	n	
Honey Brek	WTB	✗✗	?	?	✗✗	?	?	?	n	n	
Honey Nut Loops	KEL	✓✓	✓	✓✓	✓	✓	✗	✗	Y	C	
Kellogg's	KEL	✓✓	✓	✓✓	✓	✓	✗	✗	Y	C	
Marshalls Cornflakes	HIL	✗✗	?	?	✗✗	?	?	✗	n	n	
O.K. Oat Chrunchie	QOC	✗	?	?	✗✗	?	?	?	n	n	
Puffed Wheat	QOC	✗	?	?	✗✗	?	?	?	n	n	
Quakeawake	QOC	✗	?	?	✗✗	?	?	?	n	n	
Quaker Oats	QOC	✗	?	?	✗✗	?	?	?	n	n	
Raisin Splitz	KEL	✓✓	✓	✓✓	✓	✓	✗	✗	Y	C	
Ready Brek	WTB	✗✗	?	?	✗✗	?	?	?	n	n	
Rice Krispies	KEL	✓✓	✓	✓✓	✓	✓	✗	✗	Y	C	
Ricicles	KEL	✓✓	✓	✓✓	✓	✓	✗	✗	Y	C	
Rivita Cornflakes	ABF	✗✗	?	?	✗✗	?	?	✗	Y	n	a
Scotts Porage	QOC	✗	?	?	✗✗	?	?	?	n	n	
Shredded Wheat *	NES	✓	?	✗	✓✓	?	✗	✗	Y	n	a
Shreddies *	NES	✓	?	✗	✓✓	?	✗	✗	Y	n	a
Smacks	KEL	✓✓	✓	✓✓	✓	✓	✗	✗	Y	C	
Special K	KEL	✓✓	✓	✓✓	✓	✓	✗	✗	Y	C	
Start	KEL	✓✓	✓	✓✓	✓	✓	✗	✗	Y	C	
Sugar Frosted Cnflks	WTB	✗✗	?	?	✗✗	?	?	?	n	n	
Sugar Puffs	QOC	✗	?	?	✗✗	?	?	?	n	n	
Sultana Bran	KEL	✓✓	✓	✓✓	✓	✓	✗	✗	Y	C	
Summer Orchard	KEL	✓✓	✓	✓✓	✓	✓	✗	✗	Y	C	
Top Bran	WTB	✗✗	?	?	✗✗	?	?	?	n	n	
Toppas	KEL	✓✓	✓	✓✓	✓	✓	✗	✗	Y	C	
Variety	KEL	✓✓	✓	✓✓	✓	✓	✗	✗	Y	C	
Warm Start	QOC	✗	?	?	✗✗	?	?	?	n	n	

		🔍	♀	(	🏭	🌿	🐇	🥫			Alert!
Weetabix	WTB	xx	?	?	xx	?	?	?	n	n	
Weetaflakes	WTB	xx	?	?	xx	?	?	?	n	n	
Weeto's	WTB	xx	?	?	xx	?	?	?	n	n	
CAKES											
Cadbury's	RHM	x	?	?	x	?	?	x	n	C	
Homebake	UNB	✓✓	xx	xx	✓	✓	xx	✓	n	C	
Lyons	ALL	✓	?	xx	x	✓	✓✓	x	n	C	Atg
Lyons Patisserie	ALL	✓	?	xx	x	✓	✓✓	x	n	C	Atg
Mr Kipling	RHM	x	?	?	x	?	?	x	n	C	
Park Cakes	NOR	✓	?	x	xx	xx	✓✓	?	n	n	
CARS											
Alfa Romeo	FIA	x	?	?	xx	x	✓✓	?	y	n	M
Audi	VWG	x	?	?	?	?	✓✓	?	Y	n	
Citreon	PEU	x	?	?	xx	?	✓✓	?	n	n	
Ferrari	FIA	x	?	?	xx	x	✓✓	?	y	n	M
Fiat	FIA	x	?	?	xx	x	✓✓	?	y	n	M
Ford	FOR	x	x	✓	xx	?	✓✓	x	y	n	M
Jaguar	FOR	x	x	✓	xx	?	✓✓	x	y	n	M
Lancia	FIA	x	?	?	xx	x	✓✓	?	y	n	M
Land Rover	BAE	x	?	xx	✓	?	✓✓	xx	n	n	M
Lotus	GEM	✓✓	xx	xx	x	✓	xx	x	y	n	M
Nissan	NIS	✓	?	?	✓	?	✓✓	?	y	n	M
Peugeot	PEU	x	?	?	xx	?	✓✓	?	n	n	
Renault	REN	xx	?	?	xx	?	✓✓	?	n	n	M
Rover	BAE	x	?	xx	✓	?	✓✓	xx	n	n	M
Seat	VWG	x	?	?	?	?	✓✓	?	Y	n	
Talbot	PEU	x	?	?	xx	?	✓✓	?	n	n	
Vauxhall	GEM	✓✓	xx	xx	x	✓	xx	x	y	n	M

		👤	⚥	🐭	🏭	🌳	🐾	🍼	🐑	⚙	Alert!
Volkswagen	VWG	✗	?	?	?	?	✓✓	?	Y	n	
Volvo	VOL	✓	?	?	✗✗	✓	✓✓	✓	n	n	M
CATALOGUES											
Argos	ARG	✓✓	✗✗	✗✗	✗✗	✓	✓✓	✗	Y	n	
Aspect	NEX	✗	?	✗✗	✓	?	✓✓	✗	n	n	
Brian Mills	LIT	✗	?	✓	✗✗	?	?	✓	n	n	tG
Burlington	LIT	✗	?	✓	✗✗	?	?	✓	n	n	tG
Choice	GUS	✗	?	?	✗✗	?	?	✗	Y	n	
Family Album	GUS	✗	?	?	✗✗	?	?	✗	Y	n	
Family Hampers	GUS	✗	?	?	✗✗	?	?	✗	Y	n	
Fashion Extra	GUS	✗	?	?	✗✗	?	?	✗	Y	n	
Fashion Plus	NEX	✗	?	✗✗	✓	?	✓✓	✗	n	n	
Freemans	SEA	✗	?	?	✗✗	?	✓✓	✗	n	C	at
Great Universal	GUS	✗	?	?	✗✗	?	?	✗	Y	n	
Janet Fraser	LIT	✗	?	✓	✗✗	?	?	✓	n	n	tG
John Moores	LIT	✗	?	✓	✗✗	?	?	✓	n	n	tG
John Myers	GUS	✗	?	?	✗✗	?	?	✗	Y	n	
John Noble	GUS	✗	?	?	✗✗	?	?	✗	Y	n	
Kaleidoscope	NEX	✗	?	✗✗	✓	?	✓✓	✗	n	n	
Kays	GUS	✗	?	?	✗✗	?	?	✗	Y	n	
Kit	GUS	✗	?	?	✗✗	?	?	✗	Y	n	
Littlewoods	LIT	✗	?	✓	✗✗	?	?	✓	n	n	tG
Littlewoods Index	LIT	✗	?	✓	✗✗	?	?	✓	n	n	tG
Look Again	NEX	✗	?	✗✗	✓	?	✓✓	✗	n	n	
Next Directory	NEX	✗	?	✗✗	✓	?	✓✓	✗	n	n	
Peter Craig	LIT	✗	?	✓	✗✗	?	?	✓	n	n	tG
Scotcade	NEX	✗	?	✗✗	✓	?	✓✓	✗	n	n	
Trafford	GUS	✗	?	?	✗✗	?	?	✗	Y	n	

		🔑	♀	👁	🏭	🌱	🐇	🍯	🌡	🔬	Alert!
You and Yours	NEX	✗	?	✗✗	✓	?	✓✓	✗	n	n	

CLOTHING											
'NBG'	NEX	✗	?	✗✗	✓	?	✓✓	✗	n	n	
Aertex	CVI	✓	?	✗	✗✗	?	✓✓	✗	Y	C	m
Allen Solly	CVI	✓	?	✗	88	?	✓✓	✗	Y	C	m
Amanda Blake	BUR	✗✗	?	?	✗	?	?	✗	n	n	
Angelo Litrico	CAA	✗	?	?	?	✗	✓✓	✓	n	n	
Anne Brooks	BUR	✗✗	?	?	✗	?	?	✗	n	n	
Aristoc	COT	✗	?	?	✗✗	✗	✓✓	✗	Y	n	
Associates	BUR	✗✗	?	?	✗	?	?	✗	n	n	
Avanti	CAA	✗	?	?	?	✗	✓✓	✓	n	n	
Avon	AVN	✓	✗	✗✗	✓	✓	✓✓	?	n	n	
Babywise	CWS	✓✓	✓	✗	✓✓	✓	✓✓	4	n	L	at
Ballito	COT	✗	?	?	✗✗	✗	✓✓	✗	Y	n	
Berlei	COT	✗	?	?	✗✗	✗	✓✓	✗	Y	n	
Burton Classics	BUR	✗✗	?	?	✗	?	?	✗	n	n	
Byford	CVI	✓	?	✗	✗✗	?	✓✓	✗	Y	C	m
Canda	CAA	✗	?	?	?	✗	✓✓	✓	n	n	
Casual Club	BUR	✗✗	?	?	✗	?	?	✗	n	n	
Clockhouse	CAA	✗	?	?	?	✗	✓✓	✓	n	n	
Club 15	CAA	✗	?	?	?	✗	✓✓	✓	n	n	
Club Azur	CAA	✗	?	?	?	✗	✓✓	✓	n	n	
Dim	SAL	✗✗	?	?	✗✗	?	?	✗	Y	n	
Essence	BUR	✗✗	?	?	✗	?	?	✗	n	n	
Expressions	BUR	✗✗	?	?	✗	?	?	✗	n	n	
Gallery	BUR	✗✗	?	?	✗	?	?	✗	n	n	
George	ASD	✓	✗✗	✗	✗✗	✓	✓✓	✗	n	n	at
George Rech	COT	✗	?	?	✗✗	✗	✓✓	✗	Y	n	

											Alert!
Gossard	COT	✗	?	?	✗✗	✗	✓✓	✗	Y	n	
Interface	CAA	✗	?	?	?	✗	✓✓	✓	n	n	
J Taylor	BUR	✗✗	?	?	✗	?	?	✗	n	n	
Jane Hamilton	BUR	✗✗	?	?	✗	?	?	✗	n	n	
Jinglers	CAA	✗	?	?	?	✗	✓✓	✓	n	n	
Jockey	COT	✗	?	?	✗✗	✗	✓✓	✗	Y	n	
Jonelle	JLP	✗	?	✗✗	✓	?	✓✓	✗	n	n	
Kayser	COT	✗	?	?	✗✗	✗	✓✓	✗	Y	n	
Ladybird	CVI	✓	?	✗	✗✗	?	✓✓	✗	Y	C	m
Louis Phillipe	CVI	✓	?	✗	✗✗	?	✓✓	✗	Y	C	m
Lyle & Scott	COT	✗	?	?	✗✗	✗	✓✓	✗	Y	n	
Matchplay	CVI	✓	?	✗	✗✗	?	✓✓	✗	Y	C	m
New World	BUR	✗✗	?	?	✗	?	?	✗	n	n	
Nico	BUR	✗✗	?	?	✗	?	?	✗	n	n	
Nuage	BUR	✗✗	?	?	✗	?	?	✗	n	n	
Originals	NEX	✗	?	✗✗	✓	?	✓✓	✗	n	n	
Palomino	CAA	✗	?	?	?	✗	✓✓	✓	n	n	
Peter England	CVI	✓	?	✗	✗✗	?	✓✓	✗	Y	C	m
Portfolio	BUR	✗✗	?	?	✗	?	?	✗	n	n	
Premier	BUR	✗✗	?	?	✗	?	?	✗	n	n	
Profiles	BUR	✗✗	?	?	✗	?	?	✗	n	n	
Rob Roy	COT	✗	?	?	✗✗	✗	✓✓	✗	Y	n	
Rocola	CVI	✓	?	✗	✗✗	?	✓✓	✗	Y	C	m
Rodeo	CAA	✗	?	?	?	✗	✓✓	✓	n	n	
Rohan Designs	CJC	✗✗	?	?	✗✗	?	?	✗	y	n	
Secrets	BUR	✗✗	?	?	✗	?	?	✗	n	n	
Set & Match	BUR	✗✗	?	?	✗	?	?	✗	n	n	
St Michael	MKS	✗	✗	✗✗	✓	✓	✓✓	✗	n	C	a

											Alert!
Style	BUR	xx	?	?	x	?	?	x	n	n	
Top Notch	BUR	xx	?	?	x	?	?	x	n	n	
Trader	BUR	xx	?	?	x	?	?	x	n	n	
Van Heusen	CVI	✔	?	x	xx	?	✔✔	x	Y	C	m
Vivre	BUR	xx	?	?	x	?	?	x	n	n	
Viyella	CVI	✔	?	x	xx	?	✔✔	x	Y	C	m
Westbury	CAA	x	?	?	?	x	✔✔	✔	n	n	
Wolsey	COT	x	?	?	xx	x	✔✔	x	Y	n	
Yessica	CAA	x	?	?	?	x	✔✔	✔	n	n	
Your Sixth Sense	CAA	x	?	?	?	x	✔✔	✔	n	n	
CLOTHING RETAILERS											
Adams	SEA	x	?	?	xx	?	✔✔	x	n	C	at
BhS	STH	xx	?	?	✔	?	xx	x	n	n	
Blazer	STH	xx	?	?	✔	?	xx	x	n	n	
Bradleys	SEA	x	?	?	xx	?	✔✔	x	n	C	at
Burton	BUR	xx	?	?	x	?	?	x	n	n	
Chloe	RTH	xx	?	?	xx	?	?	x	Y	C	T
Contessa	COT	x	?	?	xx	x	✔✔	x	Y	n	
Dormie	SEA	x	?	?	xx	?	✔✔	x	n	C	at
Dorothy Perkins	BUR	xx	?	?	x	?	?	x	n	n	
Dunhill	RTH	xx	?	?	xx	?	?	x	Y	C	T
Evans Collection	BUR	xx	?	?	x	?	?	x	n	n	
Fosters Menswear	SEA	x	?	?	xx	?	✔✔	x	n	C	at
Harvey Nichols	BUR	xx	?	?	x	?	?	x	n	n	
Horne Brothers	SEA	x	?	?	xx	?	✔✔	x	n	C	at
Jaeger	CVI	✔	?	x	xx	?	✔✔	x	Y	C	m
Jaeger Man	CVI	✔	?	x	xx	?	✔✔	x	Y	C	m
Marks & Spencer	MKS	x	x	xx	✔	✔	✔✔	x	n	C	a

											Alert!
McIlroys	COT	✗	?	?	✗✗	✗	✓✓	✗	Y	n	
Miss Erika	SEA	✗	?	?	✗✗	?	✓✓	✗	n	C	at
Miss Selfridge	SEA	✗	?	?	✗✗	?	✓✓	✗	n	C	at
Next	NEX	✗	?	✗✗	✓	?	✓✓	✗	n	n	
Next Originals	NEX	✗	?	✗✗	✓	?	✓✓	✗	n	n	
Primark	ABF	✗✗	?	?	✗✗	?	?	✗	Y	n	a
Principles	BUR	✗✗	?	?	✗	?	?	✗	n	n	
Principles for Men	BUR	✗✗	?	?	✗	?	?	✗	n	n	
Richards Shops	STH	✗✗	?	?	✓	?	✗✗	✗	n	n	
Top Man	BUR	✗✗	?	?	✗	?	?	✗	n	n	
Top Shop	BUR	✗✗	?	?	✗	?	?	✗	n	n	
Viyella	CVI	✓	?	✗	✗✗	?	✓✓	✗	Y	C	m
Wallis	SEA	✗	?	?	✗✗	?	✓✓	✗	n	C	at
Warehouse	SEA	✗	?	?	✗✗	?	✓✓	✗	n	C	at
Your Price	SEA	✗	?	?	✗✗	?	✓✓	✗	n	C	at
COFFEE (GROUND)											
Blend 37	NES	✓	?	✗	✓✓	?	✗	✗	Y	n	a
Douwe Egberts	SAL	✗✗	?	?	✗✗	?	?	✗	Y	n	
Gold Blend	NES	✓	?	8	✓✓	?	✗	✗	Y	n	a
Kenco	PHM	✗	?	?	✗✗	?	✗✗	✗	y	n	AT
Lavazza	ABF	✗✗	?	?	✗✗	?	?	✗	Y	n	a
Lyons	ALL	✓	?	✗✗	✗	✓	✓✓	✗	n	C	Atg
Master Blend	PHM	✗	?	?	✗✗	?	✗✗	✗	y	n	AT
Pickwick	SAL	✗✗	?	?	✗✗	?	?	✗	Y	n	
Rombouts	RHM	✗	?	?	✗	?	?	✗	n	C	
Twinings	ABF	✗✗	?	?	✗✗	?	?	✗	Y	n	a
Van Nelle	SAL	✗✗	?	?	✗✗	?	?	✗	Y	n	

		♀		🏠	🌳		☕			Alert!
COFFEE (INSTANT)											
Alta Rica	NES	✔	?	✗	✔✔	?	✗	✗	Y	n	a
Blend 37	NES	✔	?	✗	✔✔	?	✗	✗	Y	n	a
Brim	PHM	✗	?	?	✗✗	?	✗✗	✗	y	n	AT
Brooke Bond	UNL	✔✔	✔	✔✔	✔	✔	✗	✔✔	Y	n	AT
Cafe Hag	PHM	✗	?	?	✗✗	?	✗✗	✗	y	n	AT
Cafe Mountain	UNL	✔✔	✔	✔✔	✔	✔	✗	✔✔	Y	n	AT
Cap Colombie	NES	✔	?	✗	✔✔	?	✗	✗	Y	n	a
Choice	UNL	✔✔	✔	✔✔	✔	✔	✗	✔✔	Y	n	AT
Coffee Time	UNL	✔✔	✔	✔✔	✔	✔	✗	✔✔	Y	n	AT
Elevenses	NES	✔	?	✗	✔✔	?	✗	✗	Y	n	a
Fine Blend	NES	✔	?	✗	✔✔	?	✗	✗	Y	n	a
Gold Blend	NES	✔	?	✗	✔✔	?	✗	✗	Y	n	a
Kenco	PHM	✗	?	?	✗✗	?	✗✗	✗	y	n	AT
Lyons	ALL	✔	?	✗✗	✗	✔	✔✔	✗	n	C	Atg
Master Blend	PHM	✗	?	?	✗✗	?	✗✗	✗	y	n	AT
Maxpax	PHM	✗	?	?	✗✗	?	✗✗	✗	y	n	AT
Maxwell House	PHM	✗	?	?	✗✗	?	✗✗	✗	y	n	AT
Mellow Bird's	PHM	✗	?	?	✗✗	?	✗✗	✗	y	n	AT
Nescafe	NES	✔	?	8	✔✔	?	✗	✗	Y	n	a
Nescore	NES	✔	?	8	✔✔	?	✗	✗	Y	n	a
Red Mountain	UNL	✔✔	✔	✔✔	✔	✔	✗	✔✔	Y	n	AT
CONDIMENTS, PICKLES AND SAUCES											
Bonjour	NES	✔	?	✗	✔✔	?	✗	✗	Y	n	a
Bonne Cuisine	NES	✔	?	✗	✔✔	?	✗	✗	Y	n	a
Branston	NES	✔	?	✗	✔✔	?	✗	✗	Y	n	a
C & B	NES	✔	?	✗	✔✔	?	✗	✗	Y	n	a
Cerebos	RHM	✗	?	?	✗	?	?	✗	n	C	

		🐰	♀	🚪	🏠	🌳	🐑	🐟	🐇	⚗	Alert!
Colman's	REC	✗	?	✗	✗✗	?	✗	?	Y	C	
Cook-in-Sauce	DAL	✓✓	✓	✗	✗✗	✓✓	✗✗	n	n	n	
Cook-in-the-Pot	NES	✓	?	✗	44	?	✗	✗	Y	n	a
Daddies	BSN	✗	?	?	✓	?	?	✗	n	n	A
Dolmio	MAR	✓	✓	?	?	✓	✓✓	✗	n	n	
Dufrais	NES	✓	?	✗	✓✓	?	✗	✗	Y	n	a
Epicure	BSN	✗	?	?	4	?	?	✗	n	n	A
Four Seasons	NES	✓	?	✗	✓✓	?	✗	✗	Y	n	a
HP	BSN	✗	?	?	✓	?	?	✗	n	n	A
Hammonds	DAL	✓✓	✓	✗	✗✗	✓✓	✗✗	n	n	n	
Haywards	HIL	✗✗	?	?	✗✗	?	?	✗	n	n	
Healthy Balance	NES	✓	?	✗	✓✓	?	✗	✗	Y	n	a
Heinz	HEN	✓✓	✗	✗✗	✓	✓	✓✓	✓✓	n	n	
Hellmanns	CPC	✗	?	?	✗✗	?	✓✓	✗	n	n	
Homepride	DAL	✓✓	✓	✗	✗✗	✓✓	✗✗	n	n	n	
Ice Magic	PHM	✗	?	?	✗✗	?	✗✗	✗	y	n	AT
Jif	REC	✗	?	✗	✗✗	?	✗	?	Y	C	
Kauffman	BOK	✗✗	?	?	✗✗	?	?	?	n	n	
Knorr	CPC	✗	?	?	✗✗	?	✓✓	✗	n	n	
L Noel	BOK	✗✗	?	?	✗✗	?	?	?	n	n	
Lea & Perrins	BSN	✗	?	?	✓	?	?	✗	n	n	A
Maille	BSN	✗	?	?	✓	?	?	✗	n	n	A
Mrs Elswood's	BOK	✗✗	?	?	✗✗	?	?	?	n	n	
Napolina	CPC	✗	?	?	✗✗	?	✓✓	✗	n	n	
OK Sauce	REC	✗	?	✗	✗✗	?	✗	?	Y	C	
Pan Yan	NES	✓	?	✗	✓✓	?	✗	✗	Y	n	a
Patak's	BOK	✗✗	?	?	✗✗	?	?	?	n	n	
Paxo	RHM	✗	?	?	✗	?	?	✗	n	C	

											Alert!
Ploughman's	HEN	✓✓	✗	✗✗	✓	✓	✓✓	✓✓	n	n	
Prego	CAM	✗	?	?	8	?	?	?	n	n	
Ragu	UNL	✓✓	✓	✓✓	✓	✓	✗	✓✓	Y	n	AT
Sarsons	NES	✓	?	✗	✓✓	?	✗	✗	Y	n	a
Saxa	RHM	✗	?	?	✗	?	?	✗	n	C	
Sharwood's	RHM	✗	?	?	✗	?	?	✗	n	C	
Toast Toppers	HEN	✓✓	✗	✗✗	✓	✓	✓✓	✓✓	n	n	
Waistline	NES	✓	?	✗	✓✓	?	✗	✗	Y	n	a
Weight Watchers	HEN	✓✓	✗	✗✗	✓	✓	✓✓	✓✓	n	n	
CONFECTIONERY											
99 Flake	CAD	✓✓	✓	✓	✗	✓	✓✓	✗	Y	n	
Aero	NES	✓	?	✗	✓✓	?	✗	✗	Y	n	a
After Eight	NES	✓	?	✗	✓✓	?	✗	✗	Y	n	a
All Gold	UNB	✓✓	✗✗	✗✗	✓	✓	✗✗	✓	n	C	
Anglo Bellamy	CAD	✓✓	✓	✓	✗	✓	✓✓	✗	Y	n	
Animal Bar	NES	✓	?	✗	✓✓	?	✗	✗	Y	n	a
Applause	MAR	✓	✓	?	?	✓	✓✓	✗	n	n	
Balisto	MAR	✓	✓	?	?	✓	✓✓	✗	n	n	
Bar Six	CAD	✓✓	✓	✓	✗	✓	✓✓	✗	Y	n	
Barratt	CAD	✓✓	✓	✓	✗	✓	✓✓	✗	Y	n	
Bassett	CAD	✓✓	✓	✓	✗	✓	✓✓	✗	Y	n	
Beechnut	CAD	✓✓	✓	✓	✗	✓	✓✓	✗	Y	n	
Biarritz	CAD	✓✓	✓	✓	✗	✓	✓✓	✗	Y	n	
Bitz	UNB	✓✓	✗✗	✗✗	✓	✓	✗✗	✓	n	C	
Black Magic	NES	✓	?	✗	✓✓	?	✗	✗	Y	n	a
Black Magic Bar	NES	✓	?	✗	✓✓	?	✗	✗	Y	n	a
Boost	CAD	✓✓	✓	✓	✗	✓	✓✓	✗	Y	n	
Bouchee	PHM	✗	?	?	✗✗	?	✗✗	✗	y	n	AT

											Alert!
Bounty	MAR	✔	✔	?	?	✔	✔✔	✗	n	n	
Bournville	CAD	✔✔	✔	✔	✗	✔	✔✔	✗	Y	n	
Burton's	ABF	✗✗	?	?	✗✗	?	?	✗	Y	n	a
Cabana	NES	✔	?	✗	✔✔	?	✗	✗	Y	n	a
Cadbury	CAD	✔✔	✔	✔	✗	✔	✔✔	✗	Y	n	
Callard & Bowser	UNB	✔✔	✗✗	✗✗	✔	✔	✗✗	✔	n	C	
Candytots	NES	✔	?	✗	✔✔	?	✗	✗	Y	n	a
Caramac	NES	✔	?	✗	✔✔	?	✗	✗	Y	n	a
Caramel	CAD	✔✔	✔	✔	✗	✔	44	✗	Y	n	
Carousel	UNB	✔✔	✗✗	✗✗	✔	✔	✗✗	✔	n	C	
Chapelet Humphries	CAD	✔✔	✔	✔	✗	✔	✔✔	✗	Y	n	
Chocolate Orange	UNB	✔✔	✗✗	✗✗	✔	✔	✗✗	✔	n	C	
Clarnico	CAD	✔✔	✔	✔	✗	✔	✔✔	✗	Y	n	
Connoisseurs	UNB	✔✔	✗✗	✗✗	✔	✔	✗✗	✔	n	C	
Contrast	CAD	✔✔	✔	✔	✗	✔	✔✔	✗	Y	n	
Cote d'Or	PHM	✗	?	?	✗✗	?	✗✗	✗	y	n	AT
Crystal	CAD	✔✔	✔	✔	✗	✔	✔✔	✗	Y	n	
Dairy Box	NES	✔	?	✗	✔✔	?	✗	✗	Y	n	a
Dairy Crunch	NES	✔	?	✗	✔✔	?	✗	✗	Y	n	a
Dairy Milk	CAD	✔✔	✔	✔	✗	✔	✔✔	✗	Y	n	
Dime	UNB	✔✔	✗✗	✗✗	✔	✔	✗✗	✔	n	C	
Double Decker	CAD	✔✔	✔	✔	✗	✔	✔✔	✗	Y	n	
Drifter	NES	✔	?	✗	✔✔	?	✗	✗	Y	n	a
Eclipse	NES	✔	?	✗	✔✔	?	✗	✗	Y	n	a
Faam	CAD	✔✔	✔	✔	✗	✔	✔✔	✗	Y	n	
Festival	NES	✔	?	✗	✔✔	?	✗	✗	Y	n	a
Flake	CAD	✔✔	✔	✔	✗	✔	✔✔	✗	Y	n	
Fox's Glacier	NES	✔	?	✗	✔✔	?	✗	✗	Y	n	a

		⚲	♀	⟨	🏭	🌳	🐇	🥊	🐈	🎞	Alert!
Frisia	CAD	✔✔	✔	✔	✗	✔	✔✔	✗	Y	n	
Fruit & Nut	CAD	✔✔	✔	✔	✗	✔	✔✔	✗	Y	n	
Fruit Gums	NES	✔	?	✗	✔✔	?	✗	✗	Y	n	a
Fruit Pastilles	NES	✔	?	✗	✔✔	?	✗	✗	Y	n	a
Fry's	CAD	✔✔	✔	✔	✗	✔	✔✔	✗	Y	n	
Fudge	CAD	✔✔	✔	✔	✗	✔	✔✔	✗	Y	n	
Galaxy	MAR	✔	✔	?	?	✔	✔✔	✗	n	Y	
Galaxy Dove Bar	MAR	✔	✔	?	?	✔	✔✔	✗	n	n	
Galaxy Gold	MAR	✔	✔	?	?	✔	✔✔	✗	n	n	
Galaxy Minstrels	MAR	✔	✔	?	?	✔	✔✔	✗	n	n	
Galaxy Ripple	MAR	✔	✔	?	?	✔	✔✔	✗	n	n	
Galaxy Rondos	MAR	✔	✔	?	?	✔	✔✔	✗	n	n	
Godiva	CAM	✗	?	?	✗	?	?	?	n	n	
Golden Crisp	CAD	✔✔	✔	✔	✗	✔	✔✔	✗	Y	n	
Golden Cup	NES	✔	?	✗	✔✔	?	✗	✗	Y	n	a
Hazelnut Cup	NES	✔	?	✗	✔✔	?	✗	✗	Y	n	a
Henri Nestle Colltn	NES	✔	?	✗	✔✔	?	✗	✗	Y	n	a
Hueso	CAD	✔✔	✔	✔	✗	✔	✔✔	✗	Y	n	
Inspiration	CAD	✔✔	✔	✔	✗	✔	✔✔	✗	Y	n	
Jamesons	CAD	✔✔	✔	✔	✗	✔	✔✔	✗	Y	n	
Jellytots	NES	✔	?	✗	✔✔	?	✗	✗	Y	n	a
Kassalic	NES	✔	?	✗	✔✔	?	✗	✗	Y	n	a
Keelers	UNB	✔✔	✗✗	✗✗	✔	✔	✗✗	✔	n	C	
Kit Kat	NES	✔	?	✗	✔✔	?	✗	✗	Y	n	a
Le Box	UNB	✔✔	✗✗	✗✗	✔	✔	✗✗	✔	n	C	
Leo	PHM	✗	?	?	✗✗	?	✗✗	✗	y	n	AT
Lila Pause	PHM	✗	?	?	✗✗	?	✗✗	✗	y	n	AT
Lion	CAD	✔✔	✔	✔	✗	✔	✔✔	✗	Y	n	

											Alert!
Lion Bar	NES	✔	?	✘	✔✔	?	✘	✘	Y	n	a
Lockets	MAR	✔	✔	?	?	✔	✔✔	✘	n	n	
Logger	UNB	✔✔	✘✘	✘✘	✔	✔	✘✘	✔	n	C	
M & M's	MAR	✔	✔	?	?	✔	✔✔	✘	n	n	
MacRobertson	CAD	✔✔	✔	✔	✘	✔	✔✔	✘	Y	n	
Maltesers	MAR	✔	✔	?	?	✔	✔✔	✘	n	n	
Marabou	UNB	✔✔	✘✘	✘✘	✔	✔	✘✘	✔	n	C	
Mars	MAR	✔	✔	?	?	✔	✔✔	✘	n	n	
Matchmakers	NES	✔	?	✘	✔✔	?	✘	✘	Y	n	a
Maynard	CAD	✔✔	✔	✔	✘	✔	✔✔	✘	Y	n	
Milk Tray	CAD	✔✔	✔	✔	✘	✔	✔✔	✘	Y	n	
Milka	PHM	✘	?	?	✘✘	?	✘✘	✘	y	n	AT
Milky Way	MAR	✔	✔	?	?	✔	✔✔	✘	n	n	
Minties	NES	✔	?	✘	✔✔	?	✘	✘	Y	n	a
Mintola	NES	✔	?	✘	✔✔	?	✘	✘	Y	n	a
Mix-o-choc	NES	✔	?	✘	✔✔	?	✘	✘	Y	n	a
Moments	UNB	✔✔	✘✘	✘✘	✔	✔	✘✘	✔	n	C	
Moonlight	UNB	✔✔	✘✘	✘✘	✔	✔	✘✘	✔	n	C	
Moro	CAD	✔✔	✔	✔	✘	✔	✔✔	✘	Y	n˜	
Munchies	NES	✔	?	8	✔✔	?	✘	✘	Y	n	a
Murray Mints	CAD	✔✔	✔	✔	✘	✔	✔✔	✘	Y	n	
Neapolitans	UNB	✔✔	✘✘	✘✘	✔	✔	✘✘	✔	n	C	
Nerds	CAD	✔✔	✔	✔	✘	✔	✔✔	✘	Y	n	
Nestle's Milky Bar	NES	✔	?	✘	✔✔	?	✘	✘	Y	n	a
Novo	NES	✔	?	✘	✔✔	?	✘	✘	Y	n	a
Nussini	PHM	✘	?	?	✘✘	?	✘✘	✘	y	n	AT
Nutcracker	UNB	✔✔	✘✘	✘✘	✔	✔	✘✘	✔	n	C	
Nuttals	UNB	✔✔	✘✘	✘✘	✔	✔	✘✘	✔	n	C	

		![]	![]	![]	![]	![]	![]	![]	![]	![]	Alert!
Old Jamaica	CAD	✓✓	✓	✓	✗	✓	✓✓	✗	Y	n	
Opal Fruits	MAR	✓	✓	?	?	✓	✓✓	✗	n	n	
Pascall	CAD	✓✓	✓	✓	✗	✓	✓✓	✗	Y	n	
Picnic	CAD	✓✓	✓	✓	✗	✓	✓✓	✗	Y	n	
Pointers	MAR	✓	✓	?	?	✓	✓✓	✗	n	n	
Polo	NES	✓	?	✗	✓✓	?	✗	✗	Y	n	a
Poulain	CAD	✓✓	✓	✓	✗	✓	✓✓	✗	Y	n	
Pyramint	UNB	✓✓	✗✗	✗✗	✓	✓	✗✗	✓	n	C	
Quality Street	NES	✓	?	✗	✓✓	?	✗	✗	Y	n	a
Red Tulip	CAD	✓✓	✓	✓	✗	✓	✓✓	✗	Y	n	
Revels	MAR	✓	✓	?	?	✓	✓✓	✗	n	n	
Rolo	NES	✓	?	✗	✓✓	?	✗	✗	Y	n	a
Roses	CAD	✓✓	✓	✓	✗	✓	✓✓	✗	Y	n	
Rowntree	NES	✓	?	✗	✓✓	?	✗	✗	Y	n	a
Royal Mint	CAD	✓✓	✓	✓	✗	✓	✓✓	✗	Y	n	
Secret	NES	✓	?	✗	✓✓	?	✗	✗	Y	n	a
Sharp	CAD	✓✓	✓	✓	✗	✓	✓✓	✗	Y	n	
Shortcake Snack	CAD	✓✓	✓	✓	✗	✓	✓✓	✗	Y	n	
Silk	CAD	✓✓	✓	✓	✗	✓	✓✓	✗	Y	n	
Skittles	MAR	✓	✓	?	?	✓	✓✓	✗	n	n	
Smarties	NES	✓	?	✗	✓✓	?	✗	✗	Y	n	a
Smith Kendon	UNB	✓✓	✗✗	✗✗	✓	✓	✗✗	✓	n	C	
Snickers	MAR	✓	✓	?	?	✓	✓✓	✗	n	n	
Spartan	UNB	✓✓	✗✗	✗✗	✓	✓	✗✗	✓	n	C	
Spira	CAD	✓✓	✓	✓	✗	✓	✓✓	✗	Y	n	
Strollers	CAD	✓✓	✓	✓	✗	✓	✓✓	✗	Y	n	
Suchard	PHM	✗	?	?	✗✗	?	✗✗	✗	y	n	AT
Terry's of York	UNB	✓✓	✗✗	✗✗	✓	✓	✗✗	✓	n	C	

			♀								Alert!
Tiffin	CAD	✓✓	✓	✓	✗	✓	✓✓	✗	Y	n	
Toblerone	PHM	✗	?	?	✗✗	?	✗✗	✗	y	n	AT
Toffee Crisp	NES	✓	?	✗	✓✓	?	✗	✗	Y	n	a
Toffo	NES	✓	?	✗	44	?	✗	✗	Y	n	a
Tooty Frooties	NES	✓	?	✗	✓✓	?	✗	✗	Y	n	a
Topic	MAR	✓	✓	?	?	✓	✓✓	✗	n	n	
Touch of Class	UNB	✓✓	✗✗	✗✗	✓	✓	✗✗	✓	n	C	
Tracker	MAR	✓	✓	?	?	✓	✓✓	✗	n	n	
Trebor Mints	CAD	✓✓	✓	✓	✗	✓	✓✓	✗	Y	n	
Trebor Refreshers	CAD	✓✓	✓	✓	✗	✓	✓✓	✗	Y	n	
Triple X	NES	✓	?	✗	✓✓	?	✗	✗	Y	n	a
Tunes	MAR	✓	✓	?	?	✓	✓✓	✗	n	n	
Turkish Delight	CAD	✓✓	✓	✓	✗	✓	✓✓	✗	Y	n	
Twilight	PHM	✗	?	?	✗✗	?	✗✗	✗	y	n	AT
Twirl	CAD	✓✓	✓	✓	✗	✓	✓✓	✗	Y	n	
Twix	MAR	✓	✓	?	?	✓	✓✓	✗	n	n	
Velvet	UNB	✓✓	✗✗	✗✗	✓	✓	✗✗	✓	n	C	
Waifa	UNB	✓✓	✗✗	✗✗	✓	✓	✗✗	✓	n	C	
Walnut Whips	NES	✓	?	✗	✓✓	?	✗	✗	Y	n	a
Weekend	NES	✓	?	✗	✓✓	?	✗	✗	Y	n	a
Wholenut	CAD	✓✓	✓	✓	✗	✓	✓✓	✗	Y	n	
Wildlife Bar	CAD	✓✓	✓	✓	✗	✓	✓✓	✗	Y	n	
Wispa	CAD	✓✓	✓	✓	✗	✓	✓✓	✗	Y	n	
York Fruits	UNB	✓✓	✗✗	✗✗	✓	✓	✗✗	✓	n	C	
Yorkie	NES	✓	?	✗	✓✓	?	✗	✗	Y	n	a
COOKING APPLIANCES											
Ariston	MRL	✗✗	?	?	✗✗	?	✓✓	?	n	n	
British Gas	BRG	✓✓	✓	✗	✓	✓	✓✓	✗	n	n	

											Alert!
Cannon	GEC	✓✓	✓	✓	✗	✓	✓✓	✗	Y	n	M
Creda	GEC	✓✓	✓	✓	✗	✓	✓✓	✗	Y	n	M
Indesit	MRL	✗✗	?	?	✗✗	?	✓✓	?	n	n	
Main	ELE	✗	?	?	✗✗	?	✓✓	?	n	n	
Moffat	ELE	✗	?	?	✗✗	?	✓✓	?	n	n	
New World	BCI	✓	✗	✗✗	✗	✓	✓✓	✗	Y	n	
Parkinson Cowan	ELE	✗	?	?	✗✗	?	✓✓	?	n	n	
Philips/Whirlpool	PHI	✗	?	?	✓	✓	✓✓	✗	Y	n	M
Tricity	ELE	✗	?	?	✗✗	?	✓✓	?	n	n	
Zanussi	ELE	✗	?	?	✗✗	?	✓✓	?	n	n	
COSMETICS AND SKIN CARE											
2nd Debut	SKB	✗	?	?	✓	?	✓	?	Y	C	
All Fresh Wipes	SKB	✗	?	?	✓	?	✓	?	Y	C	
Almay	MCF	✗✗	?	?	✗✗	?	✓✓	?	y	n	
Ambre Solaire	LOR	✓	✓	✗✗	✓	✓	✗	?	y	n	
Astral	UNL	✓✓	✓	✓✓	✓	✓	✗	✓✓	Y	n	AT
Atrixo	SMN	✗	?	?	✗	✗	✓	✗	Y	n	
Avon	AVN	✓	✗	✗✗	✓	✓	✓✓	?	n	n	
Biactol	PAG	✓✓	✓	✓✓	✗	✓	✗	✓	y	n	
Cacharel	LOR	✓	✓	✗✗	✓	✓	✗	?	y	n	
Clearasil	PAG	✓✓	✓	✓✓	✗	✓	✗	✓	y	n	
Cleopatra	COP	✓✓	✗	✗	✗✗	✓	✗	✓	Y	n	
Colourings	BOD	✓✓	✗	✗✗	✓✓	✓	✓✓	✓✓	n	n	
Cutex	UNL	✓✓	✓	✓✓	✓	✓	✗	✓✓	Y	n	AT
Delph	PAG	✓✓	✓	✓✓	✗	✓	✗	✓	y	n	
Dermacare	UNL	✓✓	✓	✓✓	✓	✓	✗	✓✓	Y	n	AT
Helena Rubinstein	LOR	✓	✓	✗✗	✓	✓	✗	?	y	n	
L'Oréal	LOR	✓	✓	✗✗	✓	✓	✗	?	y	n	

		⚷	♀	〔	🏭	🌳	🐷	🐰	☕	⊗	Alert!
Lancome	LOR	✓	✓	✗✗	✓	✓	✗	?	y	n	
Max Factor	PAG	✓✓	✓	✓✓	✗	✓	✗	✓	y	n	
Natural Collection	BOO	✗	?	?	✗	✗✗	✓	✗	Y	n	
Nature's Choice	TES	✓✓	✗	✗✗	✓✓	✓✓	✓✓	✗	n	n	at
Nature's Compliments	JSA	✓✓	✓✓	✓✓	✓	✓✓	✓✓	✗	n	n	at
Nivea	SMN	✗	?	?	✗	✗	✓	✗	Y	n	
No 17	BOO	✗	?	?	✗	✗✗	✓	✗	Y	n	
No 7	BOO	✗	?	?	✗	✗✗	✓	✗	Y	n	
Noxelle	PAG	✓✓	✓	✓✓	✗	✓	✗	✓	y	n	
Oil of Ulay	PAG	✓✓	✓	✓✓	✗	✓	✗	✓	y	n	
Ponds	UNL	✓✓	✓	✓✓	✓	✓	✗	✓✓	Y	n	AT
Pure & Simple	SKB	✗	?	?	✓	?	✓	?	Y	C	
Quickies	SKB	✗	?	?	✓	?	✓	?	Y	C	
ROC*	GUI	✓	✗✗	✗✗	✓✓	?	?	?	y	n	A
Revlon	MCF	✗✗	?	?	✗✗	?	✓✓	?	y	n	
Rimmel	UNL	✓✓	✓	✓✓	✓	✓	✗	✓✓	Y	n	AT
Simple	SMN	✗	?	?	✗	✗	✓	✗	Y	n	
Soltan	BOO	✗	?	?	✗	✗✗	✓	✗	Y	n	
The Body Shop	BOD	✓✓	✗	✗✗	✓✓	✓	✓✓	✓✓	n	n	
Timotei	UNL	✓✓	✓	✓✓	✓	✓	✗	✓✓	Y	n	AT
Vaseline	UNL	✓✓	✓	✓✓	✓	✓	✗	✓✓	Y	n	AT
Veet	REC	✗	?	✗	✗✗	?	✗	?	Y	C	
Vichy	LOR	✓	✓	✗✗	✓	✓	✗	?	y	n	
j	JSA	✓✓	✓✓	✓✓	✓	✓✓	✓✓	✗	n	n	at
DIY AND GARDENING PRODUCTS											
Acorn	WIH	✗✗	?	?	✗✗	?	✓✓	?	Y	C	M
Actellic	ICI	✓	✓	✗✗	✓✓	✓	✗	✗	Y	n	M
Anaglypta	WIH	✗✗	?	?	✗✗	?	✓✓	?	Y	C	M

											Alert!
Ant Gun	ICI	✓	✓	✗✗	✓✓	✓	✗	✗	Y	n	M
Aquaseal	BRP	✓	✓	✓✓	✓	✗	✗	✗	Y	n	tM
Atco	BCI	✓	✗	✗✗	✗	✓	✓✓	✗	Y	n	
Benlate	DUP	✓	?	?	✗✗	✗	✗	✗	n	n	tm
Bolt	SCJ	✓	✗	✗✗	✓✓	✓	✗	✓✓	Y	n	
Bop Insecticide	BRP	✓	✓	✓✓	✓	✗	✗	✗	Y	n	tM
Clariflow	BCI	✓	✗	✗✗	✗	✓	✓✓	✗	Y	n	
Clean Up	ICI	✓	✓	✗✗	✓✓	✓	✗	✗	Y	n	M
Cuprinol	WIH	✗✗	?	?	✗✗	?	✓✓	?	Y	C	M
Dulux	ICI	✓	✓	✗✗	✓✓	✓	✗	✗	Y	n	M
Ferrocrete	BCI	✓	✗	✗✗	✗	✓	✓✓	✗	Y	n	
Floret	REC	✗	?	✗	✗✗	?	✗	?	Y	C	
Flymo	ELE	✗	?	?	✗✗	?	✓✓	?	n	n	
Greensward	ICI	✓	✓	✗✗	✓✓	✓	✗	✗	Y	n	M
Homestyle By Fads	BOO	✗	?	?	✗	✗✗	✓	✗	Y	n	
Husqvarna	ELE	✗	?	?	✗✗	?	✓✓	?	n	n	
Imperator	ICI	✓	✓	✗✗	✓✓	✓	✗	✗	Y	n	M
Jonelle	JLP	✗	?	✗✗	✓	?	✓✓	✗	n	n	
Keri-root	ICI	✓	✓	✗✗	✓✓	✓	✗	✗	Y	n	M
Larch-Lap	WIH	✗✗	?	?	✗✗	?	✓✓	?	Y	C	M
Lawnweed	ICI	✓	✓	✗✗	✓✓	✓	✗	✗	Y	n	M
Lifeguard Fly Killer	SCJ	✓	✗	✗✗	✓✓	✓	✗	✓✓	Y	n	
Lightening	BCI	✓	✗	✗✗	✗	✓	✓✓	✗	Y	n	
Mason Master	WIH	✗✗	?	?	✗✗	?	✓✓	?	Y	C	M
Mouser	ICI	✓	✓	✗✗	✓✓	✓	✗	✗	Y	n	M
Nimrod	ICI	✓	✓	✗✗	✓✓	✓	✗	✗	Y	n	M
Norlett	ELE	✗	?	?	✗✗	?	✓✓	?	n	n	
Pathclear	ICI	✓	✓	✗✗	✓✓	✓	✗	✗	Y	n	M

		![binoculars]	![female]	![monkey]	![house]	![tree]	![rabbit]	![bowl]	![bottle]	![ring]	Alert!
Pheonix	BCI	✔	✘	✘✘	✘	✔	✔✔	✘	Y	n	
Polycell	WIH	✘✘	?	?	✘✘	?	✔✔	?	Y	C	M
Polyfilla	WIH	✘✘	?	?	✘✘	?	✔✔	?	Y	C	M
Portland	BCI	✔	✘	✘✘	✘	✔	✔✔	✘	Y	n	
Punch	DUP	✔	?	?	✘✘	✘	✘	✘	n	n	tm
Qualcast	BCI	✔	✘	✘✘	✘	✔	✔✔	✘	Y	n	
Raid	SCJ	✔	✘	✘✘	✔✔	✔	✘	✔✔	Y	n	
Rawlplug	WIH	✘✘	?	?	✘✘	?	✔✔	?	Y	C	M
Roseclear	ICI	✔	✔	✘✘	✔✔	✔	✘	✘	Y	n	M
Sherley's	SAL	✘✘	?	?	✘✘	?	?	✘	Y	n	
Snowcrete	BCI	✔	✘	✘✘	✘	✔	✔✔	✘	Y	n	
Strike	ICI	✔	✔	✘✘	✔✔	✔	✘	✘	Y	n	M
Sulfacrete	BCI	✔	✘	✘✘	✘	✔	✔✔	✘	Y	n	
Superglypta	WIH	✘✘	?	?	✘✘	?	✔✔	?	Y	C	M
Suttons	VOL	✔	?	?	✘✘	✔	✔✔	✔	n	n	M
Swish	WIH	✘✘	?	?	✘✘	?	✔✔	?	Y	C	M
Texas Homecare	LAD	✘	?	?	✘	✔	✔✔	✘	n	n	atG
Vamoose	SAL	✘✘	?	?	✘✘	?	?	✘	Y	n	
Vapona	SAL	✘✘	?	?	✘✘	?	?	✘	Y	n	
Verdone	ICI	✔	✔	✘✘	✔✔	✔	✘	✘	Y	n	M
Walcrete	BCI	✔	✘	✘✘	✘	✔	✔✔	✘	Y	n	
Weed Gun	ICI	✔	✔	✘✘	✔✔	✔	✘	✘	Y	n	M
Weedol	ICI	✔	✔	✘✘	✔✔	✔	✘	✘	Y	n	M
Yale	WIH	✘✘	?	?	✘✘	?	✔✔	?	Y	C	M
DIY RETAILERS											
A G Stanley	BOO	✘	?	?	✘	✘✘	✔	✘	Y	n	
B & Q	KIN	✔✔	✔✔	✘	✔	✔	✔✔	✘	n	C	t
Do It All *	BOO	✘	?	?	✘	✘✘	✔	✘	Y	n	

											Alert!
Do It All *	WHS	✗	?	?	✔	?	✔✔	✗	n	n	
FADS	BOO	✗	?	?	✗	✗✗	✔	✗	Y	n	
Halfords	BOO	✗	?	?	✗	✗✗	✔	✗	Y	n	
Homebase	JSA	✔✔	✔✔	✔✔	✔	✔✔	✔✔	✗	n	n	at
Texas	LAD	✗	?	?	✗	✔	✔✔	✗	n	n	atG
DAIRY PRODUCTS											
Anchor	NZD	✗✗	?	?	✗✗	?	?	?	n	n	
Balance	UGT	✔	?	✗	✗✗	?	✔✔	?	n	C	
Biovita	NES	✔	?	✗	✔✔	?	✗	✗	Y	n	a
Boursin	UNL	✔✔	✔	✔✔	✔	✔	✗	✔✔	Y	n	AT
Bressot	UNL	✔✔	✔	✔✔	✔	✔	✗	✔✔	Y	n	AT
Calcia	UGT	✔	?	✗	✗✗	?	✔✔	?	n	C	
Chambourcy	NES	✔	?	✗	✔✔	?	✗	✗	Y	n	a
Channel Islands	UGT	✔	?	✗	✗✗	?	✔✔	?	n	C	
Cheddarie	PHM	✗	?	?	✗✗	?	✗✗	✗	y	n	AT
Clover	MMB	✗✗	?	?	✗✗	?	✗✗	?	n	n	
Country Life	MMB	✗✗	?	?	✗✗	?	✗✗	?	n	n	
Cracker Barrel	PHM	✗	?	?	✗✗	?	✗✗	✗	y	n	AT
Dairylea	PHM	✗	?	?	✗✗	?	✗✗	✗	y	n	AT
Dale Farm	NOR	✔	?	✗	✗✗	✗✗	✔✔	?	n	n	
Danone	BSN	✗	?	?	✔	?	?	✗	n	n	A
Delight	UNL	✔✔	✔	✔✔	✔	✔	✗	✔✔	Y	n	AT
Eden Vale	GRM	✔✔	✔	✗	✔	✔	✔✔	✗	Y	n	Atg
Elmlea	UNL	✔✔	✔	✔✔	✔	✔	✗	✔✔	Y	n	AT
Express Dairy	GRM	✔✔	✔	✗	✔	✔	✔✔	✗	Y	n	Atg
Farmers Wife	UGT	✔	?	✗	✗✗	?	✔✔	?	n	C	
Fiendish Feet	UGT	✔	?	✗	✗✗	?	✔✔	?	n	C	
Fernleaf	NZD	✗✗	?	?	✗✗	?	?	?	n	n	

		🐇♀		🏠	🌳	🐇	🥁	🔫	⚙	Alert!
Flo-lite	NES	✔	?	✗	✔✔	?	✗	✗	Y	n	a
Fromage Frais	NES	✔	?	✗	✔✔	?	✗	✗	Y	n	a
Gold	UGT	✔	?	✗	✗✗	?	✔✔	?	n	C	
Golden Fern	NZD	✗✗	?	?	✗✗	?	?	?	n	n	
Hippopota	NES	✔	?	✗	✔✔	?	✗	✗	Y	n	a
Kraft	PHM	✗	?	?	✗✗	?	✗✗	✗	y	n	AT
Lockerbie	GRM	✔✔	✔	✗	✔	✔	✔✔	✗	Y	n	Atg
Mountain Maid	NZD	✗✗	?	?	✗✗	?	?	?	n	n	
Mr Cheese	MMB	✗✗	?	?	✗✗	?	✗✗	?	n	n	
Munch Bunch	GRM	✔✔	✔	✗	✔	✔	✔✔	✗	Y	n	Atg
Northern Dairies	NOR	✔	?	✗	✗✗	✗✗	✔✔	?	n	n	
Nouvelle	NES	✔	?	✗	✔✔	?	✗	✗	Y	n	a
Philadelphia	PHM	✗	?	?	✗✗	?	✗✗	✗	y	n	AT
Prize	UGT	✔	?	✗	✗✗	?	✔✔	?	n	C	
Real	UGT	✔	?	✗	✗✗	?	✔✔	?	n	C	
Shape	UGT	✔	?	✗	✗✗	?	✔✔	?	n	C	
Singles	PHM	✗	?	?	✗✗	?	✗✗	✗	y	n	AT
Ski	GRM	✔✔	✔	✗	✔	✔	✔✔	✗	Y	n	Atg
St Ivel	UGT	✔	?	✗	✗✗	?	✔✔	?	n	C	
Stripes	GRM	✔✔	✔	✗	✔	✔	✔✔	✗	Y	n	Atg
Thick & Creamy	MMB	✗✗	?	?	✗✗	?	✗✗	?	n	n	
Top C	MMB	✗✗	?	?	✗✗	?	✗✗	?	n	n	
Tuxford & Tebbutt	GRM	✔✔	✔	✗	✔	✔	✔✔	✗	Y	n	Atg
Unigate	UGT	✔	?	✗	✗✗	?	✔✔	?	n	C	
Wholemilk	UGT	✔	?	✗	✗✗	?	✔✔	?	n	C	
Willow	MMB	✗✗	?	?	✗✗	?	✗✗	?	n	n	
DEODORANTS AND FRAGRANCES											
Audace	UNL	✔✔	✔	✔✔	✔	✔	✗	✔✔	Y	n	AT

		🐾	♀	🔪	🏭	🌳	🐇	🧴	🧪	🥨	Alert!
Avon •	AVN	✓	✗	✗✗	✓	✓	✓✓	?	n	n	
Blue Grass	UNL	✓✓	✓	✓✓	✓	✓	✗	✓✓	Y	n	AT
Body Check Plus	SKB	✗	?	?	✓	?	✓	?	Y	C	
Body Mist	SKB	✗	?	?	✓	?	✓	?	Y	C	
Brut	UNL	✓✓	✓	✓✓	✓	✓	✗	✓✓	Y	n	AT
Brylcreem	SKB	✗	?	?	✓	?	✓	?	Y	C	
C'est la Vie *	GUI	✓	✗✗	✗✗	✓✓	?	?	?	y	n	A
Cachet	UNL	✓✓	✓	✓✓	✓	✓	✗	✓✓	Y	n	AT
Calvin	UNL	✓✓	✓	✓✓	✓	✓	✗	✓✓	Y	n	AT
Chloe	UNL	✓✓	✓	✓✓	✓	✓	✗	✓✓	Y	n	AT
Denim	UNL	✓✓	✓	✓✓	✓	✓	✗	✓✓	Y	n	AT
Dry	PZO	✗	?	?	✗✗	?	✓✓	✗	n	n	
Eau Fraiche	UNL	✓✓	✓	✓✓	✓	✓	✗	✓✓	Y	n	AT
Elizabeth Arden	UNL	✓✓	✓	✓✓	✓	✓	✗	✓✓	Y	n	AT
Eternity	UNL	✓✓	✓	✓✓	✓	✓	✗	✓✓	Y	n	AT
Fahrenheit *	GUI	✓	✗✗	✗✗	✓✓	?	?	?	y	n	A
Fendi	UNL	✓✓	✓	✓✓	✓	✓	✗	✓✓	Y	n	AT
Fendi Uomo	UNL	✓✓	✓	✓✓	✓	✓	✗	✓✓	Y	n	AT
Fenjal	SKB	✗	?	?	✓	?	✓	?	Y	C	
Giorgio	AVN	✓	✗	✗✗	✓	✓	✓✓	?	n	n	
Hero	UNL	✓✓	✓	✓✓	✓	✓	✗	✓✓	Y	n	AT
Impulse	UNL	✓✓	✓	✓✓	✓	✓	✗	✓✓	Y	n	AT
KL	UNL	✓✓	✓	✓✓	✓	✓	✗	✓✓	Y	n	AT
Kyomi	UNL	✓✓	✓	✓✓	✓	✓	✗	✓✓	Y	n	AT
Largerfield for Men	UNL	✓✓	✓	✓✓	✓	✓	✗	✓✓	Y	n	AT
Limara	SMN	✗	?	?	✗	✗	✓	✗	Y	n	
Lynx	UNL	✓✓	✓	✓✓	✓	✓	✗	✓✓	Y	n	AT
Natrel Plus	GIL	✗	?	?	✓	?	✗	?	Y	n	

		![]	♀	![]	![]	![]	![]	![]	![]	![]	Alert!
Noir Essentials	UNL	✓✓	✓	✓✓	✓	✓	✗	✓✓	Y	n	AT
Obsession	UNL	✓✓	✓	✓✓	✓	✓	✗	✓✓	Y	n	AT
Old Spice	PAG	✓✓	✓	✓✓	✗	✓	✗	✓	y	n	
Passion	UNL	✓✓	✓	✓✓	✓	✓	✗	✓✓	Y	n	AT
Poison *	GUI	✓	✗✗	✗✗	✓✓	?	?	?	y	n	A
Red Door	UNL	✓✓	✓	✓✓	✓	✓	✗	✓✓	Y	n	AT
Right Guard	GIL	✗	?	?	✓	?	✗	?	Y	n	
Sante Fe	PAG	✓✓	✓	✓✓	✗	✓	✗	✓	y	n	
Simple	SMN	✗	?	?	✗	✗	✓	✗	Y	n	
Sixth Sense	SKB	✗	?	?	✓	?	✓	?	Y	C	
Slazenger Sport	SKB	✗	?	?	✓	?	✓	?	Y	C	
Soft & Dry	GIL	✗	?	?	✓	?	✗	?	Y	n	
Soft & Gentle	COP	✓✓	✗	✗	✗✗	✓	✗	✓	Y	n	
Sure	UNL	✓✓	✓	✓✓	✓	✓	✗	✓✓	Y	n	AT
Ysatis *	GUI	✓	✗✗	✗✗	✓✓	?	?	?	y	n	A
DEPARTMENT AND VARIETY STORES											
Argos	ARG	✓✓	✗✗	✗✗	✗✗	✓	✓✓	✗	n	n	
Army & Navy Stores	HOU	✗✗	?	?	✓	?	?	✗	n	n	
Arnotts	HOU	✗✗	?	?	✓	?	?	✗	n	n	
Astral Sports & Leis	HOU	✗✗	?	?	✓	?	?	✗	n	n	
Bainbridge	JLP	✗	?	✗✗	✓	?	✓✓	✗	n	n	
Barkers	HOU	✗✗	?	?	✓	?	?	✗	n	n	
Best Sellers	ARG	✓✓	✗✗	✗✗	✗✗	✓	✓✓	✗	n	n	
BhS	STH	✗✗	?	?	✓	?	✗✗	✗	n	n	
Binns	HOU	✗✗	?	?	✓	?	?	✗	n	n	
Bonds	JLP	✗	?	✗✗	✓	?	✓✓	✗	n	n	
Boots	BOO	✗	?	?	✗	✗✗	✓	✗	Y	n	
Burberrys	GUS	✗	?	?	✗✗	?	?	✗	Y	n	

		🔍	♀	⟨	🏭	🌲	🐰	🧴	👁	🐾	Alert!
C & A	CAA	✗	?	?	?	✗	✓✓	✓	n	n	
Caleys	JLP	✗	?	✗✗	✓	?	✓✓	✗	n	n	
Cavendish House	HOU	✗✗	?	?	✓	?	?	✗	n	n	
Chanelle	HOU	✗✗	?	?	✓	?	?	✗	n	n	
Childrens World	BOO	✗	?	?	✗	✗✗	✓	✗	Y	n	
Cole Brothers	JLP	✗	?	✗✗	✓	?	✓✓	✗	n	n	
Concepts	CWS	✓✓	✓	✗	✓✓	✓	✓✓	✓	n	L	at
David Evans	HOU	✗✗	?	?	✓	?	?	✗	n	n	
Debenhams	BUR	✗✗	?	?	✗	?	?	✗	n	n	
Dingles	HOU	✗✗	?	?	✓	?	?	✗	n	n	
Discount Drug Co	BOO	✗	?	?	✗	✗✗	✓	✗	Y	n	
Fortnum & Masons	ABF	✗✗	?	?	✗✗	?	?	✗	Y	n	a
Frasers	HOU	✗✗	?	?	✓	?	?	✗	n	n	
George Henry Lee	JLP	✗	?	✗✗	✓	?	✓✓	✗	n	n	
Habitat	STH	✗✗	?	?	✓	?	✗✗	✗	n	n	
Hammonds	HOU	✗✗	?	?	✓	?	?	✗	n	n	
Harrods	HOU	✗✗	?	?	✓	?	?	✗	n	n	
Heelas	JLP	✗	?	✗✗	✓	?	✓✓	✗	n	n	
Homewise	CWS	✓✓	✓	✗	✓✓	✓	✓✓	✓	n	L	at
Index	LIT	✗	?	✓	✗✗	?	?	✓	n	n	tG
Jessop & Son	JLP	✗	?	✗✗	✓	?	✓✓	✗	n	n	
John Lewis	JLP	✗	?	✗✗	✓	?	✓✓	✗	n	n	
Jollys	HOU	✗✗	?	?	✓	?	?	✗	n	n	
Kendals	HOU	✗✗	?	?	✓	?	?	✗	n	n	
Knight & Lee	JLP	✗	?	✗✗	✓	?	✓✓	✗	n	n	
Lillywhites	THF	✗	?	?	✗✗	?	✓✓	?	n	C	at
Littlewoods	LIT	✗	?	✓	✗✗	?	?	✓	n	n	tG
Marks & Spencer	MKS	✗	✗	✗✗	✓	✓	✓✓	✗	n	C	a

											Alert!
Millets Leisure	SEA	✗	?	?	✗✗	?	✓✓	✗	n	C	at
Mothercare	STH	✗✗	?	?	✓	?	✗✗	✗	n	n	
Mowells	HOU	✗✗	?	?	✓	?	?	✗	n	n	
Olympus Outdoor Wrld	SEA	✗	?	?	✗✗	?	✓✓	✗	n	C	at
Olympus Sport	SEA	✗	?	?	✗✗	?	✓✓	✗	n	C	at
Peter Jones	JLP	✗	?	✗✗	✓	?	✓✓	✗	n	n	
Rackhams	HOU	✗✗	?	?	✓	?	?	✗	n	n	
Robert Sayle	JLP	✗	?	✗✗	✓	?	✓✓	✗	n	n	
Savacentre	JSA	✓✓	✓✓	✓✓	✓	✓✓	✓✓	✗	n	n	at
Schofields	HOU	✗✗	?	?	✓	?	?	✗	n	n	
Scotch House	GUS	✗	?	?	✗✗	?	?	✗	Y	n	
Selfridges	SEA	✗	?	?	✗✗	?	✓✓	✗	n	C	at
Shopping Giant	CWS	✓✓	✓	✗	✓✓	✓	✓✓	✓	n	L	at
Superdrug	KIN	✓✓	✓✓	✗	✓	✓	✓✓	✗	n	C	t
Taylor Drug	BOO	✗	?	?	✗	✗✗	✓	✗	Y	n	
Trewin Brothers	JLP	✗	?	✗✗	✓	?	✓✓	✗	n	n	
Tyrell & Green	JLP	✗	?	✗✗	✓	?	✓✓	✗	n	n	
Underwoods	BOO	✗	?	?	✗	✗✗	✓	✗	Y	n	
W H Smith	WHS	✗	?	?	✓	?	✓✓	✗	n	n	
Woolworths	KIN	✓✓	✓✓	✗	✓	✓	✓✓	✗	n	C	t
DESSERTS											
Ambrosia	CPC	✗	?	?	✗✗	?	✓✓	✗	n	n	
Angel Delight	PHM	✗	?	?	✗✗	?	✗✗	✗	y	n	AT
Best Foods	CPC	✗	?	?	✗✗	?	✓✓	✗	n	n	
Bird's	PHM	✗	?	?	✗✗	?	✗✗	✗	y	n	AT
Creamola	NES	✓	?	✗	✓✓	?	✗	✗	Y	n	a
Heinz	HEN	✓✓	✗	✗✗	✓	✓	✓✓	✓✓	n	n	
Instant Whip	PHM	✗	?	?	✗✗	?	✗✗	✗	y	n	AT

			♀	{	🏠	🌳	🐰	☕	⚥	🌍	Alert!
Lite Mousse	PHM	x	?	?	xx	?	xx	x	y	n	AT
Mr Kipling	RHM	x	?	?	x	?	?	x	n	C	
Mrs Peek's	BSN	x	?	?	✔	?	?	x	n	n	A
Pickerings	HIL	xx	?	?	xx	?	?	x	n	n	
Rowntree's Jelly	NES	✔	?	x	✔✔	?	x	x	Y	n	a
EGGS											
Daylay	HIL	xx	?	?	xx	?	?	x	n	n	
Deans Farm Eggs	DAL	✔✔	✔	x	xx	✔✔	xx	n	n	n	
Goldenlay	DAL	✔✔	✔	x	xx	✔✔	xx	n	n	n	
ELECTRICAL RETAILERS & RENTAL											
Atlantis	TEM	✔	x	✔	x	✔	✔✔	x	Y	n	M
Comet	KIN	✔✔	✔✔	x	✔	✔	✔✔	x	n	C	t
Concessions	TEM	✔	x	✔	x	✔	✔✔	x	Y	n	M
Currys	DIX	x	†	x	x	?	✔✔	x	n	n	
DER	TEM	✔	x	✔	x	✔	✔✔	x	Y	n	M
Dixons	DIX	x	?	x	x	?	✔✔	x	n	n	
Easiview	TEM	✔	x	✔	x	✔	✔✔	x	Y	n	M
Electronic Rentals	GRA	✔	xx	✔	x	?	✔✔	?	n	n	
Focus	TEM	✔	x	✔	x	✔	✔✔	x	Y	n	M
HMV	TEM	✔	x	✔	x	✔	✔✔	x	Y	n	M
Ketts	TEM	✔	x	✔	x	✔	✔✔	x	Y	n	M
Multibroadcast	TEM	✔	x	✔	x	✔	✔✔	x	Y	n	M
NSI	TEM	✔	x	✔	x	✔	✔✔	x	Y	n	M
Option 3	TEM	✔	x	✔	x	✔	✔✔	x	Y	n	M
Options	TEM	✔	x	✔	x	✔✔	✔✔	x	Y	n	M
Osaki	TEM	✔	x	✔	x	✔	✔✔	x	Y	n	M
Radio Rentals	TEM	✔	x	✔	x	✔	✔✔	x	Y	n	M
Rediffusion	GRA	✔	xx	✔	x	?	✔✔	?	n	n	

											Alert!
Rumbelows	TEM	✓	✗	✓	✗	✓	✓✓	✗	Y	n	M
Telerent	TEM	✓	✗	✓	✗	✓	✓✓	✗	Y	n	M
Value Vision	TEM	✓	✗	✓	✗	✓	✓✓	✗	Y	n	M
Videozone	TEM	✓	✗	✓	✗	✓	✓✓	✗	Y	n	M
Visionhire	GRA	✓	✗✗	✓	✗	?	✓✓	?	n	n	
ENTERTAINMENT											
1O	VIR	✗✗	?	?	✗	?	✓✓	?	n	n	
Circa	VIR	✗✗	?	?	✗	?	✓✓	?	n	n	
Columbia Pictures	SON	✓	✗	✗✗	✓	✓	✓✓	✓	n	n	
Goldcrest	BWG	✓	?	?	✗	✗✗	✓✓	n	n	C	AtG
Granada Television	GRA	✓	✗✗	✓	✗	?	✓✓	?	n	n	
Melody Radio	HAN	✗	?	?	✗	?	?	✗	Y	C	Tm
Odeon	TEM	✓	✗	✓	✗	✓	✓✓	✗	Y	n	M
Picture Music Am.	TEM	✓	✗	✓	✗	✓	✓✓	✗	Y	n	M
Picture Music Intl.	TEM	✓	✗	✓	✗	✓	✓✓	✗	Y	n	M
Satellite Television	WHS	✗	?	?	✓	?	✓✓	✗	n	n	
Sinclair	AMS	✗	?	✗✗	✗✗	✗✗	✓✓	✗	n	n	
Siren	VIR	✗✗	?	?	✗	?	✓✓	?	n	n	
Technicolor	MCF	✗✗	?	?	✗✗	?	✓✓	?	y	n	
Thames Television	TEM	✓	✗	✓	✗	✓	✓✓	✗	Y	n	M
Venture	VIR	✗✗	?	?	✗	?	✓✓	?	n	n	
WEA	TIW	✗✗	?	?	✗	?	?	?	y	n	
Warner Brothers	TIW	✗✗	?	?	✗	?	?	?	y	n	
Yorkshire Television	WHS	✗	?	?	✓	?	✓✓	✗	n	n	
EXTRACTS, GRAVY AND STOCK											
Bisto	RHM	✗	?	?	✗	?	?	✗	n	C	
Bovril	CPC	✗	?	?	✗✗	?	✓✓	✗	n	n	
Chicken Oxo	UNL	✓✓	✓	✓✓	✓	✓	✗	✓✓	Y	n	AT

		♁♀	⚤	🏠	🌱	🐇	🍲			Alert!
Gravy Boat	UNL	✓✓	✓	✓✓	✓	✓	✗	✓✓	Y	n	AT
Maggi	NES	✓	?	✗	✓✓	?	✗	✗	Y	n	a
Marmite	CPC	✗	?	?	✗✗	?	✓✓	✗	n	n	
Oxo	UNL	✓✓	✓	✓✓	✓	✓	✗	✓✓	Y	n	AT
FAST FOOD											
Boulangerie Francais	NOR	✓	?	✗	✗✗	✗✗	✓✓	?	n	n	
Burger King	GRM	✓✓	✓	✗	✓	✓	✓✓	✗	Y	n	Atg
Dunkin' Donuts	ALL	✓	?	✗✗	✗	✓	✓✓	✗	n	C	Atg
Kentucky Fried Chkn.	THF	✗	?	?	✗✗	?	✓✓	?	n	C	at
La Baguette Doree	NOR	✓	?	✗	✗✗	✗✗	✓✓	?	n	n	
McDonald's	MCD	✗✗	?	?	✗✗	?	✓✓	?	n	n	
Mister Donut	ALL	✓	?	✗✗	✗	✓	✓✓	✗	n	C	Atg
Panifico Italiano	NOR	✓	?	✗	✗✗	✗✗	✓✓	?	n	n	
FATS AND OILS											
Benedicta	BOK	✗✗	?	?	✗✗	?	?	?	n	n	
Blue Band	UNL	✓✓	✓	✓✓	✓	✓	✗	✓✓	Y	n	AT
Cookeen	UNL	✓✓	✓	✓✓	✓	✓	✗	✓✓	Y	n	AT
Crisp'n Dry	UNL	✓✓	✓	✓✓	✓	✓	✗	✓✓	Y	n	AT
Dante	UNL	✓✓	✓	✓✓	✓	✓	✗	✓✓	Y	n	AT
Delight	UNL	✓✓	✓	✓✓	✓	✓	✗	✓✓	Y	n	AT
Echo	UNL	✓✓	✓	✓✓	✓	✓	✗	✓✓	Y	n	AT
Flora	UNL	✓✓	✓	✓✓	✓	✓	✗	✓✓	Y	n	AT
Golden Crown	PHM	✗	?	?	✗✗	?	✗✗	✗	y	n	AT
Krona	UNL	✓✓	✓	✓✓	✓	✓	✗	✓✓	Y	n	AT
Lupin	PHM	✗	?	?	✗✗	?	✗✗	✗	y	n	AT
Mazola	CPC	✗	?	?	✗✗	?	✓✓	✗	n	n	
Mello	PHM	✗	?	?	✗✗	?	✗✗	✗	y	n	AT
Outline	UNL	✓✓	✓	✓✓	✓	✓	✗	✓✓	Y	n	AT

		🔍	♀	〈	🏭	🌳	🐇	☕	⑂	⊕	Alert!
Stork	UNL	✓✓	✓	✓✓	✓	✓	✗	✓✓	Y	n	AT
Summer County	UNL	✓✓	✓	✓✓	✓	✓	✗	✓✓	Y	n	AT
Vitalite	PHM	✗	?	?	✗✗	?	✗✗	✗	y	n	AT
White Cap	UNL	✓✓	✓	✓✓	✓	✓	✗	✓✓	Y	n	AT
FEMININE HYGIENE											
Bodyform	SCT	✓	✗✗	✗✗	✗✗	✓	✓✓	?	n	n	
Depend	KMB	✗✗	?	?	✗✗	✗	?	?	Y	n	
Dr. White's	SMN	✗	?	?	✗	✗	✓	✗	Y	n	
Ecosense	SMN	✗	?	?	✗	✗	✓	✗	Y	n	
Hi-Dri	KMB	✗✗	?	?	✗✗	✗	?	?	Y	n	
Kimdri	KMB	✗✗	?	?	✗✗	✗	?	?	Y	n	
Kimnet	KMB	✗✗	?	?	✗✗	✗	?	?	Y	n	
Kotex	KMB	✗✗	?	?	✗✗	✗	?	?	Y	n	
Libra	SCT	✓	✗✗	✗✗	✗✗	✓	✓✓	?	n	n	
Lightdays	KMB	✗✗	?	?	✗✗	✗	?	?	Y	n	
Lil-lets	SMN	✗	?	?	✗	✗	✓	✗	Y	n	
Lilia	SMN	✗	?	?	✗	✗	✓	✗	Y	n	
New Freedom	KMB	✗✗	?	?	✗✗	✗	?	?	Y	n	
Pennywise	SCT	✓	✗✗	✗✗	✗✗	✓	✓✓	?	n	n	
Poise	SMN	✗	?	?	✗	✗	✓	✗	Y	n	
Promise	KMB	✗✗	?	?	✗✗	✗	?	?	Y	n	
Pull-ups	KMB	✗✗	?	?	✗✗	✗	?	?	Y	n	
Simplicity	KMB	✗✗	?	?	✗✗	✗	?	?	Y	n	
Tampax	TAM	✗✗	?	?	✗✗	?	?	?	n	n	
FISH (CANNED AND SMOKED)											
Bluecrest	BOK	✗✗	?	?	✗✗	?	?	?	n	n	
Channel Foods	HIL	✗✗	?	?	✗✗	?	?	✗	n	n	
Clearwater	HIL	✗✗	?	?	✗✗	?	?	✗	n	n	

											Alert!
Gilchris	BOK	✗✗	?	?	✗✗	?	?	?	n	n	
John West	UNL	✓✓	✓	✓✓	✓	✓	✗	✓✓	Y	n	AT
Lochinvar	UNL	✓✓	✓	✓✓	✓	✓	✗	✓✓	Y	n	AT
Maconochies	HIL	✗✗	?	?	✗✗	?	?	✗	n	n	
Manx Seafoods	BOK	✗✗	?	?	✗✗	?	?	?	n	n	
Marine Harvest	UNL	✓✓	✓	✓✓	✓	✓	✗	✓✓	Y	n	AT
Newforge	BOK	✗✗	?	?	✗✗	?	?	?	n	n	
Pinneys	HIL	✗✗	?	?	✗✗	?	?	✗	n	n	
Richter	BOK	✗✗	?	?	✗✗	?	?	?	n	n	
Rob Roy	HIL	✗✗	?	?	✗✗	?	?	✗	n	n	
Rossfish	BOK	✗✗	?	?	✗✗	?	?	?	n	n	
StarKist	HEN	✓✓	✗	✗✗	✓	✓	✓✓	✓✓	n	n	
FISH (FROZEN)											
Birds Eye	UNL	✓✓	✓	✓✓	✓	✓	✗	✓✓	Y	n	AT
Captain's Table	UNL	✓✓	✓	✓✓	✓	✓	✗	✓✓	Y	n	AT
Lyons Seafoods	ALL	✓	?	✗✗	✗	✓	✓✓	✗	n	C	Atg
Young's	UNB	✓✓	✗✗	✗✗	✓	✓	✗✗	✓	n	C	
FLOOR COVERINGS											
Antron	DUP	✓	?	?	✗✗	✗	✗	✗	n	n	tm
C V Carpets	CVI	✓	?	✗	✗✗	?	✓✓	✗	Y	C	m
Donaghadee Carpets	CVI	✓	?	✗	✗✗	?	✓✓	✗	Y	C	m
Jonelle	JLP	✗	?	✗✗	✓	?	✓✓	✗	n	n	
Lancaster Carpets	CVI	✓	?	✗	✗✗	?	✓✓	✗	Y	C	m
Royal Ascot	CVI	✓	?	✗	✗✗	?	✓✓	✗	Y	C	m
Stainmaster	DUP	✓	?	?	✗✗	✗	✗	✗	n	n	tm
Wilton Royal Carpets	CVI	✓	?	✗	✗✗	?	✓✓	✗	Y	C	m
FOOD DRINKS											
Bournvita	HIL	✗✗	?	?	✗✗	?	?	✗	n	n	

											Alert!
Build-Up	NES	✔	?	✘	✔✔	?	✘	✘	Y	n	a
Cadburys	HIL	✘✘	?	?	✘✘	?	?	✘	n	n	
Cappuccino	NES	✔	?	✘	✔✔	?	✘	✘	Y	n	a
Caro Instant	NES	✔	?	✘	✔✔	?	✘	✘	Y	n	a
Choc-break	NES	✔	?	✘	✔✔	?	✘	✘	Y	n	a
Chococino	NES	✔	?	✘	✔✔	?	✘	✘	Y	n	a
Complan	BOO	✘	?	?	✘	✘✘	✔	✘	Y	n	
Dextro-Energy	CPC	✘	?	?	✘✘	?	✔✔	✘	n	n	
Flavia	MAR	✔	✔	?	?	✔	✔✔	✘	n	n	
Horlicks	SKB	✘	?	?	✔	?	✔	?	Y	C	
Klix	MAR	✔	✔	?	?	✔	✔✔	✘	n	n	
Mars Milk Drink	MAR	✔	✔	?	?	✔	✔✔	✘	n	n	
Milo	NES	✔	?	✘	✔✔	?	✘	✘	Y	n	a
Nesquik	NES	✔	?	✘	✔✔	?	✘	✘	Y	n	a
Shapers	BOO	✘	?	?	✘	✘✘	✔	✘	Y	n	
Slender	NES	✔	?	✘	✔✔	?	✘	✘	Y	n	a
Superquik	NES	✔	?	✘	✔✔	?	✘	✘	Y	n	a
FOOTWEAR											
Birthday	SEA	✘	?	?	✘✘	?	✔✔	✘	n	C	at
Carvela	HOU	✘✘	?	?	✔	?	?	✘	n	n	
Clarks	CJC	✘✘	?	?	✘✘	?	?	✘	y	n	
Dolcis	SEA	✘	?	?	✘✘	?	✔✔	✘	n	C	at
Hush Puppies	CJC	✘✘	?	?	✘✘	?	?	✘	y	n	
K Shoes	CJC	✘✘	?	?	✘✘	?	?	✘	y	n	
Manfield	SEA	✘	?	?	✘✘	?	✔✔	✘	n	C	at
Ravel	CJC	✘✘	?	?	✘✘	?	?	✘	y	n	
Roland Cartier	SEA	✘	?	?	✘✘	?	✔✔	✘	n	C	at
Saxone	SEA	✘	?	?	✘✘	?	✔✔	✘	n	C	at

											Alert!
Tuf	BOO	x	?	?	x	xx	✓	x	Y	n	
FOOTWEAR RETAILERS											
Cable & Co.	SEA	x	?	?	xx	?	✓✓	x	n	C	at
Clarks	CJC	xx	?	?	xx	?	?	x	y	n	
Dolcis	SEA	x	?	?	xx	?	✓✓	x	n	C	at
Freeman Hardy Willis	SEA	x	?	?	xx	?	✓✓	x	n	C	at
K Shoes	CJC	xx	?	?	xx	?	?	x	y	n	
Lilley & Skinner	SEA	x	?	?	xx	?	✓✓	x	n	C	at
Lord & Farmer	CJC	xx	?	?	xx	?	?	x	y	n	
Manfield	SEA	x	?	?	xx	?	✓✓	x	n	C	at
Peter Lord	CJC	xx	?	?	xx	?	?	x	y	n	
Pro Performance	SEA	x	?	?	xx	?	✓✓	x	n	C	at
Ravel	CJC	xx	?	?	xx	?	?	x	y	n	
Saxone	SEA	x	?	?	xx	?	✓✓	x	n	C	at
Shoe City	SEA	x	?	?	xx	?	✓✓	x	n	C	at
Shoe Express	SEA	x	?	?	xx	?	✓✓	x	n	C	at
Shoefayre	CWS	✓✓	✓	x	✓✓	✓	✓✓	✓	n	L	at
FRIDGES AND FREEZERS											
Ariston	MRL	xx	?	?	xx	?	✓✓	?	n	n	
Electrolux	ELE	x	?	?	xx	?	✓✓	?	n	n	
Hotpoint	GEC	✓✓	✓	✓	x	✓	✓✓	x	Y	n	M
Indesit	MRL	xx	?	?	xx	?	✓✓	?	n	n	
Lec	LEC	x	?	?	xx	?	✓✓	?	n	n	
Philips/Whirlpool	PHI	x	?	?	✓	✓	✓✓	x	Y	n	M
Zanussi	ELE	x	?	?	xx	?	✓✓	?	n	n	
FROZEN BAKED GOODS											
Home Bake	UNL	✓✓	✓	✓✓	✓	✓	x	✓✓	Y	n	AT
Jus-rol	GRM	✓✓	✓	x	✓	✓	✓✓	x	Y	n	Atg

		🔑	♀	{	🏭	🌳	🐰	👶	▽	🐾	Alert!
FROZEN DESSERTS											
Creme Vienna	NES	✔	?	✘	✔✔	?	✘	✘	Y	n	a
Fleur de Lys	GRM	✔✔	✔	✘	✔	✔	✔✔	✘	Y	n	Atg
Freshbake Foods	CAM	✘	?	?	✘	?	?	?	n	n	
Haagen-Dazs	GRM	✔✔	✔	✘	✔	✔	✔✔	✘	Y	n	Atg
Heinzel's	RHM	✘	?	?	✘	?	?	✘	n	C	
Mr Kipling	RHM	✘	?	?	✘	?	?	✘	n	C	
Sara Lee	SAL	✘✘	?	?	✘✘	?	?	✘	Y	n	
Sweet Trolley	UNL	✔✔	✔	✔✔	✔	✔	✘	✔✔	Y	n	AT
Thayer's	GRM	✔✔	✔	✘	✔	✔	✔✔	✘	Y	n	Atg
Weight Watchers	HEN	✔✔	✘	✘✘	✔	✔	✔✔	✔✔	n	n	
FROZEN PREPARED FOOD											
Healthy Options	UNL	✔✔	✔	✔✔	✔	✔	✘	✔✔	Y	n	AT
Heinz	HEN	✔✔	✘	✘✘	✔	✔	✔✔	✔✔	n	n	
Lean Cuisine	NES	✔	?	✘	✔✔	?	✘	✘	Y	n	a
Menu Master	UNL	✔✔	✔	✔✔	✔	✔	✘	✔✔	Y	n	AT
San Marco	UNB	✔✔	✘✘	✘✘	✔	✔	✘✘	✔	n	C	
Sharwood's	RHM	✘	?	?	✘	?	?	✘	n	C	
Steakhouse	UNL	✔✔	✔	✔✔	✔	✔	✘	✔✔	Y	n	AT
Tiffany	RHM	✘	?	?	✘	?	?	✘	n	C	
Weight Watchers	HEN	✔✔	✘	✘✘	✔	✔	✔✔	✔✔	n	n	
FROZEN VEGETABLES											
Birds Eye	UNL	✔✔	✔	✔✔	✔	✔	✘	✔✔	Y	n	AT
Country Club	UNL	✔✔	✔	✔✔	✔	✔	✘	✔✔	Y	n	AT
Findus	NES	✔	?	✘	✔✔	?	✘	✘	Y	n	a
Fleur de Lys	GRM	✔✔	✔	✘	✔	✔	✔✔	✘	Y	n	Atg
Green Giant	GRM	✔✔	✔	✘	✔	✔	✔✔	✘	Y	n	Atg
Peter's	GRM	✔✔	✔	✘	✔	✔	✔✔	✘	Y	n	Atg

		🔍	♀	〈	🏭	🌳	🐇	🦅	🌱	⚙	Alert!
Pullman Foods	BOK	✗✗	?	?	✗✗	?	?	?	n	n	
Ross	UNB	✓✓	✗✗	✗✗	✓	✓	✗✗	✓	n	C	
Thayer's	GRM	✓✓	✓	✗	✓	✓	✓✓	✗	Y	n	Atg
Young's	UNB	✓✓	✗✗	✗✗	✓	✓	✗✗	✓	n	C	
FRUIT AND VEGETABLES (CANNED)											
57 Varieties	HEN	✓✓	✗	✗✗	✓	✓	✓✓	✓✓	n	n	
Batchelors	UNL	✓✓	✓	✓✓	✓	✓	✗	✓✓	Y	n	AT
Bean Street Kids	HEN	✓✓	✗	✗✗	✓	✓	✓✓	✓✓	n	n	
Chesswood	RHM	✗	?	?	✗	?	?	✗	n	C	
Farrows	UNL	✓✓	✓	✓✓	✓	✓	✗	✓✓	Y	n	AT
Green Giant	GRM	✓✓	✓	✗	✓	✓	✓✓	✗	Y	n	Atg
HP Baked Beans	BSN	✗	?	?	✓	?	?	✗	n	n	A
Hartley	HIL	✗✗	?	?	✗✗	?	?	✗	n	n	
Haunted House	HEN	✓✓	✗	✗✗	✓	✓	✓✓	✓✓	n	n	
John West	UNL	✓✓	✓	✓✓	✓	✓	✗	✓✓	Y	n	AT
Lockwoods	HIL	✗✗	?	?	✗✗	?	?	✗	n	n	
Morrell	HIL	✗✗	?	?	✗✗	?	?	✗	n	n	
Morton	HIL	✗✗	?	?	✗✗	?	?	✗	n	n	
Noodle Doodles	HEN	✓✓	✗	✗✗	✓	✓	✓✓	✓✓	n	n	
Pickerings	HIL	✗✗	?	?	✗✗	?	?	✗	n	n	
Smedley's	HIL	✗✗	?	?	✗✗	?	?	✗	n	n	
FURNITURE RETAILERS											
Allied Maples	ASD	✓	✗✗	✗	✗✗	✓	✓✓	✗	n	n	at
Christie-Tyler	HIL	✗✗	?	?	✗✗	?	?	✗	n	n	
G-Plan	HIL	✗✗	?	?	✗✗	?	?	✗	n	n	
Habitat	STH	✗✗	?	?	✓	?	✗✗	✗	n	n	
Homer	HIL	✗✗	?	?	✗✗	?	?	✗	n	n	
Hygena	MFI	✗✗	?	?	✓	?	✓✓	✗	n	n	

			♀	![](	🏠	![](	🐰	![](	![](	![](	Alert!
Maxirace Furniture	MFI	xx	?	?	✔	?	✔✔	x	n	n	
Schreiber	MFI	xx	?	?	✔	?	✔✔	x	n	n	
Smallbone	WIH	xx	?	?	xx	?	✔✔	?	Y	C	M
Walker	HIL	xx	?	?	xx	?	?	x	n	n	
Williams Furniture	ASD	✔	xx	x	xx	✔	✔✔	x	n	n	at
HAIR CARE											
Alberto	ALB	xx	?	?	xx	?	x	?	y	n	
Alberto Balsam	ALB	xx	?	?	xx	?	x	?	y	n	
Alberto-Culver	ALB	xx	?	?	xx	?	x	?	y	n	
All Clear	UNL	✔✔	✔	✔✔	✔	✔	x	✔✔	Y	n	AT
Amami	SKB	x	?	?	✔	?	✔	?	Y	C	
Avon	AVN	✔	x	xx	✔	✔	✔✔	?	n	n	
Bristows	SKB	x	?	?	✔	?	✔	?	Y	C	
Brylcreem	SKB	x	?	?	✔	?	✔	?	Y	C	
Cossack	REC	x	?	x	xx	?	x	?	Y	C	
Cream Silk	UNL	✔✔	✔	✔✔	✔	✔	x	✔✔	Y	n	AT
Dimension	UNL	✔✔	✔	✔✔	✔	✔	x	✔✔	Y	n	AT
Dynasty	GIL	x	?	?	✔	?	x	?	Y	n	
Eclipse	GIL	x	?	?	✔	?	x	?	Y	n	
Elida Gibbs	UNL	✔✔	✔	✔✔	✔	✔	x	✔✔	Y	n	AT
Epic Waves	GIL	x	?	?	✔	?	x	?	Y	n	
Eugene	SAL	xx	?	?	xx	?	?	x	Y	n	
Falcon	SKB	x	?	?	✔	?	✔	?	Y	C	
Good News	GIL	x	?	?	✔	?	x	?	Y	n	
Harmony	UNL	✔✔	✔	✔✔	✔	✔	x	✔✔	Y	n	AT
Head and Shoulders	PAG	✔✔	✔	✔✔	x	✔	x	✔	y	n	
Herbelle	GIL	x	?	?	✔	?	x	?	Y	n	
Jafra	GIL	x	?	?	✔	?	x	?	Y	n	

		🔧	♀	⟨	🏭	🌳	🐰	🥫				Alert!
Natural Silk	ALB	✗✗	?	?	✗✗	?	✗	?		y	n	
Nature's Choice	TES	✓✓	✗	✗✗	✓✓	✓	✓✓	✓✓	✗	n	n	at
Nivea	SMN	✗	?	?	✗	✗	✓	✗		Y	n	
Once	REC	✗	?	✗	✗✗	?	✗	?		Y	C	
Palmolive	COP	✓✓	✗	✗	✗✗	✓	✗	✓		Y	n	
Pantene	PAG	✓✓	✓	✓✓	✗	✓	✗	✓		y	n	
Pears	UNL	✓✓	✓	✓✓	✓	✓	✗	✓✓		Y	n	AT
Pin-Up	UNL	✓✓	✓	✓✓	✓	✓	✗	✓✓		Y	n	AT
Pure & Clear	ALB	✗✗	?	?	✗✗	?	✗	?		y	n	
Restoria	SKB	✗	?	?	✓	?	✓	?		Y	C	
Salon Formula	PAG	✓✓	✓	✓✓	✗	✓	✗	✓		y	n	
Sebbix	SAL	✗✗	?	?	✗✗	?	?	✗		Y	n	
Shine	UNL	✓✓	✓	✓✓	✓	✓	✗	✓✓		Y	n	AT
Silvikrin	SKB	✗	?	?	✓	?	✓	?		Y	C	
Simple	SMN	✗	?	?	✗	✗	✓	✗		Y	n	
Slazenger Sport	SKB	✗	?	?	✓	?	✓	?		Y	C	
Sunsilk	UNL	✓✓	✓	✓✓	✓	✓	✗	✓✓		Y	n	AT
Supersoft	REC	✗	?	✗	✗✗	?	✗	?		Y	C	
Talisman	GIL	✗	?	?	✓	?	✗	?		Y	n	
The Body Shop	BOD	✓✓	✗	✗✗	✓✓	✓	✓✓	✓✓		n	n	
The Dry Look	GIL	✗	?	?	✓	?	✗	?		Y	n	
Timotei	UNL	✓✓	✓	✓✓	✓	✓	✗	✓✓		Y	n	AT
Toni	GIL	✗	?	?	✓	?	✗	?		Y	n	
Trugel	SAL	✗✗	?	?	✗✗	?	?	✗		Y	n	
VO5	ALB	✗✗	?	?	✗✗	?	✗	?		y	n	
Vidal Sassoon	PAG	✓✓	✓	✓✓	✗	✓	✗	✓		y	n	
Vitapoint	SAL	✗✗	?	?	✗✗	?	?	✗		Y	n	
Vosene	SKB	✗	?	?	✓	?	✓	?		Y	C	

		🔧♀	♀	🧴	🏭	🌲	🐇	🧪	▽	🔍	Alert!
Wash & Go	PAG	✓✓	✓	✓✓	✗	✓	✗	✓	y	n	
White Rain	GIL	✗	?	?	✓	?	✗	?	Y	n	
Wood Nymph	UNL	✓✓	✓	✓✓	✓	✓	✗	✓✓	Y	n	AT
HEALTH FOOD RETAILERS											
Gilberts Health Foods	HAN	✗	?	?	✗	?	?	✗	Y	C	Tm
Höfels	HAN	✗	?	?	✗	?	?	✗	Y	C	Tm
HEATING APPLIANCES/SYSTEMS											
Berry Magicoal	HAN	✗	?	?	✗	?	?	✗	Y	C	Tm
British Gas	BRG	✓✓	✓	✗	✓	✓	✓✓	✗	n	n	
Heatrae Sadia	WIH	✗✗	?	?	✗✗	?	✓✓	?	Y	C	M
Myson	BCI	✓	✗	✗✗	✗	✓	✓✓	✗	Y	n	
Potterton	BCI	✓	✗	✗✗	✗	✓	✓✓	✗	Y	n	
Robinson Willey	HAN	✗	?	?	✗	?	?	✗	Y	C	Tm
Valor	WIH	✗✗	?	?	✗✗	?	✓✓	?	Y	C	M
HOTELS											
Brent Walker Hotels	BWG	✓	?	?	✗	✗✗	✓✓	n	n	C	AtG
Country Club	WBR	✗	?	?	✗	?	✓✓	?	n	C	Atg
Country Lodge	BWG	✓	?	?	✗	✗✗	✓✓	n	n	C	AtG
Forte Crest	THF	✗	?	?	✗✗	?	✓✓	?	n	C	at
Forte Grand	THF	✗	?	?	✗✗	?	✓✓	?	n	C	at
Forte Heritage	THF	✗	?	?	✗✗	?	✓✓	?	n	C	at
Forte Posthouse	THF	✗	?	?	✗✗	?	✓✓	?	n	C	at
Forte Travelodge	THF	✗	?	?	✗✗	?	✓✓	?	n	C	at
Gleneagles Hotels	GUI	✓	✗✗	✗✗	✓✓	?	?	?	y	n	A
Granada Lodge	GRA	✓	✗✗	✓	✗	?	✓✓	?	n	n	
Hilton Hotels	LAD	✗	?	?	✗	✓	✓✓	✗	n	n	atG
Holiday Inns	BAS	✗	?	✗	✗✗	✓	✓✓	✗	y	n	AtG
Landsbury Hotels	WBR	✗	?	?	✗	?	✓✓	?	n	C	Atg

											Alert!
Metropole Hotels	LON	xx	?	?	xx	?	?	x	Y	n	AT
Osprey Hotels	BAS	x	?	x	xx	✔	✔✔	x	y	n	AtG
Toby Hotels	BAS	x	?	x	xx	✔	✔✔	x	y	n	AtG
Travel Inns	WBR	x	?	?	x	?	✔✔	?	n	C	Atg
Voyager Hotels	VIR	xx	?	?	x	?	✔✔	?	n	n	
Welcome Break	THF	x	?	?	xx	?	✔✔	?	n	C	at
HOUSEHOLD CLEANERS											
1001	PZO	x	?	?	xx	?	✔✔	x	n	n	
Airwick	REC	x	?	x	xx	?	x	?	Y	C	
Ajax	COP	✔✔	x	x	xx	✔	x	✔	Y	n	
Beaucare	SAL	xx	?	?	xx	?	?	x	Y	n	
Brillo	SCJ	✔	x	xx	✔✔	✔	x	✔✔	Y	n	
Classic	KMB	xx	?	?	xx	x	?	?	Y	n	
Cleen-o-Pine	REC	x	?	x	xx	?	x	?	Y	C	
Dabitoff	SAL	xx	?	?	xx	?	?	x	Y	n	
Dettol	REC	x	?	x	xx	?	x	?	Y	C	
Dettox	REC	x	?	x	xx	?	x	?	Y	C	
Dip	SAL	xx	?	?	xx	?	?	x	Y	n	
Domestos	UNL	✔✔	✔	✔✔	✔	✔	x	✔✔	Y	n	AT
Dual	UNL	✔✔	✔	✔✔	✔	✔	x	✔✔	Y	n	AT
Ecologic	AGY	x	?	?	xx	✔	✔✔	x	n	C	at
Fairy	PAG	✔✔	✔	✔✔	x	✔	x	✔	y	n	
Flash	PAG	✔✔	✔	✔✔	x	✔	x	✔	y	n	
Frish	UNL	✔✔	✔	✔✔	✔	✔	x	✔✔	Y	n	AT
Glade	SCJ	✔	x	xx	✔✔	✔	x	✔✔	Y	n	
Glade Shake 'N Vac	SCJ	✔	x	xx	✔✔	✔	x	✔✔	Y	n	
Goldilocks	REC	x	?	x	xx	?	x	?	Y	C	
Greencare	JSA	✔✔	✔✔	✔✔	✔	✔✔	✔✔	x	n	n	at

											Alert!
Greenforce	BRP	✔	✔	✔✔	✔	✗	✗	✗	Y	n	tM
Gumption	REC	✗	?	✗	✗✗	?	✗	?	Y	C	
Harpic	REC	✗	?	✗	✗✗	?	✗	?	Y	C	
Haze	REC	✗	?	✗	✗✗	?	✗	?	Y	C	
Jif	UNL	✔✔	✔	✔✔	✔	✔	✗	✔✔	Y	n	AT
Jonelle	JLP	✗	?	✗✗	✔	?	✔✔	✗	n	n	
Kimguard	KMB	✗✗	?	?	✗✗	✗	?	?	Y	n	
Kleenguard	KMB	✗✗	?	?	✗✗	✗	?	?	Y	n	
Lifebuoy	UNL	✔✔	✔	✔✔	✔	✔	✗	✔✔	Y	n	AT
Lifeguard	SCJ	✔	✗	✗✗	✔✔	✔	✗	✔✔	Y	n	
Liquid Soda Crystals	ICI	✔	✔	✗✗	✔✔	✔	✗	✗	Y	n	M
Lux	UNL	✔✔	✔	✔✔	✔	✔	✗	✔✔	Y	n	AT
Morning Fresh	PZO	✗	?	?	✗✗	?	✔✔	✗	n	n	
Mothaks	SAL	✗✗	?	?	✗✗	?	?	✗	Y	n	
Nilodor	PZO	✗	?	?	✗✗	?	✔✔	✗	n	n	
Nocturne	SAL	✗✗	?	?	✗✗	?	?	✗	Y	n	
Oven Pad	REC	✗	?	✗	✗✗	?	✗	?	Y	C	
Palmolive	COP	✔✔	✗	✗	✗✗	✔	✗	✔	Y	n	
Parador	SAL	✗✗	?	?	✗✗	?	?	✗	Y	n	
Persil	UNL	✔✔	✔	✔✔	✔	✔	✗	✔✔	Y	n	AT
Racalet	PZO	✗	?	?	✗✗	?	✔✔	✗	n	n	
Radion	UNL	✔✔	✔	✔✔	✔	✔	✗	✔✔	Y	n	AT
Rumours	PZO	✗	?	?	✗✗	?	✔✔	✗	n	n	
Soda Crystals	ICI	✔	✔	✗✗	✔✔	✔	✗	✗	Y	n	M
Spring	PZO	✗	?	?	✗✗	?	✔✔	✗	n	n	
Sqezy	UNL	✔✔	✔	✔✔	✔	✔	✗	✔✔	Y	n	AT
Sun	UNL	✔✔	✔	✔✔	✔	✔	✗	✔✔	Y	n	AT
Sunlight	UNL	✔✔	✔	✔✔	✔	✔	✗	✔✔	Y	n	AT

			♀		🏠	🌳	🐇			®	Alert!
Tesco Cares	TES	✓✓	✗	✗✗	✓✓	✓✓	✓✓	✗	n	n	at
Toilet Duck	SCJ	✓	✗	✗✗	✓✓	✓	✗	✓✓	Y	n	
Vortex	PAG	✓✓	✓	✓✓	✗	✓	✗	✓	y	n	
Waitrose	JLP	✗	?	✗✗	✓	?	✓✓	✗	n	n	
Windolene	REC	✗	?	✗	✗✗	?	✗	?	Y	C	
Wisk	UNL	✓✓	✓	✓✓	✓	✓	✗	✓✓	Y	n	AT
ICE CREAM											
Baskin-Robbins	ALL	✓	?	✗✗	✗	✓	✓✓	✗	n	C	Atg
Bertorelli	ALL	✓	?	✗✗	✗	✓	✓✓	✗	n	C	Atg
Bounty Ice Cream	MAR	✓	✓	?	?	✓	✓✓	✗	n	n	
Carte d'Or	UNL	✓✓	✓	✓✓	✓	✓	✗	✓✓	Y	n	AT
Cello	NES	✓	?	✗	✓✓	?	✗	✗	Y	n	a
Cornetto	UNL	✓✓	✓	✓✓	✓	✓	✗	✓✓	Y	n	AT
Dream	UNL	✓✓	✓	✓✓	✓	✓	✗	✓✓	Y	n	AT
Eskimo	NES	✓	?	✗	✓✓	?	✗	✗	Y	n	a
Favourite Centres	ALL	✓	?	✗✗	✗	✓	✓✓	✗	n	C	Atg
Feast	UNL	✓✓	✓	✓✓	✓	✓	✗	✓✓	Y	n	AT
Fresta	UNL	✓✓	✓	✓✓	✓	✓	✗	✓✓	Y	n	AT
Galaxy Dove Bar	MAR	✓	✓	?	?	✓	✓✓	✗	n	n	
Galaxy Rondos	MAR	✓	✓	?	?	✓	✓✓	✗	n	n	
Gino Ginelli	UNL	✓✓	✓	✓✓	✓	✓	✗	✓✓	Y	n	AT
Gold Seal	ALL	✓	?	✗✗	✗	✓	✓✓	✗	n	C	Atg
Häagen-Dazs	GRM	✓✓	✓	✗	✓	✓	✓✓	✗	Y	n	Atg
King Cone	ALL	✓	?	✗✗	✗	✓	✓✓	✗	n	C	Atg
Lyons Maid	ALL	✓	?	✗✗	✗	✓	✓✓	✗	n	C	Atg
Magnum	UNL	✓✓	✓	✓✓	✓	✓	✗	✓✓	Y	n	AT
Mars Ice Cream	MAR	✓	✓	?	?	✓	✓✓	✗	n	n	
Midland Counties	ALL	✓	?	✗✗	✗	✓	✓✓	✗	n	C	Atg

										Alert!
Milkmaid	NES	✔	?	✗	✔✔	?	✗	✗	Y	n	a
Milky Way Ice Cream	MAR	✔	✔	?	?	✔	✔✔	✗	n	n	
Monsoon	ALL	✔	?	✗✗	✗	✔	✔✔	✗	n	C	Atg
Mr Softee	ALL	✔	?	✗✗	✗	✔	✔✔	✗	n	C	Atg
Romantica	UNL	✔✔	✔	✔✔	✔	✔	✗	✔✔	Y	n	AT
Sky	UNL	✔✔	✔	✔✔	✔	✔	✗	✔✔	Y	n	AT
Snickers Ice Cream	MAR	✔	✔	?	?	✔	✔✔	✗	n	n	
Viennetta	UNL	✔✔	✔	✔✔	✔	✔	✗	✔✔	Y	n	AT
Wall's	UNL	✔✔	✔	✔✔	✔	✔	✗	✔✔	Y	n	AT
Weight Watchers	HEN	✔✔	✗	✗✗	✔	✔	✔✔✔	✔✔	n	n	
Winner	UNL	✔✔	✔	✔✔	✔	✔	✗	✔✔	Y	n	AT

KITCHEN PRODUCTS

											Alert!
Elizabeth Ann	BCI	✔	✗	✗✗	✗	✔	✔✔	✗	Y	n	
Prestige	AMB	✗	?	?	✗✗	✗	✔✔	✗	y	n	AT
Teflon	DUP	✔	?	?	✗✗	✗	✗	✗	n	n	tm

LAUNDRY PRODUCTS

											Alert!
Ariel	PAG	✔✔	✔	✔✔	✗	✔	✗	✔	y	n	
Bold 3	PAG	✔✔	✔	✔✔	✗	✔	✗	✔	y	n	
Bounce	PAG	✔✔	✔	✔✔	✗	✔	✗	✔	y	n	
Comfort	UNL	✔✔	✔	✔✔	✔	✔	✗	✔✔	Y	n	AT
Daz	PAG	✔✔	✔	✔✔	✗	✔	✗	✔	y	n	
Dreft	PAG	✔✔	✔	✔✔	✗	✔	✗	✔	y	n	
Fabulon	REC	✗	?	✗	✗✗	?	✗	?	Y	C	
Fairy	PAG	✔✔	✔	✔✔	✗	✔	✗	✔	y	n	
Frend	REC	✗	?	✗	✗✗	?	✗	?	Y	C	
Greencare	JSA	✔✔	✔✔	✔✔	✔	✔✔	✔✔	✗	n	n	at
Lenor	PAG	✔✔	✔	✔✔	✗	✔	✗	✔	y	n	
Liquid Soda Crystals	ICI	✔	✔	✗✗	✔✔	✔	✗	✗	Y	n	M

		⚙♀	♀	〈	🏭	🌳	🐑	🥫	🍶	🐰	Alert!
Lux	UNL	✓✓	✓	✓✓	✓	✓	✗	✓✓	Y	n	AT
Persil	UNL	✓✓	✓	✓✓	✓	✓	✗	✓✓	Y	n	AT
Reckitt's Blue	REC	✗	?	✗	✗✗	?	✗	?	Y	C	
Robin	REC	✗	?	✗	✗✗	?	✗	?	Y	C	
Shout	SCJ	✓	✗	✗✗	✓✓	✓	✗	✓✓	Y	n	
Soda Crystals	ICI	✓	✓	✗✗	✓✓	✓	✗	✗	Y	n	M
Softlan	COP	✓✓	✗	✗	✗✗	✓	✗	✓	Y	n	
Surf	UNL	✓✓	✓	✓✓	✓	✓	✗	✓✓	Y	n	AT
LEISURE											
Brent Walker Leisure	BWG	✓	?	?	✗	✗✗	✓✓	n	n	C	AtG
Champneys	GUI	✓	✗✗	✗✗	✓✓	?	?	?	y	n	A
Coral Entertainments	BAS	✗	?	✗	✗✗	✓	✓✓	✗	y	n	AtG
Coral Racing	BAS	✗	?	✗	✗✗	✓	✓✓	✗	y	n	AtG
Coral Snooker Club	BAS	✗	?	✗	✗✗	✓	✓✓	✗	y	n	AtG
Coral Social Clubs	BAS	✗	?	✗	✗✗	✓	✓✓	✗	y	n	AtG
Granada Bingo	BAS	✗	?	✗	✗✗	✓	✓✓	✗	y	n	AtG
Ladbroke Racing	LAD	✗	?	?	✗	✓	✓✓	✗	n	n	atG
Littlewoods	LIT	✗	?	✓	✗✗	?	?	✓	n	n	tG
Vernons Pools	LAD	✗	?	?	✗	✓	✓✓	✗	n	n	atG
William Hill	BWG	✓	?	?	✗	✗✗	✓✓	n	n	C	AtG
MEAT											
Bingham's	NOR	✓	?	✗	✗✗	✗✗	✓✓	?	n	n	
Bowyers	NOR	✓	?	✗	✗✗	✗✗	✓✓	?	n	n	
Culrose	HIL	✗✗	?	?	✗✗	?	?	✗	n	n	
Fray Bentos	UNL	✓✓	✓	✓✓	✓	✓	✗	✓✓	Y	n	AT
Harris Gold	HIL	✗✗	?	?	✗✗	?	?	✗	n	n	
Herta	NES	✓	?	✗	✓✓	?	✗	✗	Y	n	a
Holland's	NOR	✓	?	✗	✗✗	✗✗	✓✓	?	n	n	

											Alert
Lawson	UNL	✓✓	✓	✓✓	✓	✓	✗	✓✓	Y	n	AT
Mattessons	UNL	✓✓	✓	✓✓	✓	✓	✗	✓✓	Y	n	AT
Mecia	BOK	✗✗	?	?	✗✗	?	?	?	n	n	
Peperami	UNL	✓✓	✓	✓✓	✓	✓	✗	✓✓	Y	n	AT
Peter's Sav. Prods.	GRM	✓✓	✓	✗	✓	✓	✓✓	✗	Y	n	Atg
Pork Farms	NOR	✓	?	✗	✗✗	✗✗	✓✓	?	n	n	
Richmond	UNL	✓✓	✓	✓✓	✓	✓	✗	✓✓	Y	n	AT
Spam	BOK	✗✗	?	?	✗✗	?	?	?	n	n	
Steakhouse	UNL	✓✓	✓	✓✓	✓	✓	✗	✓✓	Y	n	AT
Sutherlands	HIL	✗✗	?	?	✗✗	?	?	✗	n	n	
Tyne Brand	MAR	✓	✓	?	?	✓	✓✓	✗	n	n	
Upper Crust	RHM	✗	?	?	✗	?	?	✗	n	C	
Wall's	UNL	✓✓	✓	✓✓	✓	✓	✗	✓✓	Y	n	AT
Wilsons	HIL	✗✗	?	?	✗✗	?	?	✗	n	n	
MILK (CANNED AND POWDERED)											
Carnation	NES	✓	?	✗	✓✓	?	✗	✗	Y	n	a
Coffee-Mate	NES	✓	?	✗	✓✓	?	✗	✗	Y	n	a
Dream Topping	PHM	✗	?	?	✗✗	?	✗✗	✗	y	n	AT
Fussell's	NES	✓	?	✗	✓✓	?	✗	✗	Y	n	a
Ideal	NES	✓	?	8	✓✓	?	✗	✗	Y	n	a
Marvel	HIL	✗✗	?	?	✗✗	?	†	✗	n	n	
Tip Top	NES	✓	?	✗	✓✓	?	✗	✗	Y	n	a
MINERAL WATER											
Ashbourne Water	NES	✓	?	✗	✓✓	?	✗	✗	Y	n	a
Badoit	BSN	✗	?	?	✓	?	?	✗	n	n	A
Evian	BSN	✗	?	?	✓	?	?	✗	n	n	A
Hepburn Spa	CAD	✓✓	✓	✓	✗	✓	✓✓	✗	Y	n	
Malvern	CAD	✓✓	✓	✓	✗	✓	✓✓	✗	Y	n	

											Alert!
Mountain Dew	PEP	✗	?	?	✗✗	✓	✗	✗	y	n	
Prysg	BWG	✓	?	?	✗	✗✗	✓✓	n	n	C	AtG
Pure Spring	CAD	✓✓	✓	✓	✗	✓	✓✓	✗	Y	n	
Vittel	NES	✓	?	✗	✓✓	?	✗	✗	Y	n	a
MISCELLANEOUS PRODUCTS											
Aero	CVI	✓	?	✗	✗✗	?	✓✓	✗	Y	C	m
Anchor	CVI	✓	?	✗	✗✗	?	✓✓	✗	Y	C	m
Aptan	CVI	✓	?	✗	✗✗	?	✓✓	✗	Y	C	m
Beehive	CVI	✓	?	✗	✗✗	?	✓✓	✗	Y	C	m
Chain	CVI	✓	?	✗	✗✗	?	✓✓	✗	Y	C	m
Cyclone	CVI	✓	?	✗	✗✗	?	✓✓	✗	Y	C	m
Drima	CVI	✓	?	✗	✗✗	?	✓✓	✗	Y	C	m
Dryad	REC	✗	?	✗	✗✗	?	✗	?	Y	C	
Dual Duty	CVI	✓	?	✗	✗✗	?	✓✓	✗	Y	C	m
Duet	CVI	✓	?	✗	✗✗	?	✓✓	✗	Y	C	m
Fisher Price	QOC	✗	?	?	✗✗	?	?	?	n	n	
Glasgow Herald	LON	✗✗	?	?	✗✗	?	?	✗	Y	n	AT
Koban	CVI	✓	?	✗	✗✗	?	✓✓	✗	y	C	m
Marie Claire	LOR	✓	✓	✗✗	✓	✓	✗	?	y	n	
Methuen	TOC	✗✗	?	?	✓	?	✓✓	✗	n	n	
Milwards	CVI	✓	?	✗	✗✗	?	✓✓	✗	Y	C	m
New Cavendish Books	TOC	✗✗	?	?	✓	?	✓✓	✗	n	n	
Nomotta	CVI	✓	?	✗	✗✗	?	✓✓	✗	Y	C	m
Observer	LON	✗✗	?	?	✗✗	?	?	✗	Y	n	AT
Patons	CVI	✓	?	✗	✗✗	?	✓✓	✗	Y	C	m
Penelope	CVI	✓	?	✗	✗✗	?	✓✓	✗	Y	C	m
Playbox Toys	ASD	✓	✗✗	✗	✗✗	✓	✓✓	✗	n	n	at
Red Heart	CVI	✓	?	✗	✗✗	?	✓✓	✗	Y	C	m

		👥	♀	〈	🏭	🌳	🍶	☕	🔊	Alert.
Reeves	REC	✗	?	✗	✗✗	?	✗	?	Y	C	
Routledge	TOC	✗✗	?	?	✔	?	✔✔	✗	n	n	
Slipspun	CVI	✔	?	✗	✗✗	?	✔✔	✗	Y	C	m
Sunny Jim	REC	✗	?	✗	✗✗	?	✗	?	Y	C	
Thomson Newspapers	TOC	✗✗	?	?	✔	?	✔✔	✗	n	n	
Trend	BRP	✔	✔	✔✔	✔	✗	✗	✗	Y	n	tM
Trident	CVI	✔	?	✗	✗✗	?	✔✔	✗	Y	C	m
Winton	REC	✗	?	✗	✗✗	?	✗	?	Y	C	
Zip Firelighters	REC	✗	?	✗	✗✗	?	✗	?	Y	C	
MISCELLANEOUS RETAILERS											
Bakers Oven	ABF	✗✗	?	?	✗✗	?	?	✗	Y	n	a
Cartier	RTH	✗✗	?	?	✗✗	?	?	✗	Y	C	T
Champion Sport	BUR	✗✗	?	?	✗	?	?	✗	n	n	
Children's World	BOO	✗	?	?	✗	✗✗	✔	✗	Y	n	
Dollond & Aitchison	AMB	✗	?	?	✗✗	✗	✔✔	✗	y	n	AT
Dunhill	RTH	✗✗	?	?	✗✗	?	?	✗	Y	C	T
Elizabeth Duke	ARG	✔✔	✗✗	✗✗	✗✗	✔	✔✔	✗	n	n	
HMV	TEM	✔	✗	✔	✗	✔	✔✔	✗	Y	n	M
Our Price	WHS	✗	?	?	✔	?	✔✔	✗	n	n	
Paper Chase	WHS	✗	?	?	✔	?	✔✔	✗	n	n	
Sherrat & Hughes	WHS	✗	?	?	✔	?	✔✔	✗	n	n	
Supasnaps	DIX	✗	?	✗	✗	?	✔✔	✗	n	n	
Virgin	VIR	✗✗	?	?	✗	?	✔✔	?	n	n	
Waterstone	WHS	✗	?	?	✔	?	✔✔	✗	n	n	
OFF LICENCES, PUBS AND TOBACCONISTS											
Augustus Barnett	BAS	✗	?	✗	✗✗	✔	✔✔	✗	y	n	AtG
Bass	BAS	✗	?	✗	✗✗	✔	✔✔	✗	y	n	AtG
Best of Cellars	KWK	✗	?	✗✗	✗✗	✔	✔✔	✗	n	n	at

		💰	♀	{	🏭	🌳	🐇	👁	🍾	🌐	Alert!
Bottoms Up	GRM	✔✔	✔	✗	✔	✔	✔✔	✗	Y	n	Atg
Brent Walker Inns	BWG	✔	?	?	✗	✗✗	✔✔	n	n	C	AtG
Charrington	BAS	✗	?	✗	✗✗	✔	✔✔	✗	y	n	AtG
Coaching Inns	WBR	✗	?	?	✗	?	✔✔	?	n	C	Atg
Forbuoys	AMB	✗	?	?	✗✗	✗	✔✔	✗	y	n	AT
Haddows	ALL	✔	?	✗✗	✗	✔	✔✔	✗	n	C	Atg
Liquorsave	ASD	✔	✗✗	✗	✗✗	✔	✔✔	✗	n	n	at
Marshell Group	AMB	✗	?	?	✗✗	✗	✔✔	✗	y	n	AT
Mitchells & Butler	BAS	✗	?	✗	✗✗	✔	✔✔	✗	y	n	AtG
Peter Dominic	GRM	✔✔	✔	✗	✔	✔	✔✔	✗	Y	n	Atg
Tap & Spile	BWG	✔	?	?	✗	✗✗	✔✔	n	n	C	AtG
Tates Off Licence	KWK	✗	?	✗✗	✗✗	✔	✔✔	✗	n	n	at
Tennents	BAS	✗	?	✗	✗✗	✔	✔✔	✗	y	n	AtG
Threshers	WBR	✗	?	?	✗	?	✔✔	?	n	C	Atg
Victoria Wine	ALL	✔	?	✗✗	✗	✔	✔✔	✗	n	C	Atg
Waverley Vintners	SCN	✗	?	?	✗	?	✔✔	?	n	C	Atg
Wayside Inns	WBR	✗	?	?	✗	?	✔✔	?	n	C	Atg
Welsh Brewers	BAS	✗	?	✗	✗✗	✔	✔✔	✗	y	n	AtG
Whitbread Inns	WBR	✗	?	?	✗	?	✔✔	?	n	C	Atg
Wine Rack	WBR	✗	?	?	✗	?	✔✔	?	n	C	Atg
ORAL HYGIENE											
Actibrush Mouthwash	COP	✔✔	✗	✗	✗✗	✔	✗	✔	Y	n	
Aquafresh	SKB	✗	?	?	✔	?	✔	?	Y	C	
Colgate	COP	✔✔	✗	✗	✗✗	✔	✗	✔	Y	n	
Colgate-Hoyt	COP	✔✔	✗	✗	✗✗	✔	✗	✔	Y	n	
Crest	PAG	✔✔	✔	✔✔	✗	✔	✗	✔	y	n	
Denclen	PAG	✔✔	✔	✔✔	✗	✔	✗	✔	y	n	
Gordon Moore's	SAL	✗✗	?	?	✗✗	?	?	✗	Y	n	

		🐦♀		🏭	🌳	🐇					Alert!
Interdens	SAL	xx	?	?	xx	?	?	x	Y	n	
Jordan	ALB	xx	?	?	xx	?	x	?	y	n	
Macleans	SKB	x	?	?	✓	?	✓	?	Y	C	
Mentadent P	UNL	✓✓	✓	✓✓	✓	✓	x	✓✓	Y	n	AT
Oral-B	GIL	x	?	?	✓	?	x	?	Y	n	
Pearl Drops	ALB	xx	?	?	xx	?	x	?	y	n	
Plax	BOO	x	?	?	x	xx	✓	x	Y	n	
Punch & Judy	SAL	xx	?	?	xx	?	?	x	Y	n	
SR	UNL	✓✓	✓	✓✓	✓	✓	x	✓✓	Y	n	AT
Sensiq	UNL	✓✓	✓	✓✓	✓	✓	x	✓✓	Y	n	AT
Sensitive	SKB	x	?	?	✓	?	✓	?	Y	C	
Signal	UNL	✓✓	✓	✓✓	✓	✓	x	✓✓	Y	n	AT
Steradent	REC	x	?	x	xx	?	x	?	Y	C	
Superdent	REC	x	?	x	xx	?	x	?	Y	C	
Ultra Brite	COP	✓✓	x	x	xx	✓	x	✓	Y	n	
PACKAGE HOLIDAYS											
Alta Holidays	BAW	✓	✓	✓	xx	x	✓✓	x	y	C	atM
British Airways	BAW	✓	✓	✓	xx	x	✓✓	x	y	C	atM
Centre Parcs	SCN	x	?	?	x	?	✓✓	?	n	C	Atg
Concorde International	BAW	✓	✓	✓	xx	x	✓✓	x	y	C	atM
Granada Travel	GRA	✓	xx	✓	x	?	✓✓	?	n	n	
HCI	TOC	xx	?	?	✓	?	✓✓	x	n	n	
Horizon Holidays	TOC	xx	?	?	✓	?	✓✓	x	n	n	
Lunn Poly	TOC	xx	?	?	✓	?	✓✓	x	n	n	
OSL	TOC	xx	?	?	✓	?	✓✓	x	n	n	
Overseas Air Travel	BAW	✓	✓	✓	xx	x	✓✓	x	y	C	atM
Pontins	SCN	x	?	?	x	?	✓✓	?	n	C	Atg
Portland Holidays	TOC	xx	?	?	✓	?	✓✓	x	n	n	

		♂	♀	🏭	🌳	🐇	🍲	✌	🌐		Alert!
Skytours	TOC	✗✗	?	?	✓	?	✓✓	✗	n	n	
Thomson Holidays	TOC	✗✗	?	?	✓	?	✓✓	✗	n	n	
Virgin Holidays	VIR	✗✗	?	?	✗	?	✓✓	?	n	n	
W H Smith Travel	WHS	✗	?	?	✓	?	✓✓	✗	n	n	
Wings	TOC	✗✗	?	?	✓	?	✓✓	✗	n	n	
PAPER PRODUCTS											
Andrex	SCT	✓	✗✗	✗✗	✗✗	✓	✓✓	?	n	n	
Ballet	KMB	✗✗	?	?	✗✗	✗	?	?	Y	n	
Delsey	KMB	✗✗	?	?	✗✗	✗	?	?	Y	n	
Fiesta	SCT	✓	✗✗	✗✗	✗✗	✓	✓✓	?	n	n	
Flair	GIL	✗	?	?	✓	?	✗	?	Y	n	
Greencare	JSA	✓✓	✓✓	✓✓	✓	✓✓	✓✓	✗	n	n	at
Handy Andies	SCT	✓	✗✗	✗✗	✗✗	✓	✓✓	?	n	n	
Hot Liner	GIL	✗	?	?	✓	?	✗	?	Y	n	
Just for Copies	GIL	✗	?	?	✓	?	✗	?	Y	n	
Kimcel	KMB	✗✗	?	?	✗✗	✗	?	?	Y	n	
Kimtex	KMB	✗✗	?	?	✗✗	✗	?	?	Y	n	
Kimwipes	KMB	✗✗	?	?	✗✗	✗	?	?	Y	n	
Kleenex Boutique	KMB	✗✗	?	?	✗✗	✗	?	?	Y	n	
Kleenex Pocket Pack	KMB	✗✗	?	?	✗✗	✗	?	?	Y	n	
Kleenex Tissues	KMB	✗✗	?	?	✗✗	✗	?	?	Y	n	
Kleenex Travel Tissues	KMB	✗✗	?	?	✗✗	✗	?	?	Y	n	
Kleenex Velvet	KMB	✗✗	?	?	✗✗	✗	?	?	Y	n	
Liquid Paper	GIL	✗	?	?	✓	?	✗	?	Y	n	
Mansize	SCT	✓	✗✗	✗✗	✗✗	✓	✓✓	?	n	n	
Mistake Out	GIL	✗	?	?	✓	?	✗	?	Y	n	
Mobil Foodwrap	MOB	✗	?	?	✓	✗	?	?	n	n	tM
Paper Mate	GIL	✗	?	?	✓	?	✗	?	Y	n	

											Alert!
Pen & Ink	GIL	✗	?	?	✔	?	✗	?	Y	n	
Scotties	SCT	✔	✗✗	✗✗	✗✗	✔	✔✔	?	n	n	
Scottissues	SCT	✔	✗✗	✗✗	✗✗	✔	✔✔	?	n	n	
Scottowels	SCT	✔	✗✗	✗✗	✗✗	✔	✔✔	?	n	n	
Sylvapen	GIL	✗	?	?	✔	?	✗	?	Y	n	
Tempo	GIL	✗	?	?	✔	?	✗	?	Y	n	
PET PRODUCTS											
9-Lives	HEN	✔✔	✗	✗✗	✔	✔	✔✔	✔✔	n	n	
Aquarian	MAR	✔	✔	?	?	✔	✔✔	✗	n	n	
Atlantis	MAR	✔	✔	?	?	✔	✔✔	✗	n	n	
Balance	QOC	✗	?	?	✗✗	?	?	?	n	n	
Biscrok	MAR	✔	✔	?	?	✔	✔✔	✗	n	n	
Black Cat	BRP	✔	✔	✔✔	✔	✗	✗	✗	Y	n	tM
Bob Martin	HEN	✔✔	✗	✗✗	✔	✔	✔✔	✔✔	n	n	
Bonio	DAL	✔✔	✔	✗	✗✗	✔✔	✗✗		n	n	
Bonus	DAL	✔✔	✔	✗	✗✗	✔✔	✗✗		n	n	
Bounce	MAR	✔	✔	?	?	✔	✔✔	✗	n	n	
Brekkies	MAR	✔	✔	?	?	✔	✔✔	✗	n	n	
Butch	HIL	✗✗	?	?	✗✗	?	?	✗	n	n	
Cats Choice	HIL	✗✗	?	?	✗✗	?	?	✗	n	n	
Catsan	MAR	✔	✔	?	?	✔	✔✔	✗	n	n	
Cesar	MAR	✔	✔	?	?	✔	✔✔	✗	n	n	
Champ	BRP	✔	✔	✔✔	✔	✗	✗	✗	Y	n	tM
Chappie	MAR	✔	✔	?	?	✔	✔✔	✗	n	n	
Choice	DAL	✔✔	✔	✗	✗✗	✔✔	✗✗		n	n	
Choosy	DAL	✔✔	✔	✗	✗✗	✔✔	✗✗		n	n	
Chunky	QOC	✗	?	?	✗✗	?	?	?	n	n	
Delikat	QOC	✗	?	?	✗✗	?	?	?	n	n	

												Alert!
Duo	BRP	✔	✔	✔✔	✔	✗	✗	✗		Y	n		tM
Felix Supreme	QOC	✗	?	?	✗✗	?	?	?		n	n		
Friskies	NES	✔	?	✗	✔✔	?	✗	✗		Y	n		a
Frolic	MAR	✔	✔	?	?	✔	✔✔	✗		n	n		
Gaines	QOC	✗	?	?	✗✗	?	?	?		n	n		
Gala Dog Food	HIL	✗✗	?	?	✗✗	?	?	✗		n	n		
Go-Cat	NES	✔	?	✗	✔✔	?	✗	✗		Y	n		a
Go-Dog	NES	✔	?	✗	✔✔	?	✗	✗		Y	n		a
Goldstar	BRP	✔	✔	✔✔	✔	✗	✗	✗		Y	n		tM
Katkins	MAR	✔	✔	?	?	✔	✔✔	✗		n	n		
Kattomeat	DAL	✔✔	✔	✗	✗✗	✔✔	✗✗			n	n	n	
Ken-l-ration	QOC	✗	?	?	✗✗	?	?	?		n	n		
Kibbles n' bits	QOC	✗	?	?	✗✗	?	?	?		n	n		
Kitekat	MAR	✔	✔	?	?	✔	✔✔	✗		n	n		
Kosy Kittens	HEN	✔✔	✗	✗✗	✔	✔	✔✔	✔✔		n	n	n	
Markies	MAR	✔	✔	?	?	✔	✔✔	✗		n	n		
Marrobone	MAR	✔	✔	?	?	✔	✔✔	✗		n	n		
Meomix	QOC	✗	?	?	✗✗	?	?	?		n	n		
Mince Morsels	QOC	✗	?	?	✗✗	?	?	?		n	n		
Nuckles	BRP	✔	✔	✔✔	✔	✗	✗	✗		Y	n		tM
Pal	MAR	✔	✔	?	?	✔	✔✔	✗		n	n		
Pal Partners	MAR	✔	✔	?	?	✔	✔✔	✗		n	n		
Pedigree Chum	MAR	✔	✔	?	?	✔	✔✔	✗		n	n		
Pedigree Formula	MAR	✔	✔	?	?	✔	✔✔	✗		n	n		
Pet Craft	MAR	✔	✔	?	?	✔	✔✔	✗		n	n		
Purrfect	DAL	✔✔	✔	✗	✗✗	✔✔	✗✗			n	n	n	
Saval	DAL	✔✔	✔	✗	✗✗	✔✔	✗✗			n	n	n	
Savour	DAL	✔✔	✔	✗	✗✗	✔✔	✗✗			n	n	n	

											Alert!
Shapes	DAL	✓✓	✓	✗	✗✗	✓✓	✗✗	n	n	n	
Sheba	MAR	✓	✓	?	?	✓	✓✓	✗	n	n	
Smackos	MAR	✓	✓	?	?	✓	✓✓	✗	n	n	
Spillers	DAL	✓✓	✓	✗	✗✗	✓✓	✗✗	n	n	n	
Spratts Choosy	DAL	✓✓	✓	✗	✗✗	✓✓	✗✗	n	n	n	
Spratts Professional	DAL	✓✓	✓	✗	✗✗	✓✓	✗✗	n	n	n	
Spratts Tailwaggers	DAL	✓✓	✓	✗	✗✗	✓✓	✗✗	n	n	n	
Style	BRP	✓	✓	✓✓	✓	✗	✗	✗	Y	n	tM
Swoop	MAR	✓	✓	?	?	✓	✓✓	✗	n	n	
Thomas Cat Litter	MAR	✓	✓	?	?	✓	✓✓	✗	n	n	
Thomas Cat Treats	MAR	✓	✓	?	?	✓	✓✓	✗	n	n	
Thomas Chocbix	MAR	✓	✓	?	?	✓	✓✓	✗	n	n	
Thomas Dog Treats	MAR	✓	✓	?	?	✓	✓✓	✗	n	n	
Thomas Dogstix	MAR	✓	✓	?	?	✓	✓✓	✗	n	n	
Thomas Kitbits	MAR	✓	✓	?	?	✓	✓✓	✗	n	n	
Thomas Kitstrips	MAR	✓	✓	?	?	✓	✓✓	✗	n	n	
Thomas Rodeo	MAR	✓	✓	?	?	✓	✓✓	✗	n	n	
Thomas Tandem	MAR	✓	✓	?	?	✓	✓✓	✗	n	n	
Top Cat	DAL	✓✓	✓	✗	✗✗	✓✓	✗✗	n	n	n	
Top Dog	DAL	✓✓	✓	✗	✗✗	✓✓	✗✗	n	n	n	
Trill	MAR	✓	✓	?	?	✓	✓✓	✗	n	n	
Trill Wild Bird Food	MAR	✓	✓	?	?	✓	✓✓	✗	n	n	
Whiskas	MAR	✓	✓	?	?	✓	✓✓	✗	n	n	
Winalot	DAL	✓✓	✓	✗	✗✗	✓✓	✗✗	n	n	n	
Winalot Prime	DAL	✓✓	✓	✗	✗✗	✓✓	✗✗	n	n	n	
PETROL AND OIL											
Alvania	SHL	✓✓	✓	✓✓	✓	✓	✗	✗	Y	n	tM
B P	BRP	✓	✓	✓✓	✓	✗	✗	✗	Y	n	tM

											Alert!
Britoil	BRP	✔	✔	✔✔	✔	✗	✗	✗	Y	n	tM
Clavus	SHL	✔✔	✔	✔✔	✔	✔	✗	✗	Y	n	tM
Conoco	DUP	✔	?	?	✗✗	✗	✗	✗	n	n	tm
Corena	SHL	✔✔	✔	✔✔	✔	✔	✗	✗	Y	n	tM
Donax	SHL	✔✔	✔	✔✔	✔	✔	✗	✗	Y	n	tM
Dromus	SHL	✔✔	✔	✔✔	✔	✔	✗	✗	Y	n	tM
Ensis	SHL	✔✔	✔	✔✔	✔	✔	✗	✗	Y	n	tM
Esso	EXX	✔✔	✗	✗	✔	✔	✗	?	n	n	tM
Formula 7	BRP	✔	✔	✔✔	✔	✗	✗	✗	Y	n	tM
Garia	SHL	✔✔	✔	✔✔	✔	✔	✗	✗	Y	n	tM
Gemini	SHL	✔✔	✔	✔✔	✔	✔	✗	✗	Y	n	tM
Havoline	TEX	✗	?	?	✗✗	✗✗	?	?	Y	n	M
Jet	DUP	✔	?	?	✗✗	✗	✗	✗	n	n	tm
Lear Petroleum	BRP	✔	✔	✔✔	✔	✗	✗	✗	Y	n	tM
Macron	SHL	✔✔	✔	✔✔	✔	✔	✗	✗	Y	n	tM
Mobil	MOB	✗	?	?	✔	✗	?	?	n	n	tM
Myrina	SHL	✔✔	✔	✔✔	✔	✔	✗	✗	Y	n	tM
Omala	SHL	✔✔	✔	✔✔	✔	✔	✗	✗	Y	n	tM
Qmatic	BRP	✔	✔	✔✔	✔	✗	✗	✗	Y	n	tM
Rimula	SHL	✔✔	✔	✔✔	✔	✔	✗	✗	Y	n	tM
Risella	SHL	✔✔	✔	✔✔	✔	✔	✗	✗	Y	n	tM
Shell	SHL	✔✔	✔	✔✔	✔	✔	✗	✗	Y	n	tM
Shell Tellus	SHL	✔✔	✔	✔✔	✔	✔	✗	✗	Y	n	tM
Spirax	SHL	✔✔	✔	✔✔	✔	✔	✗	✗	Y	n	tM
Texaco	TEX	✗	?	?	✗✗	✗✗	?	?	Y	n	M
Turbo	SHL	✔✔	✔	✔✔	✔	✔	✗	✗	Y	n	tM
Vitrea	SHL	✔✔	✔	✔✔	✔	✔	✗	✗	Y	n	tM

			♀	👤	🏭	🌳	🐇	🍼	🌐	Alert!
POLISHES											
Brasso	REC	✗	?	✗	✗✗	?	✗	?	Y	C	
Cardinal	REC	✗	?	✗	✗✗	?	✗	?	Y	C	
Cherry Blossom	REC	✗	?	✗	✗✗	?	✗	?	Y	C	
Duraglit	REC	✗	?	✗	✗✗	?	✗	?	Y	C	
Goddard's	SCJ	✔	✗	✗✗	✔✔	✔	✗	✔✔	Y	n	
Johnson Wax	SCJ	✔	✗	✗✗	✔✔	✔	✗	✔✔	Y	n	
Kiwi	SAL	✗✗	?	?	✗✗	?	?	✗	Y	n	
Klear	SCJ	✔	✗	✗✗	✔✔	✔	✗	✔✔	Y	n	
Mansion	REC	✗	?	✗	✗✗	?	✗	?	Y	C	
Meltonian	REC	✗	?	✗	✗✗	?	✗	?	Y	C	
Mr Sheen	REC	✗	?	✗	✗✗	?	✗	?	Y	C	
Onestep Shoe Shine	SCJ	✔	✗	✗✗	✔✔	✔	✗	✔✔	Y	n	
Original Wax	SCJ	✔	✗	✗✗	✔✔	✔	✗	✔✔	Y	n	
Pledge	SCJ	✔	✗	✗✗	✔✔	✔	✗	✔✔	Y	n	
Properts Saddle Soap	REC	✗	?	✗	✗✗	?	✗	?	Y	C	
Silvo	REC	✗	?	✗	✗✗	?	✗	?	Y	C	
Wax Free Sparkle	SCJ	✔	✗	✗✗	✔✔	✔	✗	✔✔	Y	n	
Wren's Dubbin	REC	✗	?	✗	✗✗	?	✗	?	Y	C	
Zebrite Grate Polish	REC	✗	?	✗	✗✗	?	✗	?	Y	C	
POULTRY											
Butterball Foods	HIL	✗✗	?	?	✗✗	?	?	✗	n	n	
Buxted	HIL	✗✗	?	?	✗✗	?	?	✗	n	n	
Harvest	HIL	✗✗	?	?	✗✗	?	?	✗	n	n	
Hermanns	HIL	✗✗	?	?	✗✗	?	?	✗	n	n	
Mayhew Chicken	NOR	✔	?	✗	✗✗	✗✗	✔✔	?	n	n	
Twydale	HIL	✗✗	?	?	✗✗	?	?	✗	n	n	

		🔧♀	👶	🏠🌳	🐄	🍶	🍷⚙			Alert!
PREPARED FOOD										
Alphabetti	NES	✓	?	✗	✓✓	?	✗	✗	Y	n	a
Armour Foods	PHM	✗	?	?	✗✗	?	✗✗	✗	y	n	AT
Batchelors	UNL	✓✓	✓	✓✓	✓	✓	✗	✓✓	Y	n	AT
Beanfeast	UNL	✓✓	✓	✓✓	✓	✓	✗	✓✓	Y	n	AT
Bemax	SKB	✗	?	?	✓	?	✓	?	Y	C	
Chef	NES	✓	?	✗	✓✓	?	✗	✗	Y	n	a
Crosse & Blackwell	NES	✓	?	✗	✓✓	?	✗	✗	Y	n	a
Dinner Jackets	QOC	✗	?	?	✗✗	?	?	?	n	n	
Fray Bentos	UNL	✓✓	✓	✓✓	✓	✓	✗	✓✓	Y	n	AT
Healthy Balance	NES	✓	?	✗	✓✓	?	✗	✗	Y	n	a
Heinz	HEN	✓✓	✗	✗✗	✓	✓	✓✓	✓✓	n	n	
John West	UNL	✓✓	✓	✓✓	✓	✓	✗	✓✓	Y	n	AT
Kitchen Classics	PHM	✗	?	?	✗✗	?	✗✗	✗	y	n	AT
Le Menu	CAM	✗	?	?	✗	?	?	?	n	n	
Microwave Ready Meals	UNL	✓✓	✓	✓✓	✓	✓	✗	✓✓	Y	n	AT
Mr Brains	PHM	✗	?	?	✗✗	?	✗✗	✗	y	n	AT
Newforge	BOK	✗✗	?	?	✗✗	?	?	?	n	n	
Parish & Fenn	BOK	✗✗	?	?	✗✗	?	?	?	n	n	
Pefect Timing	PHM	✗	?	?	✗✗	?	✗✗	✗	y	n	AT
Royal Norfolk	ABF	✗✗	?	?	✗✗	?	?	✗	Y	n	a
Slim-A-Meal	UNL	✓✓	✓	✓✓	✓	✓	✗	✓✓	Y	n	AT
Stocks Lovell	BOK	✗✗	?	?	✗✗	?	?	?	n	n	
Susi-Wan	MAR	✓	✓	?	?	✓	✓✓	✗	n	n	
Trent	BOK	✗✗	?	?	✗✗	?	?	?	n	n	
Vesta	UNL	✓✓	✓	✓✓	✓	✓	✗	✓✓	Y	n	AT
Weight Watchers	HEN	✓✓	✗	✗✗	✓	✓	✓✓	✓✓	n	n	
Wilson's	HIL	✗✗	?	?	✗✗	?	?	✗	n	n	

		🔍	♀	{	🏠	🌳	🐾	👶	🍼	⚙	Alert!
Yeoman	MAR	✔	✔	?	?	✔	✔✔	✗	n	n	
PRESERVES AND SPREADS											
Chivers	HIL	✗✗	?	?	✗✗	?	?	✗	n	n	
Frank Cooper	CPC	✗	?	?	✗✗	?	✔✔	✗	n	n	
Gale's	NES	✔	?	✗	✔✔	?	✗	✗	Y	n	a
Hartley	HIL	✗✗	?	?	✗✗	?	?	✗	n	n	
Heinz	HEN	✔✔	✗	✗✗	✔	✔	✔✔	✔✔	n	n	
Keiller Preserves	RHM	✗	?	?	✗	?	?	✗	n	C	
Nelsons of Aintree	ABF	✗✗	?	?	✗✗	?	?	✗	Y	n	a
Robertson's	RHM	✗	?	?	✗	?	?	✗	n	C	
Rose's	HIL	✗✗	?	?	✗✗	?	?	✗	n	n	
Sun-Pat	NES	✔	?	✗	✔✔	?	✗	✗	Y	n	a
Sutherlands	QOC	✗	?	?	✗✗	?	?	?	n	n	
Weight Watchers	HEN	✔✔	✗	✗✗	✔	✔	✔✔	✔✔	n	n	
Whitepot Marmalade	RHM	✗	?	?	✗	?	?	✗	n	C	
PROPRIETARY MEDICINES											
Amplex	SAL	✗✗	?	?	✗✗	?	?	✗	Y	n	
Ansaid	BOO	✗	?	?	✗	✗✗	✔	✗	Y	n	
Aspro	SAL	✗✗	?	?	✗✗	?	?	✗	Y	n	
Aspro Clear	SAL	✗✗	?	?	✗✗	?	?	✗	Y	n	
Beecham	SKB	✗	?	?	✔	?	✔	?	Y	C	
Body Plan	REC	✗	?	✗	✗✗	?	✗	?	Y	C	
Bonjela	REC	✗	?	✗	✗✗	?	✗	?	Y	C	
Buccastem	REC	✗	?	✗	✗✗	?	✗	?	Y	C	
C-VIT	SKB	✗	?	?	✔	?	✔	?	Y	C	
Casilan	BOO	✗	?	?	✗	✗✗	✔	✗	Y	n	
Chloraseptic	PAG	✔✔	✔	✔✔	✗	✔	✗	✔	y	n	
Codis	REC	✗	?	✗	✗✗	?	✗	?	Y	C	

		🔍	♀	〈	🏭	🌳	🐰	👶	🍼	🥧	Alert!
Coldcare	PAG	✓✓	✓	✓✓	✗	✓	✗	✓	y	n	
Colven	REC	✗	?	✗	✗✗	?	✗	?	Y	C	
Contact 400	SKB	✗	?	?	✓	?	✓	?	Y	C	
CoughCaps	SKB	✗	?	?	✓	?	✓	?	Y	C	
Crookes Healthcare	BOO	✗	?	?	✗	✗✗	✓	✗	Y	n	
Day Nurse	SKB	✗	?	?	✓	?	✓	?	Y	C	
Dequadin	BOO	✗	?	?	✗	✗✗	✓	✗	Y	n	
Dettol	REC	✗	?	✗	✗✗	?	✗	?	Y	C	
Diocalm	SKB	✗	?	?	✓	?	✓	?	Y	C	
Diocare	SKB	✗	?	?	✓	?	✓	?	Y	C	
Disprin	REC	✗	?	✗	✗✗	?	✗	?	Y	C	
Disprol	REC	✗	?	✗	✗✗	?	✗	?	Y	C	
E-Mycin	BOO	✗	?	?	✗	✗✗	✓	✗	Y	n	
E45	BOO	✗	?	?	✗	✗✗	✓	✗	Y	n	
Ecotrin	SKB	✗	?	?	✓	?	✓	?	Y	C	
Elastoplast	SMN	✗	?	?	✗	✗	✓	✗	Y	n	
Ellimans Embrocation	SKB	✗	?	?	✓	?	✓	?	Y	C	
Eno 'Fruit Salt'	SKB	✗	?	?	✓	?	✓	?	Y	C	
Froben S R	BOO	✗	?	?	✗	✗✗	✓	✗	Y	n	
Fybogel	REC	✗	?	✗	✗✗	?	✗	?	Y	C	
Fynnon	SKB	✗	?	?	✓	?	✓	?	Y	C	
Gaviscon	REC	✗	?	✗	✗✗	?	✗	?	Y	C	
Germolene	SKB	✗	?	?	✓	?	✓	?	Y	C	
Germoloids	SKB	✗	?	?	✓	?	✓	?	Y	C	
Glucodin	BOO	✗	?	?	✗	✗✗	✓	✗	Y	n	
Gold Spot	SAL	✗✗	?	?	✗✗	?	?	✗	Y	n	
Haliborange	REC	✗	?	✗	✗✗	?	✗	?	Y	C	
Healthcrafts	BOK	✗✗	?	?	✗✗	?	?	?	n	n	

											Alert!
Ice Mint	SAL	✗✗	?	?	✗✗	?	?	✗	Y	n	
Iron Jelloids	SKB	✗	?	?	✔	?	✔	?	Y	C	
Junifen	BOO	✗	?	?	✗	✗✗	✔	✗	Y	n	
Junior Disprol	REC	✗	?	✗	✗✗	?	✗	?	Y	C	
Junior Paraclear	SAL	✗✗	?	?	✗✗	?	?	✗	Y	n	
Karvol	BOO	✗	?	?	✗	✗✗	✔	✗	Y	n	
Krushen Salts	SAL	✗✗	?	?	✗✗	?	?	✗	Y	n	
Lemsip	REC	✗	?	✗	✗✗	?	✗	?	Y	C	
Lloyds	REC	✗	?	✗	✗✗	?	✗	?	Y	C	
Mac Losenges	SKB	✗	?	?	✔	?	✔	?	Y	C	
Maclean	SKB	✗	?	?	✔	?	✔	?	Y	C	
Medeva	BOO	✗	?	?	✗	✗✗	✔	✗	Y	n	
Medinite	PAG	✔✔	✔	✔✔	✗	✔	✗	✔	y	n	
Minadex	HAN	✗	?	?	✗	?	?	✗	Y	C	Tm
Mycil	BOO	✗	?	?	✗	✗✗	✔	✗	Y	n	
Nature's Best	BOK	✗✗	?	?	✗✗	?	?	?	n	n	
New Era Minerals	HAN	✗	?	?	✗	?	?	✗	Y	C	Tm
Night Nurse	SKB	✗	?	?	✔	?	✔	?	Y	C	
Nurofen	BOO	✗	?	?	✗	✗✗	✔	✗	Y	n	
Nylax	BOO	✗	?	?	✗	✗✗	✔	✗	Y	n	
Optrex	BOO	✗	?	?	✗	✗✗	✔	✗	Y	n	
Orovite	SKB	✗	?	?	✔	?	✔	?	Y	C	
Oxy	SKB	✗	?	?	✔	?	✔	?	Y	C	
Paraclear	SAL	✗✗	?	?	✗✗	?	?	✗	Y	n	
Peptobismol	PAG	✔✔	✔	✔✔	✗	✔	✗	✔	y	n	
Phensic	SKB	✗	?	?	✔	?	✔	?	Y	C	
Phyllosan	SKB	✗	?	?	✔	?	✔	?	Y	C	
Pripsen	REC	✗	?	✗	✗✗	?	✗	?	Y	C	

		![🔍]	![♀]	![(]	![🏭]	![🌿]	![🐰]	![]	![]	![]	Alert!
Pro Plus	SAL	✗✗	?	?	✗✗	?	?	✗	Y	n	
Prothiaden	BOO	✗	?	?	✗	✗✗	✔	✗	Y	n	
Ralgex	SKB	✗	?	?	✔	?	✔	?	Y	C	
Range 2000	BOO	✗	?	?	✗	✗✗	✔	✗	Y	n	
Rennie	SAL	✗✗	?	?	✗✗	?	?	✗	Y	n	
Resolve	SKB	✗	?	?	✔	?	✔	?	Y	C	
Senokot Laxative	REC	✗	?	✗	✗✗	?	✗	?	Y	C	
Setlers Tums	SKB	✗	?	?	✔	?	✔	?	Y	C	
Seven Seas	HAN	✗	?	?	✗	?	?	✗	Y	C	Tm
Sine-Off	SKB	✗	?	?	✔	?	✔	?	Y	C	
Sinex	PAG	✔✔	✔	✔✔	✗	✔	✗	✔	y	n	
Solmin	REC	✗	?	✗	✗✗	?	✗	?	Y	C	
Sominex	SKB	✗	?	?	✔	?	✔	?	Y	C	
Strepsils	BOO	✗	?	?	✗	✗✗	✔	✗	Y	n	
Sucrets	SKB	✗	?	?	✔	?	✔	?	Y	C	
Synthroid	BOO	✗	?	?	✗	✗✗	✔	✗	Y	n	
Tancolin	SAL	✗✗	?	?	✗✗	?	?	✗	Y	n	
Temgesic	REC	✗	?	✗	✗✗	?	✗	?	Y	C	
Tender Touch	SMN	✗	?	?	✗	✗	✔	✗	Y	n	
Timodine	REC	✗	?	✗	✗✗	?	✗	?	Y	C	
Timoped	REC	✗	?	✗	✗✗	?	✗	?	Y	C	
Vaporub	PAG	✔✔	✔	✔✔	✗	✔	✗	✔	y	n	
Veno's	SKB	✗	?	?	✔	?	✔	?	Y	C	
Vicks	PAG	✔✔	✔	✔✔	✗	✔	✗	✔	y	n	
Vykmin	SKB	✗	?	?	✔	?	✔	?	Y	C	
Yeast Vite	SKB	✗	?	?	✔	?	✔	?	Y	C	
Zubes	PZO	✗	?	?	✗✗	?	✔✔	✗	n	n	

RECORDED MUSIC		👤	♀	🐇	🏭	🌳	🐾	🥣	🍷	🔭	Alert!
Abbey Road Studios	TEM	✔	✗	✔	✗	✔	✔✔	✗	Y	n	M
Angel	TEM	✔	✗	✔	✗	✔	✔✔	✗	Y	n	M
Blue Note	TEM	✔	✗	✔	✗	✔	✔✔	✗	Y	n	M
CBS Records	SON	✔	✗	✗✗	✔	✔	✔✔	✔	n	n	
Capitol	TEM	✔	✗	✔	✗	✔	✔✔	✗	Y	n	M
Classics for Pleasure	TEM	✔	✗	✔	✗	✔	✔✔	✗	Y	n	M
Chrysalis	TEM	✔	✗	✔	✗	✔	✔✔	✗	Y	n	M
EMI	TEM	✔	✗	✔	✗	✔	✔✔	✗	Y	n	M
EMI Classics	TEM	✔	✗	✔	✗	✔	✔✔	✗	Y	n	M
EMI Emmence	TEM	✔	✗	✔	✗	✔	✔✔	✗	Y	n	M
EMI Music	TEM	✔	✗	✔	✗	✔	✔✔	✗	Y	n	M
EMI Records	TEM	✔	✗	✔	✗	✔	✔✔	✗	Y	n	M
EMO	TEM	✔	✗	✔	✗	✔	✔✔	✗	Y	n	M
Electrola	TEM	✔	✗	✔	✗	✔	✔✔	✗	Y	n	M
Encore	TEM	✔	✗	✔	✗	✔	✔✔	✗	Y	n	M
HMV	TEM	✔	✗	✔	✗	✔	✔✔	✗	Y	n	M
HMV Greensleeves	TEM	✔	✗	✔	✗	✔	✔✔	✗	Y	n	M
Harvest	TEM	✔	✗	✔	✗	✔	✔✔	✗	Y	n	M
Hispavox	TEM	✔	✗	✔	✗	✔	✔✔	✗	Y	n	M
IRS	TEM	✔	✗	✔	✗	✔	✔✔	✗	Y	n	M
Island Records	PHI	✗	?	?	✔	✔	✔✔	✗	Y	n	M
Listen for Pleasure	TEM	✔	✗	✔	✗	✔	✔✔	✗	Y	n	M
Minerva	TEM	✔	✗	✔	✗	✔	✔✔	✗	Y	n	M
Music Box	VIR	✗✗	?	?	✗	?	✔✔	?	n	n	
Music for Pleasure	TEM	✔	✗	✔	✗	✔	✔✔	✗	Y	n	M
Our Price Music	WHS	✗	?	?	✔	?	✔✔	✗	n	n	
Pampa	TEM	✔	✗	✔	✗	✔	✔✔	✗	Y	n	M

											Alert!
Parlophone	TEM	✔	✗	✔	✗	✔	✔✔	✗	Y	n	M
Pathe	TEM	✔	✗	✔	✗	✔	✔✔	✗	Y	n	M
Polygram	PHI	✗	?	?	✔	✔	✔✔	✗	Y	n	M
Regal	TEM	✔	✗	✔	✗	✔	✔✔	✗	Y	n	M
SBK Records	TEM	✔	✗	✔	✗	✔	✔✔	✗	Y	n	M
Stateside	TEM	✔	✗	✔	✗	✔	✔✔	✗	Y	n	M
Virgin Records	VIR	✗✗	?	?	✗	?	✔✔	?	n	n	
Warner	TIW	✗✗	?	?	✗	?	?	?	y	n	
Zonophone	TEM	✔	✗	✔	✗	✔	✔✔	✗	Y	n	M
RESTAURANTS											
Beefeater	WBR	✗	?	?	✗	?	✔✔	?	n	C	Atg
Biguns Ribs	CCR	✗✗	?	?	✗✗	?	✔✔	?	n	n	at
Brewers Fayre	WBR	✗	?	?	✗	?	✔✔	?	n	C	Atg
Calenders	ALL	✔	?	✗✗	✗	✔	✔✔	✗	n	C	Atg
Chandlers	SCN	✗	?	?	✗	?	✔✔	?	n	C	Atg
Chef & Brewer	GRM	✔✔	✔	✗	✔	✔	✔✔	✗	Y	n	Atg
Chiquito	CCR	✗✗	?	?	✗✗	?	✔✔	?	n	n	at
Clifton Inns	GRM	✔✔	✔	✗	✔	✔	✔✔	✗	Y	n	Atg
Country Fayre	BWG	✔	?	?	✗	✗✗	✔✔	n	n	C	AtG
Deep Pan Pizza Co	CCR	✗✗	?	?	✗✗	?	✔✔	?	n	n	at
Drummonds Cafe Bars	BAS	✗	?	✗	✗✗	✔	✔✔	✗	y	n	AtG
Exchange	ALL	✔	?	✗✗	✗	✔	✔✔	✗	n	C	Atg
Filling Station	CCR	✗✗	?	?	✗✗	?	✔✔	?	n	n	at
Garfunkel's	CCR	✗✗	?	?	✗✗	?	✔✔	?	n	n	at
Granada Services	GRA	✔	✗✗	✔	✗	?	✔✔	?	n	n	
Hanrahan's	WBR	✗	?	?	✗	?	✔✔	?	n	C	Atg
Happy Eater	THF	✗	?	?	✗✗	?	✔✔	?	n	C	at
Hartley's	WBR	✗	?	?	✗	?	✔✔	?	n	C	Atg

											Alert!
Harvester	THF	✗	?	?	✗✗	?	✓✓	?	n	C	at
Henry's	WBR	✗	?	?	✗	?	✓✓	?	n	C	Atg
Jeffersons	BAS	✗	?	✗	✗✗	✓	✓✓	✗	y	n	AtG
Little Chef	THF	✗	?	?	✗✗	?	✓✓	?	n	C	at
Manor Houses	SCN	✗	?	?	✗	?	✓✓	?	n	C	Atg
Muswell's	ALL	✓	?	✗✗	✗	✓	✓✓	✗	n	C	Atg
Old Orleans	GRM	✓✓	✓	✗	✓	✓	✓✓	✗	Y	n	Atg
Papaveros	BAS	✗	?	✗	✗✗	✓	✓✓	✗	y	n	AtG
Pizza Hut	WBR	✗	?	?	✗	?	✓✓	?	n	C	Atg
Pizzaland	UNB	✓✓	✗✗	✗✗	✓	✓	✗✗	✓	n	C	
Porterhouse	ALL	✓	?	✗✗	✗	✓	✓✓	✗	n	C	Atg
Puritan Maid	THF	✗	?	?	✗✗	?	✓✓	?	n	C	at
Roast Inn	WBR	✗	?	?	✗	?	✓✓	?	n	C	Atg
Sarah's	RHM	✗	?	?	✗	?	?	✗	n	C	
Springfields	BAS	✗	?	✗	✗✗	✓	✓✓	✗	y	n	AtG
Squires Table	BWG	✓	?	?	✗	✗✗	✓✓	n	n	C	AtG
T G I Friday's	WBR	✗	?	?	✗	?	✓✓	?	n	C	Atg
TJ's	BAS	✗	?	✗	✗✗	✓	✓✓	✗	y	n	AtG
Three Cooks	RHM	✗	?	?	✗	?	?	✗	n	C	
Toby Carving Room	BAS	✗	?	✗	✗✗	✓	✓✓	✗	y	n	AtG
Toby Grills	BAS	✗	?	✗	✗✗	✓	✓✓	✗	y	n	AtG
Wheelers	THF	✗	?	?	✗✗	?	✓✓	?	n	C	at
RICE AND PASTA											
Batchelors Savoury	UNL	✓✓	✓	✓✓	✓	✓	✗	✓✓	Y	n	AT
Buitoni	NES	✓	?	✗	✓✓	?	✗	✗	Y	n	a
Noodle-Roni	QOC	✗	?	?	✗✗	?	?	?	n	n	
Pasta Choice	NES	✓	?	✗	✓✓	?	✗	✗	Y	n	a
Record	RHM	✗	?	?	✗	?	?	✗	n	C	

											Alert!
Rice & Things	NES	✔	?	✗	✔✔	?	✗	✗	Y	n	a
Rice-a-Roni	QOC	✗	?	?	✗✗	?	?	?	n	n	
Smash	HIL	✗✗	?	?	✗✗	?	?	✗	n	n	
Super Noodles	UNL	✔✔	✔	✔✔	✔	✔	✗	✔✔	Y	n	AT
Uncle Ben's	MAR	✔	✔	?	?	✔	✔✔	✗	n	n	
SHAVING PRODUCTS											
7 O'Clock	GIL	✗	?	?	✔	?	✗	?	Y	n	
Blue II	GIL	✗	?	?	✔	?	✗	?	Y	n	
Brylcreem	SKB	✗	?	?	✔	?	✔	?	Y	C	
Contour Plus	GIL	✗	?	?	✔	?	✗	?	Y	n	
Foamy	GIL	✗	?	?	✔	?	✗	?	Y	n	
Gillette	GIL	✗	?	?	✔	?	✗	?	Y	n	
Mostly Men	BOD	✔✔	✗	✗✗	✔✔	✔	✔✔	✔✔	n	n	
Slazenger Sport	SKB	✗	?	?	✔	?	✔	?	Y	C	
SMALL ELECTRICAL APPLIANCES											
Alfalec	ELE	✗	?	?	✗✗	?	✔✔	?	n	n	
Bendix	ELE	✗	?	?	✗✗	?	✔✔	?	n	n	
Braun	GIL	✗	?	?	✔	?	✗	?	Y	n	
Breville	WIH	✗✗	?	?	✗✗	?	✔✔	?	Y	C	M
Electrolux	ELE	✗	?	?	✗✗	?	✔✔	?	n	n	
Eureka	ELE	✗	?	?	✗✗	?	✔✔	?	n	n	
Ferguson	TSA	✗✗	?	?	✗✗	?	✔✔	✗	n	n	M
Hitachi	HIT	✗	?	?	✗✗	✗	✔✔	✔	n	n	m
Hoover	MAY	✗	?	?	✗✗	?	✔✔	?	y	n	
Husqvarna	ELE	✗	?	?	✗✗	?	✔✔	?	n	n	
Jarnkonst	TEM	✔	✗	✔	✗	✔	✔✔	✗	Y	n	M
Panasonic	MAT	✔✔	✗	✗	✗	✔	✔✔	✔	y	n	
Philips	PHI	✗	?	?	✔	✔	✔✔	✗	Y	n	M

											Alert!
Progress	ELE	✗	?	?	✗✗	?	✓✓	?	n	n	
Redring	GEC	✓✓	✓	✓	✗	✓	✓✓	✗	Y	n	M
Scholten	MRL	✗✗	?	?	✗✗	?	✓✓	?	n	n	
Sodastream	CAD	✓✓	✓	✓	✗	✓	✓✓	✗	Y	n	
THORN	TEM	✓	✗	✓	✗	✓	✓✓	✗	Y	n	M
Tornado	ELE	✗	?	?	✗✗	?	✓✓	?	n	n	
Toshiba	TOS	✓	✗	✗	✓	✓	✓✓	✓	y	n	M
Volta	ELE	✗	?	?	✗✗	?	✓✓	?	n	n	
Xpelair	GEC	✓✓	✓	✓	✗	✓	✓✓	✗	Y	n	M
Zanussi	ELE	✗	?	?	✗✗	?	✓✓	?	n	n	
SNACK FOODS											
Bacon Fries	PEP	✗	?	?	✗✗	✓	✗	✗	y	n	
Big 'D' Nuts	PEP	✗	?	?	✗✗	✓	✗	✗	y	n	
Blitza Pizza	PEP	✗	?	?	✗✗	✓	✗	✗	y	n	
Brannigans	UNB	✓✓	✗✗	✗✗	✓	✓	✗✗	✓	n	C	
Cheese Snips	UNB	✓✓	✗✗	✗✗	✓	✓	✗✗	✓	n	C	
Cheeslets	BSN	✗	?	?	✓	?	?	✗	n	n	A
Cheetos	PEP	✗	?	?	✗✗	✓	✗	✗	y	n	
Chipsticks	PEP	✗	?	?	✗✗	✓	✗	✗	y	n	
Choc Dips	UNB	✓✓	✗✗	✗✗	✓	✓	✗✗	✓	n	C	
Crispy Tubes	PEP	✗	?	?	✗✗	✓	✗	✗	y	n	
Frazzles	PEP	✗	?	?	✗✗	✓	✗	✗	y	n	
French Fries	PEP	✗	?	?	✗✗	✓	✗	✗	y	n	
Golden Wonder	DAL	✓✓	✓	✗	✗✗	✓✓	✗✗	n	n	n	
Hula Hoops	UNB	✓✓	✗✗	✗✗	✓	✓	✗✗	✓	n	C	
Jackets	PEP	✗	?	?	✗✗	✓	✗	✗	y	n	
K P Crisps	UNB	✓✓	✗✗	✗✗	✓	✓	✗✗	✓	n	C	
K P Dips	UNB	✓✓	✗✗	✗✗	✓	✓	✗✗	✓	n	C	

		♂♀		🚼	🏭		🐄				Alert!
K P Discos	UNB	✓✓	✗✗	✗✗	✓	✓	✗✗	✓	n	C	
K P Frisps	UNB	✓✓	✗✗	✗✗	✓	✓	✗✗	✓	n	C	
K P Nuts	UNB	✓✓	✗✗	✗✗	✓	✓	✗✗	✓	n	C	
K P Skips	UNB	✓✓	✗✗	✗✗	✓	✓	✗✗	✓	n	C	
K P Snacks	UNB	✓✓	✗✗	✗✗	✓	✓	✗✗	✓	n	C	
K P World Snacks	UNB	✓✓	✗✗	✗✗	✓	✓	✗✗	✓	n	C	
Le Snack	UNB	✓✓	✗✗	✗✗	✓	✓	✗✗	✓	n	C	
Mini Cheddars	UNB	✓✓	✗✗	✗✗	✓	✓	✗✗	✓	n	C	
Monster Munch	PEP	✗	?	?	✗✗	✓	✗	✗	y	n	
Nibb-It	DAL	✓✓	✓	✗	✗✗	✓✓	✗✗	n	n	n	
Planters	PEP	✗	?	?	✗✗	✓	✗	✗	y	n	
Poppadum Crisps	PEP	✗	?	?	✗✗	✓	✗	✗	y	n	
Pot Noodles	DAL	✓✓	✓	✗	✗✗	✓✓	✗✗	n	n	n	
Quavers	PEP	✗	?	?	✗✗	✓	✗	✗	y	n	
Real McCoy's	UNB	✓✓	✗✗	✗✗	✓	✓	✗✗	✓	n	C	
Ringos	DAL	✓✓	✓	✗	✗✗	✓✓	✗✗	n	n	n	
Ruffles	PEP	✗	?	?	✗✗	✓	✗	✗	y	n	
Salt 'n' Shake	PEP	✗	?	?	✗✗	✓	✗	✗	y	n	
Scampie Fries	PEP	✗	?	?	✗✗	✓	✗	✗	y	n	
Smiths	PEP	✗	?	?	✗✗	✓	✗	✗	y	n	
Snaps	PEP	✗	?	?	✗✗	✓	✗	✗	y	n	
Space Raiders	UNB	✓✓	✗✗	✗✗	✓	✓	✗✗	✓	n	C	
Square Crisps	PEP	✗	?	?	✗✗	✓	✗	✗	y	n	
Tudor Crisps	PEP	✗	?	?	✗✗	✓	✗	✗	y	n	
Twiglets	BSN	✗	?	?	✓	?	?	✗	n	n	A
Walkers	PEP	✗	?	?	✗✗	✓	✗	✗	y	n	
Wotsits	DAL	✓✓	✓	✗	✗✗	✓✓	✗✗	n	n	n	

		🏭	♀	(	🏭	🌳	🐇	🚬	🍷	☢	Alert!
SOFT DRINKS AND MIXERS											
7 UP	PEP	✗	?	?	✗✗	✔	✗	✗	y	n	
Apeel	PHM	✗	?	?	✗✗	?	✗✗	✗	y	n	AT
Aqua Libra	GRM	✔✔	✔	✗	✔	✔	✔✔	✗	Y	n	Atg
Britvic 55 *	BAS	✗	?	✗	✗✗	✔	✔✔	✗	y	n	AtG
Britvic Fruit Juices *	BAS	✗	?	✗	✗✗	✔	✔✔	✗	y	n	AtG
Britvic Quencher *	BAS	✗	?	✗	✗✗	✔	✔✔	✗	y	n	AtG
C-Drinks	NES	✔	?	✗	✔✔	?	✗	✗	Y	n	a
C-Vit	SKB	✗	?	?	✔	?	✔	?	Y	C	
Canada Dry *	BAS	✗	?	✗	✗✗	✔	✔✔	✗	y	n	AtG
Capri-Sun	RHM	✗	?	?	✗	?	?	✗	n	C	
Cherry 7 UP	PEP	✗	?	?	✗✗	✔	✗	✗	y	n	
Cherry Coca-Cola	COC	✔	✗	✔	✔✔	✔	✗	✗	y	n	
Cherry Pepsi	PEP	✗	?	?	✗✗	✔	✗	✗	y	n	
Citrus Spring *	BAS	✗	?	✗	✗✗	✔	✔✔	✗	y	n	AtG
Coca-Cola	COC	✔	✗	✔	✔✔	✔	✗	✗	y	n	
Corona *	BAS	✗	?	✗	✗✗	✔	✔✔	✗	y	n	AtG
Cottee's	CAD	✔✔	✔	✔	✗	✔	✔✔	✗	Y	n	
Crush	CAD	✔✔	✔	✔	✗	✔	✔✔	✗	Y	n	
De L'Ora	RHM	✗	?	?	✗	?	?	✗	n	C	
Dexters	GRM	✔✔	✔	✗	✔	✔	✔✔	✗	Y	n	Atg
Diet 7 UP	PEP	✗	?	?	✗✗	✔	✗	✗	y	n	
Diet Coca-Cola	COC	✔	✗	✔	✔✔	✔	✗	✗	y	n	
Diet Fanta	COC	✔	✗	✔	✔✔	✔	✗	✗	y	n	
Diet Lilt	COC	✔	✗	✔	✔✔	✔	✗	✗	y	n	
Diet Pepsi	PEP	✗	?	?	✗✗	✔	✗	✗	y	n	
Diet Sprite	COC	✔	✗	✔	✔✔	✔	✗	✗	y	n	
ED Smith	CAD	✔✔	✔	✔	✗	✔	✔✔	✗	Y	n	

												Alert!
Fanta	COC	✓	✗	✓	✓✓	✓	✗	✗	y	n	
Ferguzade	SKB	✗	?	?	✓	?	✓	?	Y	C	
Five Alive	COC	✓	✗	✓	✓✓	✓	✗	✗	y	n	
Five Alive Citrus	COC	✓	✗	✓	✓✓	✓	✗	✗	y	n	
Five Alive Lite	COC	✓	✗	✓	✓✓	✓	✗	✗	y	n	
Five Alive Tropical	COC	✓	✗	✓	✓✓	✓	✗	✗	y	n	
Five Alive Tropical	COC	✓	✗	✓	✓✓	✓	✗	✗	y	n	
Gini	CAD	✓✓	✓	✓	✗	✓	✓✓	✗	Y	n	
Groosome Joosome	RHM	✗	?	?	✗	?	?	✗	n	C	
Hires	CAD	✓✓	✓	✓	✗	✓	✓✓	✗	Y	n	
Holland House	CAD	✓✓	✓	✓	✗	✓	✓✓	✗	Y	n	
Hycal	SKB	✗	?	?	✓	?	✓	?	Y	C	
Idris *	BAS	✗	?	✗	✗✗	✓	✓✓	✗	y	n	AtG
Just Juice	RHM	✗	?	?	✗	?	?	✗	n	C	
Kia-Ora	CAD	✓✓	✓	✓	✗	✓	✓✓	✗	Y	n	
Libby	NES	✓	?	✗	✓✓	?	✗	✗	Y	n	a
Lilt	COC	✓	✗	✓	✓✓	✓	✗	✗	y	n	
Lucozade	SKB	✗	?	?	✓	?	✓	?	Y	C	
Moonshine	NES	✓	?	✗	✓✓	?	✗	✗	Y	n	a
Mott's	CAD	✓✓	✓	✓	✗	✓	✓✓	✗	Y	n	
Mr & Mrs 'T'	CAD	✓✓	✓	✓	✗	✓	✓✓	✗	Y	n	
Napolina	CPC	✗	?	?	✗✗	?	✓✓	✗	n	n	
Oasis	CAD	✓✓	✓	✓	✗	✓	✓✓	✗	Y	n	
Old Colony	CAD	✓✓	✓	✓	✗	✓	✓✓	✗	Y	n	
One-Cal	RHM	✗	?	?	✗	?	?	✗	n	C	
PLJ	SKB	✗	?	?	✓	?	✓	?	Y	C	
Pepsi Cola	PEP	✗	?	?	✗✗	✓	✗	✗	y	n	
Quosh *	BAS	✗	?	✗	✗✗	✓	✓✓	✗	y	n	AtG

		⚥	⚔	🏠	🌳	🐾	🥁	💉	⚙	Alert!
R. Whites *	BAS	✗	?	✗	✗✗	✔	✔✔	✗	y	n	AtG
Ribena	SKB	✗	?	?	✔	?	✔	?	Y	C	
Robinsons	REC	✗	?	✗	✗✗	?	✗	?	Y	C	
Robinsons Barley Water	REC	✗	?	✗	✗✗	?	✗	?	Y	C	
Rose's	CAD	✔✔	✔	✔	✗	✔	✔✔	✗	Y	n	
Schloer	SKB	✗	?	?	✔	?	✔	?	Y	C	
Schweppes	CAD	✔✔	✔	✔	✗	✔	✔✔	✗	Y	n	
Shandy Bass	BAS	✗	?	✗	✗✗	✔	✔✔	✗	y	n	AtG
Shandy Pilsner	BAS	✗	?	✗	✗✗	✔	✔✔	✗	y	n	AtG
Solo	CAD	✔✔	✔	✔	✗	✔	✔✔	✗	Y	n	
Sprite	COC	✔	✗	✔	✔✔	✔	✗	✗	y	n	
St Ivel Real	UGT	✔	?	✗	✗✗	?	✔✔	†	n	C	
Sun-drop	CAD	✔✔	✔	✔	✗	✔	✔✔	✗	Y	n	
Sunkist	COC	✔	✗	✔	✔✔	✔	✗	✗	y	n	
Tango *	BAS	✗	?	✗	✗✗	✔	✔✔	✗	y	n	AtG
The Juice	MMB	✗✗	?	?	✗✗	?	✗✗	?	n	n	
Top Deck *	BAS	✗	?	✗	✗✗	✔	✔✔	✗	y	n	AtG
TriNaranjus	CAD	✔✔	✔	✔	✗	✔	✔✔	✗	Y	n	
Um Bongo	NES	✔	?	✗	✔✔	?	✗	✗	Y	n	a
V-8	CAM	✗	?	?	✗	?	?	?	n	n	
Welch's	CAD	✔✔	✔	✔	✗	✔	✔✔	✗	Y	n	
SOFT FURNISHINGS AND TEXTILES											
Accord	LON	✗✗	?	?	✗✗	?	?	✗	Y	n	AT
Brentford	LON	✗✗	?	?	✗✗	?	?	✗	Y	n	AT
Chortex	CVI	✔	?	✗	✗✗	?	✔✔	✗	Y	C	m
Christy	COT	✗	?	?	✗✗	✗	✔✔	✗	Y	n	
Diana Cowpe	CVI	✔	?	✗	✗✗	?	✔✔	✗	Y	C	m
Dorma	CVI	✔	?	✗	✗✗	?	✔✔	✗	Y	C	m

											Alert!
Greenhills	COT	✗	?	?	✗✗	✗	✓✓	✗	Y	n	
Horrockses	CVI	✓	?	✗	✗✗	?	✓✓	✗	Y	C	m
Lycra	DUP	✓	?	?	✗✗	✗	✗	✗	n	n	tm
Orlon	DUP	✓	?	?	✗✗	✗	✗	✗	n	n	tm
Vantona	CVI	✓	?	✗	✗✗	?	✓✓	✗	Y	C	m
Zorbit	COT	✗	?	?	✗✗	✗	✓✓	✗	Y	n	
SOUPS											
Batchelors	UNL	✓✓	✓	✓✓	✓	✓	✗	✓✓	Y	n	AT
Big Soups	HEN	✓✓	✗	✗✗	✓	✓	✓✓	✓✓	n	n	
Bumper Harvest	CAM	✗	?	?	✗	?	?	?	n	n	
Campbell's	CAM	✗	?	?	✗	?	?	?	n	n	
Cup-a-Soup	UNL	✓✓	✓	✓✓	✓	✓	✗	✓✓	Y	n	AT
Farmhouse Soup	HEN	✓✓	✗	✗✗	✓	✓	✓✓	✓✓	n	n	
Granny's	CAM	✗	?	?	✗	?	?	?	n	n	
Heinz	HEN	✓✓	✗	✗✗	✓	✓	✓✓	✓✓	n	n	
Invaders	HEN	✓✓	✗	✗✗	✓	✓	✓✓	✓✓	n	n	
Knorr	CPC	✗	?	?	✗✗	?	✓✓	✗	n	n	
Main Course	CAM	✗	?	?	✗	?	?	?	n	n	
Organic Soups	CAM	✗	?	?	✗	?	?	?	n	n	
Slim-a-Soup	UNL	✓✓	✓	✓✓	✓	✓	✗	✓✓	Y	n	AT
Snack-a-Soup	UNL	✓✓	✓	✓✓	✓	✓	✗	✓✓	Y	n	AT
Special Recipe	HEN	✓✓	✗	✗✗	✓	✓	✓✓	✓✓	n	n	
Spicy Soups	HEN	✓✓	✗	✗✗	✓	✓	✓✓	✓✓	n	n	
Weight Watchers	HEN	✓✓	✗	✗✗	✓	✓	✓✓	✓✓	n	n	
SPIRITS											
1900	ALL	✓	?	✗✗	✗	✓	✓✓	✗	n	C	Atg
Abbot's Choice	GUI	✓	✗✗	✗✗	✓✓	?	?	?	y	n	A
Absolut	GUI	✓	✗✗	✗✗	✓✓	?	?	?	y	n	A

		🍸	♀	〈	🏭	🌳	�골	👙	🍶	🕸	Alert!
Ainslie's	GUI	✔	✗✗	✗✗	✔✔	?	?	?	y	n	A
Aperol	ALL	✔	?	✗✗	✗	✔	✔✔	✗	n	C	Atg
Archer's	GRM	✔✔	✔	✗	✔	✔	✔✔	✗	Y	n	Atg
Aultmore	GUI	✔	✗✗	✗✗	✔✔	?	?	?	y	n	A
Baileys Original	GRM	✔✔	✔	✗	✔	✔	✔✔	✗	Y	n	Atg
Balblair	ALL	✔	?	✗✗	✗	✔	✔✔	✗	n	C	Atg
Ballantine's	ALL	✔	?	✗✗	✗	✔	✔✔	✗	n	C	Atg
Balvenie	WGT	✗	?	?	✗✗	?	✔✔	n	n	n	A
Beefeater Gin	ALL	✔	?	✗✗	✗	✔	✔✔	✗	n	C	Atg
Bell's 12 Year Old	GUI	✔	✗✗	✗✗	✔✔	?	?	?	y	n	A
Bell's 21 Year Old	GUI	✔	✗✗	✗✗	✔✔	?	?	?	y	n	A
Bell's Islander	GUI	✔	✗✗	✗✗	✔✔	?	?	?	y	n	A
Bells Extra Special	GUI	✔	✗✗	✗✗	✔✔	?	?	?	y	n	A
Black & White	GUI	✔	✗✗	✗✗	✔✔	?	?	?	y	n	A
Black Bottle	ALL	✔	?	✗✗	✗	✔	✔✔	✗	n	C	Atg
Black Velvet	GRM	✔✔	✔	✗	✔	✔	✔✔	✗	Y	n	Atg
Bladnoch	GUI	✔	✗✗	✗✗	✔✔	?	?	?	y	n	A
Blair Athol	GUI	✔	✗✗	✗✗	✔✔	?	?	?	y	n	A
Bombay Dry Gin	GRM	✔✔	✔	✗	✔	✔	✔✔	✗	Y	n	Atg
Booth's	GUI	✔	✗✗	✗✗	✔✔	?	?	?	y	n	A
Borzoi Vodka	ALL	✔	?	✗✗	✗	✔	✔✔	✗	n	C	Atg
Bulloch Lade	GUI	✔	✗✗	✗✗	✔✔	?	?	?	y	n	A
Bunnahabhain	HIG	✗✗	?	?	✗	?	✔✔	n	n	C	A
Cambus	GUI	✔	✗✗	✗✗	✔✔	?	?	?	y	n	A
Cameron Brig	GUI	✔	✗✗	✗✗	✔✔	?	?	?	y	n	A
Canadian Club	ALL	✔	?	✗✗	✗	✔	✔✔	✗	n	C	Atg
Canard Duchene	GUI	✔	✗✗	✗✗	✔✔	?	?	?	y	n	A
Cardhu	GUI	✔	✗✗	✗✗	✔✔	?	?	?	y	n	A

		♟	♀	〈	🏭	🌳	🐰	🥣	▽	🔶	Alert!
Carolans Irish Cream	ALL	✓	?	✗✗	✗	✓	✓✓	✗	n	C	Atg
Centenario	ALL	✓	?	✗✗	✗	✓	✓✓	✗	n	C	Atg
Chequers	GUI	✓	✗✗	✗✗	✓✓	?	?	?	y	n	A
Christian Brothers	GRM	✓✓	✓	✗	✓	✓	✓✓	✗	Y	n	Atg
Clynelish	GUI	✓	✗✗	✗✗	✓✓	?	?	?	y	n	A
Cognac Otard	BAS	✗	?	✗	✗✗	✓	✓✓	✗	y	n	AtG
Cossack	GUI	✓	✗✗	✗✗	✓✓	?	?	?	y	n	A
Country Satin	ALL	✓	?	✗✗	✗	✓	✓✓	✗	n	C	Atg
Courvoisier	ALL	✓	?	✗✗	✗	✓	✓✓	✗	n	C	Atg
Crabbie	GUI	✓	✗✗	✗✗	✓✓	?	?	?	y	n	A
Cragganmore	GUI	✓	✗✗	✗✗	✓✓	?	?	?	y	n	A
Crawford's	AMB	✗	?	?	✗✗	✗	✓✓	✗	y	n	AT
Dalwhinnie	GUI	✓	✗✗	✗✗	✓✓	?	?	?	y	n	A
DeKuyper	AMB	✗	?	?	✗✗	✗	✓✓	✗	y	n	AT
Denaka	ALL	✓	?	✗✗	✗	✓	✓✓	✗	n	C	Atg
Dewar's White Label	GUI	✓	✗✗	✗✗	✓✓	?	?	?	y	n	A
Dimple	GUI	✓	✗✗	✗✗	✓✓	?	?	?	y	n	A
Dufftown-Glenlivet	GUI	✓	✗✗	✗✗	✓✓	?	?	?	y	n	A
Family Reserve	WGT	✗	?	?	✗✗	?	✓✓	n	n	n	A
Frangelico	ALL	✓	?	✗✗	✗	✓	✓✓	✗	n	C	Atg
George Dickel	GUI	✓	✗✗	✗✗	✓✓	?	?	?	y	n	A
Gilbey's	GRM	✓✓	✓	✗	✓	✓	✓✓	✗	Y	n	Atg
Glen Elgan	GUI	✓	✗✗	✗✗	✓✓	?	?	?	y	n	A
Glendullan	GUI	✓	✗✗	✗✗	✓✓	?	?	?	y	n	A
Glenesk	GUI	✓	✗✗	✗✗	✓✓	?	?	?	y	n	A
Glenfiddich	WGT	✗	?	?	✗✗	?	✓✓	n	n	n	A
Glenkinchie	GUI	✓	✗✗	✗✗	✓✓	?	?	?	y	n	A
Glenordie	GUI	✓	✗✗	✗✗	✓✓	?	?	?	y	n	A

											Alert!
Glenturret	HIG	xx	?	?	x	?	✓✓	n	n	C	A
Glenury Royal	GUI	✓	xx	xx	✓✓	?	?	?	y	n	A
Gordon's Gin	GUI	✓	xx	xx	✓✓	?	?	?	y	n	A
Gordon's Twist	GUI	✓	xx	xx	✓✓	?	?	?	y	n	A
Haig Whiskies	AMB	x	?	?	xx	x	✓✓	x	y	n	AT
Hennessy	GUI	✓	xx	xx	✓✓	?	?	?	y	n	A
Heubelein Cocktails	GRM	✓✓	✓	x	✓	✓	✓✓	x	Y	n	Atg
Highland Park	HIG	xx	?	?	x	?	✓✓	n	n	C	A
Hine	GUI	✓	xx	xx	✓✓	?	?	?	y	n	A
Hiram Walker	ALL	✓	?	xx	x	✓	✓✓	x	n	C	Atg
Inchgower	GUI	✓	xx	xx	✓✓	?	?	?	y	n	A
Irish Mist	ALL	✓	?	xx	x	✓	✓✓	x	n	C	Atg
J & B Rare	GRM	✓✓	✓	x	✓	✓	✓✓	x	Y	n	Atg
J.de Malliac	ALL	✓	?	xx	x	✓	✓✓	x	n	C	Atg
Jim Beam	AMB	x	?	?	xx	x	✓✓	x	y	n	AT
John Begg	GUI	✓	xx	xx	✓✓	?	?	?	y	n	A
Johnnie Walker	GUI	✓	xx	xx	✓✓	?	?	?	y	n	A
Kahlua	ALL	✓	?	xx	x	✓	✓✓	x	n	C	Atg
Kamchatka	AMB	x	?	?	xx	x	✓✓	x	y	n	AT
King George IV	GUI	✓	xx	xx	✓✓	?	?	?	y	n	A
Knockando	GRM	✓✓	✓	x	✓	✓	✓✓	x	Y	n	Atg
Lagavulin	GUI	✓	xx	xx	✓✓	?	?	?	y	n	A
Lamb's Navy	ALL	✓	?	xx	x	✓	✓✓	x	n	C	Atg
Laphroaig Islay Malt	ALL	✓	?	xx	x	✓	✓✓	x	n	C	Atg
Lemon Hart	ALL	✓	?	xx	x	✓	✓✓	x	n	C	Atg
Linkwood	GUI	✓	xx	xx	✓✓	?	?	?	y	n	A
Logan	GUI	✓	xx	xx	✓✓	?	?	?	y	n	A
Long John	ALL	✓	?	xx	x	✓	✓✓	x	n	C	Atg

		🐝♀		⟨	🏠🌲	🐇	🍵	▽	🅐	Alert!
Maker's Mark	ALL	✔	?	✗✗	✗	✔	✔✔	✗	n	C	Atg
Malibu	GRM	✔✔	✔	✗	✔	✔	✔✔	✗	Y	n	Atg
McCallum's	GUI	✔	✗✗	✗✗	✔✔	?	?	?	y	n	A
Metaxa	GRM	✔✔	✔	✗	✔	✔	✔✔	✗	Y	n	Atg
Miltonduff	ALL	✔	?	✗✗	✗	✔	✔✔	✗	n	C	Atg
Mirage	WGT	✗	?	?	✗✗	?	✔✔	n	n	n	A
Monterez	ALL	✔	?	✗✗	✗	✔	✔✔	✗	n	C	Atg
Mortlach	GUI	✔	✗✗	✗✗	✔✔	?	?	?	y	n	A
Oban	GUI	✔	✗✗	✗✗	✔✔	?	?	?	y	n	A
Old Parr	GUI	✔	✗✗	✗✗	✔✔	?	?	?	y	n	A
Old Smuggler	ALL	✔	?	✗✗	✗	✔	✔✔	✗	n	C	Atg
Peter Dawson	GUI	✔	✗✗	✗✗	✔✔	?	?	?	y	n	A
Petite Liquorelle	GUI	✔	✗✗	✗✗	✔✔	?	?	?	y	n	A
Popov	GRM	✔✔	✔	✗	✔	✔	✔✔	✗	Y	n	Atg
Port Dundas	GUI	✔	✗✗	✗✗	✔✔	?	?	?	y	n	A
President	GUI	✔	✗✗	✗✗	✔✔	?	?	?	y	n	A
Primero	ALL	✔	?	✗✗	✗	✔	✔✔	✗	n	C	Atg
Rebel Yell	GUI	✔	✗✗	✗✗	✔✔	?	?	?	y	n	A
Relska	GRM	✔✔	✔	✗	✔	✔	✔✔	✗	Y	n	Atg
Robbie Burns	GUI	✔	✗✗	✗✗	✔✔	?	?	?	y	n	A
Rosebank	GUI	✔	✗✗	✗✗	✔✔	?	?	?	y	n	A
Royal Lochnagar	GUI	✔	✗✗	✗✗	✔✔	?	?	?	y	n	A
Rumple Minze	GRM	✔✔	✔	✗	✔	✔	✔✔	✗	Y	n	Atg
Salignac	ALL	✔	?	✗✗	✗	✔	✔✔	✗	n	C	Atg
Sambuca Romana	GRM	✔✔	✔	✗	✔	✔	✔✔	✗	Y	n	Atg
Singleton of Auchruich	GRM	✔✔	✔	✗	✔	✔	✔✔	✗	Y	n	Atg
Smirnoff	GRM	✔✔	✔	✗	✔	✔	✔✔	✗	Y	n	Atg
Snowball	ALL	✔	?	✗✗	✗	✔	✔✔	✗	n	C	Atg

											Alert!
Stewarts	ALL	✔	?	✗✗	✗	✔	✔✔	✗	n	C	Atg
Swing	GUI	✔	✗✗	✗✗	✔✔	?	?	?	y	n	A
Taboo	WGT	✗	?	?	✗✗	?	✔✔	n	n	n	A
Talisker	GUI	✔	✗✗	✗✗	✔✔	?	?	?	y	n	A
Tamdhu	HIG	✗✗	?	?	✗	?	✔✔	n	n	C	A
Tanqueray	GUI	✔	✗✗	✗✗	✔✔	?	?	?	y	n	A
Teacher's	ALL	✔	?	✗✗	✗	✔	✔✔	✗	n	C	Atg
The Antiquary	GUI	✔	✗✗	✗✗	✔✔	?	?	?	y	n	A
The Claymore	AMB	✗	?	?	✗✗	✗	✔✔	✗	y	n	AT
The Dalmore	AMB	✗	?	?	✗✗	✗	✔✔	✗	y	n	AT
The Famous Grouse	HIG	✗✗	?	?	✗	?	✔✔	n	n	C	A
The Glenronach	ALL	✔	?	✗✗	✗	✔	✔✔	✗	n	C	Atg
The Tormore	ALL	✔	?	✗✗	✗	✔	✔✔	✗	n	C	Atg
Three Barrels	GUI	✔	✗✗	✗✗	✔✔	?	?	?	y	n	A
Tia Maria	ALL	✔	?	✗✗	✗	✔	✔✔	✗	n	C	Atg
Usher's Green Stripe	GUI	✔	✗✗	✗✗	✔✔	?	?	?	y	n	A
VAT 69	GUI	✔	✗✗	✗✗	✔✔	?	?	?	y	n	A
Vladivar	AMB	✗	?	?	✗✗	✗	✔✔	✗	y	n	AT
Warninks Advocaat	ALL	✔	?	✗✗	✗	✔	✔✔	✗	n	C	Atg
White Horse	GUI	✔	✗✗	✗✗	✔✔	?	?	?	y	n	A
Whyte & Mackay	AMB	✗	?	?	✗✗	✗	✔✔	✗	y	n	AT
Windsor Canadian	AMB	✗	?	?	✗✗	✗	✔✔	✗	y	n	AT
Wiser's De Luxe	ALL	✔	?	✗✗	✗	✔	✔✔	✗	n	C	Atg
Ye Monks	GUI	✔	✗✗	✗✗	✔✔	?	?	?	y	n	A
SUGAR AND SWEETENERS											
Fowlers	TAL	✔✔	✗	✗✗	✗	✔	✗	✔	y	C	
Lyle's Black Treacle	TAL	✔✔	✗	✗✗	✗	✔	✗	✔	y	C	
Lyle's Golden Syrup	TAL	✔✔	✗	✗✗	✗	✔	✗	✔	y	C	

118

											Alert!
Lyles Pouring Syrup	TAL	✓✓	✗	✗✗	✗	✓	✗	✓		y	C	
Margetts	ALL	✓	?	✗✗	✗	✓	✓✓	✗		n	C	Atg
Silver Spoon	ABF	✗✗	?	?	✗✗	?	?	✗		Y	n	a
Sweetex	BOO	✗	?	?	✗	✗✗	✓	✗		Y	n	
Tate & Lyle	TAL	✓✓	✗	✗✗	✗	✓	✗	✓		y	C	
Tate Cubes	TAL	✓✓	✗	✗✗	✗	✓	✗	✓		y	C	
SUPERMARKETS												
Asda	ASD	✓	✗✗	✗	✗✗	✓	✓✓	✗		n	n	at
Co-op	CWS	✓✓	✓	✗	✓✓	✓	✓✓	✓		n	L	at
Crazy Prices	ABF	✗✗	?	?	✗✗	?	?	✗		Y	n	a
Galbraith	AGY	✗	?	?	✗✗	✓	✓✓	✗		n	C	at
Gateway	ISO	✗	?	✗✗	✓	?	✓✓	✗		n	n	at
Iceland	ICE	✓✓	✗	✓	✓	✓✓	✓✓		n	n	n	a
Kwik Save Stores	KWK	✗	?	✗✗	✗✗	✓	✓✓	✗		n	n	at
Late Shopper	KWK	✗	?	✗✗	✗✗	✓	✓✓	✗		n	n	at
Leo's	CWS	✓✓	✓	✗	✓✓	✓	✓✓	✓		n	L	at
Lo-Cost	AGY	✗	?	?	✗✗	✓	✓✓	✗		n	C	at
Market Fresh	CWS	✓✓	✓	✗	✓✓	✓	✓✓	✓		n	L	at
Marks & Spencer	MKS	✗	✗	✗✗	✓	✓	✓✓	✗		n	n	a
Presto	AGY	✗	?	?	✗✗	✓	✓✓	✗		n	C	at
Quinnsworth	ABF	✗✗	?	?	✗✗	?	?	✗		Y	n	a
Safeway	AGY	✗	?	?	✗✗	✓	✓✓	✗		n	C	at
Sainsbury	JSA	✓✓	✓✓	✓✓	✓✓	✓	✓✓	✓✓	✗	n	n	at
Snowking	AGY	✗	?	?	✗✗	✓	✓✓	✗		n	C	at
Somerfield	ISO	✗	?	✗✗	✓	?	✓✓	✗		n	n	at
Stewarts	ABF	✗✗	?	?	✗✗	?	?	✗		Y	n	a
Stop and Shop	CWS	✓✓	✓	✗	✓✓	✓	✓✓	✓		n	L	at
Tesco	TES	✓✓	✗	✗✗	✓✓	✓✓	✓✓	✓✓	✗	n	n	at

		♂♀	⚥	🏭	🌳	🐇	🍵	Ⓥ	⚙	Alert!
Waitrose	JLP	✗	?	✗✗	✔	?	✔✔	✗	n	n	
Wellworths	ISO	✗	?	✗✗	✔	?	✔✔	✗	n	n	at
TEA											
'D'	UNL	✔✔	✔	✔✔	✔	✔	✗	✔✔	Y	n	AT
Brooke Bond	UNL	✔✔	✔	✔✔	✔	✔	✗	✔✔	Y	n	AT
Choice Leaf	ALL	✔	?	✗✗	✗	✔	✔✔	✗	n	C	Atg
Choicest Blend	UNL	✔✔	✔	✔✔	✔	✔	✗	✔✔	Y	n	AT
Coolbrew	UNL	✔✔	✔	✔✔	✔	✔	✗	✔✔	Y	n	AT
Fresh Brew	HIL	✗✗	?	?	✗✗	?	?	✗	n	n	
Glengettie	HIL	✗✗	?	?	✗✗	?	?	✗	n	n	
Hornimans	ALL	✔	?	✗✗	✗	✔	✔✔	✗	n	C	Atg
Jacksons	ABF	✗✗	?	?	✗✗	?	?	✗	Y	n	a
London Herb & Spice	HIL	✗✗	?	?	✗✗	?	?	✗	n	n	
Lyons	ALL	✔	?	✗✗	✗	✔	✔✔	✗	n	C	Atg
Melroses	HIL	✗✗	?	?	✗✗	?	?	✗	n	n	
Natureland	HIL	✗✗	?	?	✗✗	?	?	✗	n	n	
PG Lemon Tea	UNL	✔✔	✔	✔✔	✔	✔	✗	✔✔	Y	n	AT
PG Tips	UNL	✔✔	✔	✔✔	✔	✔	✗	✔✔	Y	n	AT
Quick Brew	ALL	✔	?	✗✗	✗	✔	✔✔	✗	n	C	Atg
Ridgways	HIL	✗✗	?	?	✗✗	?	?	✗	n	n	
Secret Garden	HIL	✗✗	?	?	✗✗	?	?	✗	n	n	
Tetley	ALL	✔	?	✗✗	✗	✔	✔✔	✗	n	C	Atg
Twinings	ABF	✗✗	?	?	✗✗	?	?	✗	Y	n	a
Typhoo	HIL	✗✗	?	?	✗✗	?	?	✗	n	n	
Typhoo 'Q Tea'	HIL	✗✗	?	?	✗✗	?	?	✗	n	n	
TOBACCO											
3 Castles	HAN	✗	?	?	✗	?	?	✗	Y	C	Tm
3 Nuns	HAN	✗	?	?	✗	?	?	✗	Y	C	Tm

		⚥	♀	⚔	🏭	🐷	🐰	👁	🌸	🐒	Alert!
Benson & Hedges	AMB	✗	?	?	✗✗	✗	✓✓	✗	y	n	AT
Berkeley Superkings	AMB	✗	?	?	✗✗	✗	✓✓	✗	y	n	AT
Cadets	AMB	✗	?	?	✗✗	✗	✓✓	✗	y	n	AT
Capstan	HAN	✗	?	?	✗	?	?	✗	Y	C	Tm
Carlton	AMB	✗	?	?	✗✗	✗	✓✓	✗	y	n	AT
Cartier	RTH	✗✗	?	?	✗✗	?	?	✗	Y	C	T
Castella	HAN	✗	?	?	✗	?	?	✗	Y	C	Tm
Chargers	AMB	✗	?	?	✗✗	✗	✓✓	✗	y	n	AT
Cigarello	HAN	✗	?	?	✗	?	?	✗	Y	C	Tm
Clan	AMB	✗	?	?	✗✗	✗	✓✓	✗	y	n	AT
Classic	HAN	✗	?	?	✗	?	?	✗	Y	C	Tm
Club	AMB	✗	?	?	✗✗	✗	✓✓	✗	y	n	AT
Cocktail	AMB	✗	?	?	✗✗	✗	✓✓	✗	y	n	AT
Condor	AMB	✗	?	?	✗✗	✗	✓✓	✗	y	n	AT
Corsair	AMB	✗	?	?	✗✗	✗	✓✓	✗	y	n	AT
Customs	AMB	✗	?	?	✗✗	✗	✓✓	✗	y	n	AT
De Luxe Blue	AMB	✗	?	?	✗✗	✗	✓✓	✗	y	n	AT
Digger	HAN	✗	?	?	✗	?	?	✗	Y	C	Tm
Dunhill	RTH	✗✗	?	?	✗✗	?	?	✗	Y	C	T
Elites	AMB	✗	?	?	✗✗	✗	✓✓	✗	y	n	AT
Embassy	HAN	✗	?	?	✗	?	?	✗	Y	C	Tm
Exmoor Hunt	HAN	✗	?	?	✗	?	?	✗	Y	C	Tm
Falstaff	AMB	✗	?	?	✗✗	✗	✓✓	✗	y	n	AT
Gallaher	AMB	✗	?	?	✗✗	✗	✓✓	✗	y	n	AT
Gold Bond	AMB	✗	?	?	✗✗	✗	✓✓	✗	y	n	AT
Golden Virginia	HAN	✗	?	?	✗	?	?	✗	Y	C	Tm
Hamlet	AMB	✗	?	?	✗✗	✗	✓✓	✗	y	n	AT
Henri Wintermans	HAN	✗	?	?	✗	?	?	✗	Y	C	Tm

		🔑	♀	〈	🏭	🌳	🐇	🐄	🍷	🌀	*Alert!*
Holland House	AMB	✗	?	?	✗✗	✗	✓✓	✗	y	n	AT
Imperial Tobacco	HAN	✗	?	?	✗	?	?	✗	Y	C	Tm
John Cotton's	AMB	✗	?	?	✗✗	✗	✓✓	✗	y	n	AT
John Player Special	HAN	✗	?	?	✗	?	?	✗	Y	C	Tm
Kensitas	AMB	✗	?	?	✗✗	✗	✓✓	✗	y	n	AT
Lambert & Butler	HAN	✗	?	?	✗	?	?	✗	Y	C	Tm
Lucky Strike	AMB	✗	?	?	✗✗	✗	✓✓	✗	y	n	AT
Marlboro	PHM	✗	?	?	✗✗	?	✗✗	✗	y	n	AT
Mellow Virginia	AMB	✗	?	?	✗✗	✗	✓✓	✗	y	n	AT
Old Holborn	AMB	✗	?	?	✗✗	✗	✓✓	✗	y	n	AT
Pall Mall	AMB	✗	?	?	✗✗	✗	✓✓	✗	y	n	AT
Panama	HAN	✗	?	?	✗	?	?	✗	Y	C	Tm
Panatella	HAN	✗	?	?	✗	?	?	✗	Y	C	Tm
Peter Stuyvesant	RTH	✗✗	?	?	✗✗	?	?	✗	Y	C	T
Philip Morris	PHM	✗	?	?	✗✗	?	✗✗	✗	y	n	AT
Regal	HAN	✗	?	?	✗	?	?	✗	Y	C	Tm
Rothmans	RTH	✗✗	?	?	✗✗	?	?	✗	Y	C	T
Samson	AMB	✗	?	?	✗✗	✗	✓✓	✗	y	n	AT
Silk Cut	AMB	✗	?	?	✗✗	✗	✓✓	✗	y	n	AT
St Bruno	HAN	✗	?	?	✗	?	?	✗	Y	C	Tm
St Julian Virginia	HAN	✗	?	?	✗	?	?	✗	Y	C	Tm
Walnut	HAN	✗	?	?	✗	?	?	✗	Y	C	Tm
Weights	HAN	✗	?	?	✗	?	?	✗	Y	C	Tm
Whiskey	HAN	✗	?	?	✗	?	?	✗	Y	C	Tm
Woodbines	HAN	✗	?	?	✗	?	?	✗	Y	C	Tm
TOILETRIES											
Albion	SMN	✗	?	?	✗	✗	✓	✗	Y	n	
Atrixo	SMN	✗	?	?	✗	✗	✓	✗	Y	n	

												Alert!
Avon	AVN	✔	✗	✗✗	✔	✔	✔✔	?	n	n	
Badedas	SKB	✗	?	?	✔	?	✔	?	Y	C	
Body Mist	SKB	✗	?	?	✔	?	✔	?	Y	C	
Brylcreem	SKB	✗	?	?	✔	?	✔	?	Y	C	
Camay	PAG	✔✔	✔	✔✔	✗	✔	✗	✔	y	n	
Cidal	SMN	✗	?	?	✗	✗	✔	✗	Y	n	
Cussons	PZO	✗	?	?	✗✗	?	✔✔	✗	n	n	
Fenjal	SKB	✗	?	?	✔	?	✔	?	Y	C	
Fresh	COP	✔✔	✗	✗	✗✗	✔	✗	✔	Y	n	
Imperial Leather	PZO	✗	?	?	✗✗	?	✔✔	✗	n	n	
Knight's Castile	UNL	✔✔	✔	✔✔	✔	✔	✗	✔✔	Y	n	AT
Labello	SMN	✗	?	?	✗	✗	✔	✗	Y	n	
Lifebuoy	UNL	✔✔	✔	✔✔	✔	✔	✗	✔✔	Y	n	AT
Lux	UNL	✔✔	✔	✔✔	✔	✔	✗	✔✔	Y	n	AT
Mamatoto	BOD	✔✔	✗	✗✗	✔✔	✔	✔✔	✔✔	n	n	
Midas	SKB	✗	?	?	✔	?	✔	?	Y	C	
Mostly Men	BOD	✔✔	✗	✗✗	✔✔	✔	✔✔	✔✔	n	n	
My Fair Lady	PZO	✗	?	?	✗✗	?	✔✔	✗	n	n	
Nature's Choice	TES	✔✔	✗	✗✗	✔✔	✔✔	✔✔	✗	n	n	at
Nature's Compliments	JSA	✔✔	✔✔	✔✔	✔	✔✔	✔✔	✗	n	n	at
Nivea	SMN	✗	?	?	✗	✗	✔	✗	Y	n	
Old Spice	PAG	✔✔	✔	✔✔	✗	✔	✗	✔	y	n	
Palmolive	COP	✔✔	✗	✗	✗✗	✔	✗	✔	Y	n	
Pearl	PZO	✗	?	?	✗✗	?	✔✔	✗	n	n	
Pears	UNL	✔✔	✔	✔✔	✔	✔	✗	✔✔	Y	n	AT
Sante Fe	PAG	✔✔	✔	✔✔	✗	✔	✗	✔	y	n	
Shield	UNL	✔✔	✔	✔✔	✔	✔	✗	✔✔	Y	n	AT
Simple	SMN	✗	?	?	✗	✗	✔	✗	Y	n	

											Alert!
Slazenger Sport	SKB	✗	?	?	✓	?	✓	?	Y	C	
The Body Shop	BOD	✓✓	✗	✗✗	✓✓	✓	✓✓	✓✓	n	n	
Zest	PAG	✓✓	✓	✓✓	✗	✓	✗	✓	y	n	

WASHING MACHINES AND DISHWASHERS

											Alert!
Ariston	MRL	✗✗	?	?	✗✗	?	✓✓	?	n	n	
Electrolux	ELE	✗	?	?	✗✗	?	✓✓	?	n	n	
Hoover	MAY	✗	?	?	✗✗	?	✓✓	?	y	n	
Hotpoint	GEC	✓✓	✓	✓	✗	✓	✓✓	✗	Y	n	M
Indesit	MRL	✗✗	?	?	✗✗	?	✓✓	?	n	n	
Philips/Whirlpool	PHI	✗	?	?	✓	✓	✓✓	✗	Y	n	M
Zanussi	ELE	✗	?	?	✗✗	?	✓✓	?	n	n	

WINE

											Alert!
Almaden Wines	GRM	✓✓	✓	✗	✓	✓	✓✓	✗	Y	n	Atg
Babycham	ALL	✓	?	✗✗	✗	✓	✓✓	✗	n	C	Atg
Barwell & Jones	BWG	✓	?	?	✗	✗✗	✓✓	n	n	C	AtG
Beaulieu Vineyards	GRM	✓✓	✓	✗	✓	✓	✓✓	✗	Y	n	Atg
Black Tower	WBR	✗	?	?	✗	?	✓✓	?	n	C	Atg
Callaway	ALL	✓	?	✗✗	✗	✓	✓✓	✗	n	C	Atg
Calvet	ALL	✓	?	✗✗	✗	✓	✓✓	✗	n	C	Atg
Calvet Reserve	WBR	✗	?	?	✗	?	✓✓	?	n	C	Atg
Canard Duchene	GUI	✓	✗✗	✗✗	✓✓	?	?	?	y	n	A
Champagne Lanson	WBR	✗	?	?	✗	?	✓✓	?	n	C	Atg
Chateau Latour	ALL	✓	?	✗✗	✗	✓	✓✓	✗	n	C	Atg
Chiron De-alcohol	ALL	✓	?	✗✗	✗	✓	✓✓	✗	n	C	Atg
Christian Brothers	GRM	✓✓	✓	✗	✓	✓	✓✓	✗	Y	n	Atg
Clos du Bois	ALL	✓	?	✗✗	✗	✓	✓✓	✗	n	C	Atg
Cockburn's Ports	ALL	✓	?	✗✗	✗	✓	✓✓	✗	n	C	Atg
Concorde	ALL	✓	?	✗✗	✗	✓	✓✓	✗	n	C	Atg

		♂⚲	♀	〈	🏠	🌳	🐇	🍲	🍇	⚘	Alert!
Corrida	WBR	✗	?	?	✗	?	✔✔	?	n	C	Atg
Country Manor	ALL	✔	?	✗✗	✗	✔	✔✔	✗	n	C	Atg
Crabbie's Green Ginger	GUI	✔	✗✗	✗✗	✔✔	?	?	?	y	n	A
Croft Original	GRM	✔✔	✔	✗	✔	✔	✔✔	✗	Y	n	Atg
Croft Port	GRM	✔✔	✔	✗	✔	✔	✔✔	✗	Y	n	Atg
Delaforce Port	GRM	✔✔	✔	✗	✔	✔	✔✔	✗	Y	n	Atg
Dom Perignon	GUI	✔	✗✗	✗✗	✔✔	?	?	?	y	n	A
Domain Chandon	GUI	✔	✗✗	✗✗	✔✔	?	?	?	y	n	A
Don Cortez	WBR	✗	?	?	✗	?	✔✔	?	n	C	Atg
Eisberg	BAS	✗	?	✗	✗✗	✔	✔✔	✗	y	n	AtG
Emva Cyprus Sherry	BAS	✗	?	✗	✗✗	✔	✔✔	✗	y	n	AtG
Grants of St James's	WBR	✗	?	?	✗	?	✔✔	?	n	C	Atg
Harveys Sherries	ALL	✔	?	✗✗	✗	✔	✔✔	✗	n	C	Atg
Henriot	GUI	✔	✗✗	✗✗	✔✔	?	?	?	y	n	A
Inglenook Wines	GRM	✔✔	✔	✗	✔	✔	✔✔	✗	Y	n	Atg
J. Moreau et Fils	ALL	✔	?	✗✗	✗	✔	✔✔	✗	n	C	Atg
La Cour Pavillion	GRM	✔✔	✔	✗	✔	✔	✔✔	✗	Y	n	Atg
Lancers Wines	GRM	✔✔	✔	✗	✔	✔	✔✔	✗	Y	n	Atg
Langenbach	WBR	✗	?	?	✗	?	✔✔	?	n	C	Atg
Lanson	ALL	✔	?	✗✗	✗	✔	✔✔	✗	n	C	Atg
Le Piat D'Or	GRM	✔✔	✔	✗	✔	✔	✔✔	✗	Y	n	Atg
Mercier	GUI	✔	✗✗	✗✗	✔✔	?	?	?	y	n	A
Möet et Chandon	GUI	✔	✗✗	✗✗	✔✔	?	?	?	y	n	A
Piat Beaujolais	GRM	✔✔	✔	✗	✔	✔	✔✔	✗	Y	n	Atg
Piemontello	WBR	✗	?	?	✗	?	✔✔	?	n	C	Atg
Pierlant	GUI	✔	✗✗	✗✗	✔✔	?	?	?	y	n	A
Pimm's	GUI	✔	✗✗	✗✗	✔✔	?	?	?	y	n	A
Pimontello	ALL	✔	?	✗✗	✗	✔	✔✔	✗	n	C	Atg

		🍷♀		⟨🏭	🌳	🐰	👜	🐑	⚙	Alert!
Pink Lady	ALL	✔	?	✘✘	✘	✔	✔✔	✘	n	C	Atg
QC British Sherry	ALL	✔	?	✘✘	✘	✔	✔✔	✘	n	C	Atg
Rougemont Castle	ALL	✔	?	✘✘	✘	✔	✔✔	✘	n	C	Atg
Ruinart	GUI	✔	✘✘	✘✘	✔✔	?	?	?	y	n	A
Stowells of Chelsea	WBR	✘	?	?	✘	?	✔✔	?	n	C	Atg
Tio Mateo Sherry	ALL	✔	?	✘✘	✘	✔	✔✔	✘	n	C	Atg
Veuve Clicquot	GUI	✔	✘✘	✘✘	✔✔	?	?	?	y	n	A
Veuve du Vernay	BAS	✘	?	✘	✘✘	✔	✔✔	✘	y	n	AtG

Alberto-Culver (UK) Limited

									Alert!
XX	?	?	XX	?	X	?	y	n	

Parent: Alberto-Culver Company		USA
Size: World: £450m UK: £42m	UK employees: 448	
Activities: Manufactures and market hair care products		

- A major manufacturer and distributor of hair care products, both to consumers and to the hairdressing trade.

- Minimal social information is publicly available.

- The Chief Executive Officer of parent Alberto-Culver Company stated in the latest annual report when describing the company: 'We are a no frills outfit . . . We spend money to build sales, not monuments'.

- The company's record on charitable giving in the UK scarcely registered at £600 in 1989.

- Observed US legislation in 1978 banning CFCs, but did not modify its aerosol propellants in the UK until 1985.

- In 1989 it introduced a range of clear colourless hair care products packaged in recyclable bottles.

- Alberto-Culver contracts out its animal testing, and funds research into alternative testing through the Fund for the Replacement of Animal Experiments (FRAME) in the UK and John Hopkins University in the USA.

- One of a dozen companies targeted in the British Union for the Abolition of Vivisection's (BUAV) latest boycott campaign.

- Markets its products in many third world countries.

Lack of disclosure makes an affirmative assessment of the company's social and ethical performance difficult, though there appears to be little evidence of strong corporate responsibility.

Allied-Lyons plc

										Alert!
✔	?	✗✗	✗	✔	✔✔	✗	n	C		Atg

Size: World: £5,133m UK: £2,994m	*UK employees:* 67,215

Activities: Manufactures and sells beer, food and beverages

- One of the UK's top six brewers now diversified around foods and having substantial interests in Europe, USA and the Far East.
- Over 50 per cent of graduate recruits are women.
- Donations, in the UK, including gifts in kind were just over £1 million in 1989, 0.2 per cent of pre-tax profits. Evidence of considerable giving in the US.
- Its *Good Environmental Practice* booklet provides a detailed breakdown of environmental issues and action taken by the company.
- Environmental action includes reduction in emissions, energy, and noise, waste control measures and efforts to minimise packaging.
- Retails organic tea and coffee endorsed respectively by the Soil Association and Organic Farmers and Growers.
- Imports products including tea, coffee and seafood and has subsidiaries in 13 third world countries. It provided examples of its charitable and community involvement in the third world.
- Political donations in 1989/90 included £110,000 to the Conservative Party; one of the top six corporate donors.
- The company states it is 'dedicated to the encouragement of sensible drinking as a feature of a pleasurable social existence'.

> *The company has a philosophical commitment to the economic and social betterment of society by means of an unfettered market.*

Amstrad plc

SECRET	♀	🔊	🏠	🌳	🐰	👙	☕	⚙	Alert!
✗	?	✗✗	✗✗	✗✗	✓✓	✗	n	n	

Size: World: £577m UK: £251m	UK employees: 1,328

Activities: Manufactures and sells consumer electronics goods

- Currently the number one UK-owned supplier of computing equipment. Businessman's survey by *The Financial Times* rates Amstrad the most admired marketing company in the UK.

- Its founder and major shareholder, Alan Sugar, once remarked that Amstrad would market portable nuclear weapons if there were a market for them.

- Notably, there is no reference to corporate responsibility beyond the minimum required by law in the company's publicly available literature.

- No equal opportunities monitoring is carried out as the company believes that by not making an issue of the matter it does not discriminate.

- There is one woman on the main board of directors.

- No charitable donations have been recorded in the last three annual reports. Alan Sugar is a supporter of Business in the Community.

- Amstrad sources around 40 per cent of its electronic components and equipment from developing countries, particularly China and newly industrialised South Korea.

> *A company with a high public profile that has shown little evidence of developed corporate social responsibility policies.*

Anchor Foods Ltd

SECRET	♀	👤	🏠	🌳	🐰	🍯	💊	⚙	Alert!
XX	?	?	XX	?	?	?	n	n	

Parent: The New Zealand Dairy Board	New Zealand

Size: World: £1,268m UK: £175m	**UK employees:** 433

Activities: Manufactures and markets dairy products

- Its parent company the New Zealand Dairy Board (NZDB) supplies nearly 25 per cent of all the international trade in milk, and is the world's largest single exporter.

- In 1989, three million households in Britain bought Anchor butter every month.

- Both the company and its parent company's publicly available literature provided no social or ethical information.

- Charitable donations, in the UK amounted to £515 in 1989.

- Its parent is involved in biotechnology including the production of products to improve the immunity of new born pigs and calves.

- The NZDB has extensive operations in the third world with 21 subsidiaries in 16 countries. It is a major supplier of milk powder to developing countries.

- Over 50 per cent of Latin American imports of milk products are supplied by the NZDB.

> *The lack of social and ethical information disclosure by a major food company contrasts sharply with public demand for improved information on food and health issues.*

Argos plc

🔍SECRET	⚥	👤	🏠	🌳	🐰	👶	⚠	⚙	Alert!
✓✓	✗✗	✗✗	✗✗	✓	✓✓	✗	n	n	

Size: World: £906m UK: £906m	*UK employees:* 11,619

Activities: Retails consumer goods through catalogue stores

- Europe's leading catalogue store chain, with 272 outlets in the UK.

- Demerged from B.A.T Industries, the tobacco to insurance conglomerate, in April 1990, and independent policy formulation on certain issues is still at the formative stage.

- No women or ethnic minorities on the board of directors and no figures available for the numbers in management.

- In 1990 Argos donated £46,866 to charity (less than 0.1 per cent of pre-tax profits). It is a member of Business in the Community.

- Argos has an environmental policy statement and initiated a company wide environmental audit in 1989.

- In its current catalogue it states that it 'is against testing cosmetics on animals. None of our finished products have been tested on animals'.

- No reported policy on goods sourced from the third world.

> *The company is still in the process of establishing policies after demerger from a leading tobacco company. Whether these will emphasise social and ethical issues remains to be seen.*

Argyll Group PLC

									Alert!
✗	?	?	✗✗	✓	✓✓	✗	n	C	at

Size: World: £4,758m	UK: £4,758m	UK employees: 66,099

Activities: Supermarkets

- Better known by its principal store name Safeway, which accounts for 70 per cent of its turnover.

- The large amount of publicly available literature, particularly on environmental issues, contrasts strongly with the company's unwillingness to comment or answer questions.

- Prue Leith, food writer and restaurateur is a non-executive director.

- Argyll, as with other major supermarket chains has successfully taken on a number of environmental issues. It was the first large retailer to market organic produce on a substantial scale.

- The company's own label cosmetics, toiletries and household products have not been tested on animals. However, the company states that it 'cannot guarantee that all of the manufacturers' raw materials are not tested at any stage on animals'.

- The company has made annual donations of £30,000 to the Conservative Party in the last three years.

- In common with most other major food retailers, Argyll retails products from South Africa. It argues that it is up to consumers to choose not to buy. There is no reported policy on goods sourced from the third world.

- Through its supermarkets and off-licenses Argyll is a major alcoholic drinks retailer.

A high profile and disclosure on environmental issues is not matched in other areas of corporate responsibility.

Asda Group plc

SEC	♀	👤	🏠	🌳	🐰	🍲	💣	🌹	Alert!
✔	xx	x	xx	✔	✔✔	x	n	n	at

Size: World: £2,709m	UK: £2,709m	UK employees: 50,465

Activities: Superkarkets and furniture retailing

- A major supermarket chain and furniture retailer (Allied Maples), with a high level of disclosure.

- Although the company stated that it did monitor women and ethnic minorities centrally, it declined to supply any figures. Asda has been commended for its equal opportunities policies.

- In addition to its direct corporate donations Asda established the Asda Foundation, an independent charity, in 1988. It is a member of Business in the Community and the UK Per Cent Club.

- Like other supermarkets it has taken a wide range of environmental initiatives. It is a member of the Industry Council on Packaging and the Environment (INCPEN).

- Allied Maples is currently reviewing the sale of tropical hardwood furniture in its stores.

- Asda sells 'conservation grade meat' (meat farmed through a more traditional farming system).

- None of the company's own-label products have been tested on animals. The ingredients used are also under investigation.

- Products are sourced from South Africa when no suitable alternative source can be found either for the quantity or the quality required. All such products are clearly labelled.

- No reported policy on goods sourced from the third world.

An above average level of disclosure was supported by positive policies in several areas of corporate responsibility.

Aspro Nicholas Holdings plc

SECRET	♀	〈	🏭	🌳	🐰	👶	⚠	⚙	Alert!
✗✗	?	?	✗✗	?	?	✗	Y	n	

Parent: Sara Lee Corporation		USA

Size: World: £6,561m	UK: £94m	UK employees: 2,000

Activities: Manufactures pharmaceuticals, toiletries, polish, coffee and frozen cakes

- The US parent Sara Lee is better known as the world's largest producer of frozen desserts. Its parent's diverse interests also include Kiwi polish, ladies tights (Dim), and Douwe Egberts and Van Nelle, two Dutch coffee giants.

- Aspro Nicholas manufactures and markets pharmaceutical, household products, cosmetics and toiletries in the UK.

- Its parent company provided ample evidence about its corporate responsibility, however no corresponding public information was provided for its UK operations.

- No charitable donations were reported in its 1988 annual report. This contrasts markedly with its two per cent of pre-tax profits donations in the US.

- In the US Sara Lee is not involved in any animal testing.

- Through its ownership of Nicholas Kiwi Ltd. it sub-licenses certain trademarks to South African companies.

- No reported policy on goods sourced or operations in the third world.

> *The lack of information relating to the company's UK operations meant that its parent company's strong personnel, community giving and equal opportunities initiatives cannot be attributed to its activities here.*

Associated British Foods plc

SEC?	♀	🏠	🌳	🐰	👶	✌	⚙	Alert!
XX	?	?	XX	?	?	X	Y	n	a

Size: World: £2,775m	UK: £1,730m	UK employees: 38,743

Activities: Manufactures bread, frozen and canned products, tea and coffee

- Britain's leading bread producer and owner of Fortnum & Masons.

- The company is ultimately owned by Whittington Investments Ltd. The chairman, Canadian businessman Garry Weston, has a controlling interest.

- In 1990 it acquired British Sugar, which uses beet sugar, sourced in the UK and the European Community, as opposed to cane sugar, sourced from developing countries, as its raw material.

- Charitable donations of £100,000 were made in 1989/90, 0.04 per cent of pre-tax profits, a notably low amount. Its membership of the Per Cent Club implies significant in-kind community involvement, though no evidence to support this is presented.

- Environmental issues mentioned in its latest annual report include support for national can reclamation and bottle recycling programmes, and switching all new refrigeration from CFCs to R22 — a more environmentally friendly refrigerant.

- Overseas operations involved in livestock rearing through meat and dairy divisions. Provided no comment on issues concerning animal husbandry, or on sourcing from the third world.

- The company is the 'clear leader in sales of wines and spirits' in Northern Ireland, through its Stewarts' in-store off-licenses.

- ABF has a South African subsidiary, Talisman Holdings Ltd. The company did not comment on its activities.

> *One of Britain's largest food companies, with a poor level of disclosure and little evidence of systematic social policies.*

Avon Cosmetics Limited

							Alert!	
✓	✗	✗✗	✓	✓	✓✓	?	n	n

Parent: Avon Products Incorporated		USA
Size: World: £1,875m UK: £147m	*UK employees:* 2,131	

Activities: Manufactures and sells cosmetics, toiletries, toys and gifts

- The world's largest producer of cosmetics and toiletries, selling through a network of 1.5 million representatives.

- A high level of disclosure.

- There is only one woman non-executive director on the UK board, contrasting with three women on the US parent company's board. Although the company has strong policies in relation to disabled employees, it has few initiatives for women or ethnic minorities.

- Community involvement in the USA is stronger than in the UK, though the figures for the most recent donations show a marked increase on the previous year, rising from £7,958 in 1989 to £62,303 in 1990.

- It has set up an environmental committee. Its positive initiatives include reducing energy consumption over the last two years by 50 per cent; switching to the use of more environmentally benign chemicals; recycling initiatives; and steps to minimise packaging.

- Has manufacturing and sales operations in a number of third world countries, including more recently China, targeted as a major new market.

- In June 1989 Avon stopped all animal testing for cosmetics and toiletries. In the UK it continues to support FRAME (Fund for the Replacement of Animal in Medical Experiments) and in the US CAAT (National Center for Alternatives to Animal Testing).

> *Avon UK could move further towards adopting its parent's positive policies.*

Bass plc

![SECRET]	![female]	![knife]	![house]	![tree]	![rabbit]	![pot]	![globe]	![magnifier]	Alert!
✗	?	✗	✗✗	✓	✓✓	✗	y	n	AtG

Size: World: £4,461m	UK: £3,886m	UK employees: 98,345

Activities: Pubs, hotels, restaurants, alcohol and gambling

- Britain's largest brewer and owner of the world's largest hotel chain (Holiday Inn Worldwide).

- Holds the majority shareholding in Britannia Soft Drinks Ltd, which owns Britvic Soft Drinks Ltd.

- The most senior woman is the Company Secretary. No specific information was available about the overall number of women and ethnic minorities in management.

- Bass's latest cash charitable donations amounted to only 0.13 per cent of pre-tax profit, a low figure for the UK. It is a member of Business in the Community.

- The company has no specific written environmental policy, but has taken a number of initiatives including water and energy conservation measures, recycling and packaging initiatives, and switching its cars to unleaded petrol.

- Through its Holiday Inn Worldwide operations it operates in a number of third world countries, including China.

- Bass franchises 22 Holiday Inns in South Africa.

- Extensive gambling and leisure interests, from fruit machines and bingo (Coral Leisure, Granada Bingo) to racing (Coral Racing).

- Bass was one of the pioneers of alcohol-free/low alcohol beer. Criticised for its active marketing of extra-strength brands.

Bass's corporate responsibility programme gives the impression of being at a formative stage, with many areas to be consolidated.

Blue Circle Industries PLC

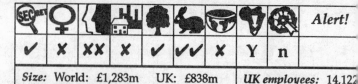

									Alert!
✔	✗	✗✗	✗	✔	✔✔	✗	Y	n	

Size: World: £1,283m UK: £838m **UK employees:** 14,122

Activities: Manufactures building materials, heating equipment and home products

- The UK's largest cement producer, with activities in homecare an environmental management.
- No information about numbers of women or ethnic minorities i staff and management were available.
- The company is a member of Business in the Community and th UK Per Cent Club. The Blue Circle Trust provides advice an support for people setting themselves up in business.
- No written environmental policy currently available, though on is in preparation. According to regulatory bodies its operations ar generally well run. It outlined a number of positive initiatives.
- Runs environmental services through its landfill operations.
- Has extensive cement producing operations in developing coun tries. The company stated that, where it can, it influences th behaviour of these subsidiaries, but did not provide any detail.
- Has a wholly owned operation and a 42 per cent interest in cement operation in South Africa, with nearly 5,000 employees i 1990.

> *A company with a major environmental impact and extensive environmental management services, yet not appearing to have any company-wide policies on these matters.*

The Body Shop International PLC

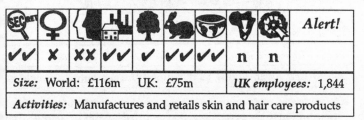

![SECRET]	♀	🏠	🌳	🐇	👶	☠	⚙	Alert!
✓✓	✗	✗✗	✓✓	✓	✓✓	✓✓	n	n	

Size: World: £116m UK: £75m	UK employees: 1,844

Activities: Manufactures and retails skin and hair care products

- A small but significant alternative cosmetics and toiletries company. No advertising, no animal testing and trade not aid policy.

- States that it 'cares about humanising the business community . . . success and profit can go hand in hand with ideals and values'.

- A very open company, providing detailed responses to requests for information.

- It still has to develop strengths in staff representation, employee profit sharing, and equal opportunities.

- High level of community and social involvement, both in terms of donations and action. It gave more than one per cent of its 1990 pre-tax profit for charitable purposes, as well as encouraging individual staff initiatives.

- It has a strong environmental profile, with cradle-to-grave audits of its own operations and those of its suppliers and service companies.

- A low level of involvement in the third world, but one of the few companies that seriously considers its sourcing policy.

- Innovative in the production and retailing of cosmetics and toiletries not tested on animals.

> *The first modern UK company to take corporate social responsibility successfully as its unique selling proposition.*

Booker plc

SECRET	♀	👤	🏠	🌳	🐇	👶	🍷	⚙	Alert!
XX	?	?	XX	?	?	?	n	n	

Size: World: £2,926m UK: £261m	UK employees: 22,762

Activities: Agribusiness, food manufacture and book copyrights

- A company with operations ranging from agriculture and food distribution to the prestigious Booker prize for authors. It owns the rights to Agatha Christie's novels and the James Bond books.

- It has formed a joint 50/50 venture, Booker Tate, with Tate & Lyle, the sugar company, to provide agricultural management and consultancy throughout the world.

- Booker claimed that it was unable to provide detailed information about the group because no centralised records are held.

- There is virtually no reference to environmental issues in publicly available information. Booker has major forestry operations in Scotland.

- Booker's subsidiaries in the third world are mainly involved in poultry production or breeding.

- Through Booker Tate it is currently working in over 30 countries, mainly as consultant to projects involved in tea, coffee, sugar, palm oil and livestock production.

- A major poultry and fish breeder. Booker mentions in its *1990 Annual Report* that it is looking into the use of biological control for fish parasites to replace use of chemicals.

- Booker retails alcohol through its cash and carry operations.

> *From the little information available, Booker appears to be addressing some corporate responsibility issues.*

The Boots Company PLC

SECRET	♀	{⟨	🏭	🌳	🐰	👶	☠	🔍	Alert!
✗	?	?	✗	✗✗	✓	✗	Y	n	

Size: World: £3,565m	UK: £3,166m	UK employees: 83,745

Activities: Manufactures and retails pharmaceuticals, DIY, toiletries and baby products

- Boots combined retail outlets serve half the women and a quarter of the men in Britain every week.

- Its disclosure was below average, providing limited information beyond general policy statements.

- Boots has one female non-executive director on the main board.

- Boots is a member of Business in the Community and gave charitable donations of just over 0.2 per cent of its 1989/90 pre-tax profit to charity, a low figure for a company of its size.

- Virtually no information was provided about any environmental initiatives or policies.

- Its large pharmaceuticals division is involved in animal testing, but no tests are conducted for the large range of own-label cosmetics and toiletries.

- A Boots subsidiary was named as one of the top six offenders by a 1989 IBFAN/IOCU report on irresponsible marketing of breast milk substitutes in third world countries.

- It has an operating subsidiary in South Africa, which manufactures and markets pharmaceutical products and employed 146 staff in 1989.

> *A unique company, being both a major manufacturer and retailer of pharmaceutical and related products. With such a high public profile, its low level of disclosure was disappointing.*

Brent Walker Group PLC

SECRET	♀	〰	🏠	🌳	🐰	🍯	👕	🔔	Alert!
✔	?	?	✗	✗✗	✔✔	n	n	C	AtG

Size: World: £527m	UK: £407m	UK employees: 6,251

Activities: Leisure development, pubs, brewing, betting, hotels

- Leisure group that expanded rapidly at the end of the 1980s and is now struggling with large debts.

- In spite of its current financial difficulties the company completed some of the latest questionnaires.

- One out of 15 members of the wider board is a woman (Mrs Jean Walker), and there are two ethnic minority representatives on the divisional boards.

- No information was provided about the overall numbers of women and ethnic minorities in managerial positions.

- Three pages of its latest annual report are devoted to describing the company's small but evolving community involvement programme.

- A regular but modest donor to the Conservative Party.

- For a company heavily involved in brewing and retailing alcohol there is, surprisingly, no reference to action on sensible drinking in any of its literature.

- It has 1,650 licensed betting offices.

> *Evidence of an evolving community/sponsorship programme is not supported by activity in other areas of corporate responsibility.*

British Aerospace PLC

🔒	♀	🔊	🏭	🌳	🐰	👶	☠	⚙	Alert!
✗	?	✗✗	✓	?	✓✓	✗✗	n	n	**M**

Size: World: £10,540m UK: £3,668m	*UK employees:* 127,900

Activities: Manufactures cars, aircraft, military and engineering products

- Britain's largest manufacturer of engineering products, and the main surviving car manufacturer.

- Declined to respond to requests for information as it felt that the subsidiary businesses were too diverse to be adequately represented under one umbrella.

- Cash donations for 1990 increased from £514,000 in 1989 to £1,365,000 (0.36 per cent of pre-tax profit). A member of Business in the Community and the UK Per Cent Club.

- Produces 'environmentally friendly' shotgun cartridges.

- Significant ethical issues arising from its operations include huge profits from the sale of Royal Ordnance assets purchased from the state. It concealed the subsidies received from the government in the purchase of the Rover Group.

- An active seller of arms to third world countries. Pressure from the Government prevented sales of £300 million of military aircraft to Iraq in autumn 1990. The company chaperoned former Chilean dictator, General Pinochet, on a visit to review the Anglo/Chilean arms project in May 1991.

- One of the leading manufacturers of military equipment in Europe, and the largest in the UK. In 1990 arms sales totalled £4,635 million, 44 per cent of turnover and contributing 83 per cent of trading profit.

A low level of disclosure and lack of publicly available information on ethical and social issues suggests the company places a low priority on corporate social responsibility.

British Airways Plc

									Alert!
✔	✔	✔	✗✗	✗	✔✔	✗	y	C	atM

Size: World: £4,937m UK: £571m	UK employees: 47,221

Activities: Airline services and tourism

- The largest carrier of international scheduled passenger traffic in the world.

- It has an extensive employee profit sharing scheme. In 1990 around 70 per cent of the workforce were BA shareholders.

- It has a company wide equal opportunities monitoring scheme. In 1990 women accounted for 21 per cent of managers and 12 per cent of senior managers.

- Charitable donations amounted to 0.13 per cent of pre-tax profits in 1989/90, below average for UK giving.

- In 1989 it appointed a Head of Environment, and subsequently provided a summary of an environmental audit to New Consumer in 1991.

- Flies to many third world destinations, also to South Africa, and has associate companies in a number of developing countries.

- Supports the Conservative Party through its annual political donations (£130,000 in 1987/90), because it believes that 'it is in the best interest of our shareholders and our future commercial success for us to operate in the free enterprise environment created by the present Government'.

- Military sales include engine maintenance contracts for non-UK airforces.

The company shows a high degree of openness and is developing interesting initiatives in a number of areas.

British Gas plc

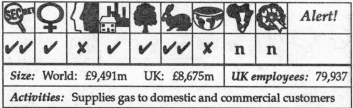

										Alert!
✔✔	✔	✘	✔	✔	✔✔	✘	n	n	

Size: World: £9,491m UK: £8,675m	**UK employees:** 79,937

Activities: Supplies gas to domestic and commercial customers

- British Gas is the near monopoly supplier of domestic and commercial gas in the UK.

- An open company, providing both published and internal literature as well as specific information.

- There is one woman non-executive director on the board, Baroness Platt of Writtle, a former chair of the Equal Opportunities Commission from 1983-1988.

- Ten per cent of managers were women in 1990. The company stated that it monitors both women and ethnic minorities though unable to supply figures for ethnic minorities in management.

- Produced a booklet, *A Sense of Commitment*, which outlines its extensive community involvement. In 1990 its total community involvement amounted to £6 million, 0.57 pre-tax profit.

- As a major energy supplier it has a statutory obligation to promote efficient use of gas. BG reduced its own energy usage by ten per cent during 1988/89.

- Most gas is transported through pipelines. The company carries out environmental impact assessments before laying pipes.

- Through its oil exploration BG is involved in operations in tropical rainforest in Gabon and Ecuador. It claims that these are run to standards aimed to minimise environmental impact, contrary to the views of FoE in August 1990, but this is still under review.

General openness, with a high level of understanding and responsiveness to most corporate social responsibility issues.

The British Petroleum Company p.l.c.

🔐	♀	👄	🏠	🌳	🐰	🍯	🛡	🔍	*Alert!*
✓	✓	✓✓	✓	✗	✗	✗	Y	n	tM

Size: World: £33,039m UK: £12,209m	*UK employees:* 30,850

Activities: Oil, gas, petroleum, chemicals, pet foods and cleaners

- One of the top five oil and petroleum suppliers in the UK.

- Seventy seven per cent of employees in share ownership schemes.

- Although only two per cent of managerial staff are women and one per cent are members of ethnic minorities, the company recognises the need to provide opportunities for these groups and has taken steps to do so.

- Notable as one of only four companies in survey to provide figures for the number of registered disabled employees.

- Charitable donations in the UK amounted to £13.5 million (0.49 per cent of pre-tax profits) in 1990.

- It owns the Robert McBride Group which produces Green Force 'environmentally friendly' cleaning products.

- BP owns the Olympic Dam uranium mine in Australia which supplies ore for nuclear power generation. The company does not accept accusations of differing environmental standards in third world countries. In 1989 BP subsidiaries in South Africa employed 3,110 staff.

- As well as being a major fuel supplier to the MoD, a subsidiary of BP Chemicals supplies composite materials for the defence industry worth £50-100 million in 1988/89.

> *The company was very open about a number of social and ethical issues, with a strong commitment to action in a number of areas, particularly equal opportunities and community involvement.*

The Burton Group plc

SECRET	♀	🧍	🏠	🌳	🐰	🍼	🐄	⚙️	Alert!
xx	?	?	x	?	?	x	n	n	

Size: World: £1,801m	UK: £1,801m	UK employees: 38,054

Activities: Clothing retailers, department stores, property and finance

- A major high street fashion retailer.
- Showed a very low level of disclosure, and declined to take part in any New Consumer survey.
- Exceptionally high top executives' pay and golden handshakes.
- Operated employee profit sharing and savings-related share schemes for senior staff only in 1989/90.
- Burton's say 'Principles for Women's target customers are confident aspirational working women', but there is little evidence of actively promoting equal opportunities for women in management.
- Charitable donations have declined from £565,000 (0.31 per cent of pre-tax profit) in 1986/87 to £320,100 (0.24 per cent of pre-tax profit) in 1989/90. Burton is a member of Business in the Community and the UK Per Cent Club.
- In 1989 Burton ran a promotional campaign in which it donated £1 from each of a range of t-shirts sold to three environmental charities. It appears to have taken no other environmental initiatives.
- It declined to respond to questions about its sourcing of garments from third world countries, or any related policy.

> *A market-led company which offered no acknow-ledgement of a responsibility to provide information about its social and ethical behaviour.*

C&A

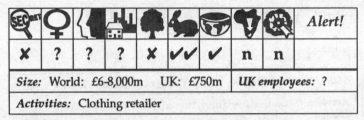

									Alert!
✗	?	?	?	✗	✓✓	✓	n	n	

Size: World: £6-8,000m UK: £750m	**UK employees:** ?

Activities: Clothing retailer

- Has a unique status for a large company, as it is both private and unlimited. This means that the owners, members of a Dutch family, are personally financially liable for the company.

- The company is not obliged to disclose any financial details.

- C&A pioneered the five-day week in retailing and is a major supporter of the Keep Sunday Special Campaign, which campaigns against shops opening on Sundays.

- Working conditions, pay, holiday entitlement and benefits are considered to be good for the retail sector.

- The company states that it monitors its equal opportunities policy, but was not prepared to supply figures.

- C&A makes its charitable donations through the C&A Charitable Trust. The Trust gave £189,287 in donations in 1989.

- The company sources clothing from various third world countries, and claims to be opposed to any form of poor working conditions or exploitation by its suppliers.

- C&A indicated that it intends to adopt a number of initiatives to address problems of exploitation, including training buyers to be aware of potential problems and a revision of the standard order form to incorporate legally binding terms and conditions. If they are applied, these appear to be positive moves.

C&A has been at the leading edge in some areas of social responsibility, particularly personnel policy, though it is reticent about information concerning ownership and control.

Cadbury Schweppes p.l.c.

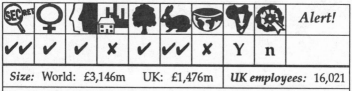

									Alert!
✓✓	✓	✓	✗	✓	✓✓	✗	Y	n	

Size: World: £3,146m	UK: £1,476m	*UK employees:* 16,021

Activities: Manufactures and markets confectionery and soft drinks

- One of the UK's leading manufacturers of branded confectionery and beverages including a 51 per cent stake in Coca-Cola's marketing subsidiary in the UK.

- Cadbury's original philanthropic foundations were laid in the exemplary late-19th century 'model' factory and workers estate at Bournville.

- It has a strong public commitment to disclosure, which was matched by its response to requests for detailed information.

- Cadbury has modest charitable and community programmes for a company of its size. In 1990 its charitable giving amounted to 0.15 per cent of pre-tax profits.

- The company has taken a number of positive environmental initiatives. These including a notable policy to ensure that its raw material suppliers minimise the use of pesticides.

- It has subsidiaries in nine third world countries, and is a major purchaser of commodities produced in the third world.

- The company has substantial interests in South Africa, and is involved in the manufacture and sale of confectionery and beverages. In 1989 it employed a total of 2,745 workers there.

NB The 'Cadbury' name and interests are currently held in biscuits and drinking chocolate by Hillsdown Holdings, and in cakes by Ranks Hovis McDougall.

An early reputation gained as a leading socially concerned employer appears to be reflected in current operations.

Campbell's UK Limited

SECRET	♀	〈	🏠	🌳	🐰	🍯	🎖	⚙	Alert!
✗	?	?	✗	?	?	?	n	n	

Parent: Campbell Soup Company		USA

Size: World: £3,508m UK: £47m	UK employees: 654

Activities: Food manufacturer: soup and convenience food

- The US parent company maintains a strong reputation for social concern in its home country. It is one of America's oldest and most powerful food companies.

- Operations in the UK have recently undergone a major restructuring, which may have been a contributory factor to the lack of response to New Consumer.

- Campbell's UK Ltd's latest charitable donations are reasonable for the UK, but low in comparison to its parent company's extensive community programmes in the USA. There is little evidence of any other community involvement.

- The company claims to have progressive environmental policies in the USA, but has had a number of complaints filed against it by the Environmental Protection Agency (EPA).

- Campbell's in the USA has been criticised for excessive use of packaging for its microwavable food.

> A strong reputation for openness and for well-developed social and ethical programmes in the US does not appear to be mirrored in the UK operations.

City Centre Restaurants plc

![SECRET]	♀	🥤	🏠	🌳	🐇	👶	🍷	⚙	Alert!
XX	?	?	XX	?	✓✓	?	n	n	at

Size: World: £63m	UK: £63m	UK employees: 2,746

Activities: Restaurants

- Formally known as Belhaven plc, it is better known by its restaurant chains: Garfunkels, Deep Pan Pizza Company, Biguns Ribs and Filling Station.

- It made no response to any requests for information, and produces very little publicly available information.

- There are no women or ethnic minorities on the main board of directors.

- Charitable donations in the latest annual report were £2,452 (0.03 per cent of pre-tax profit), a notably low figure.

- There was no evidence of any environmental policies or initiatives.

> *One of the smallest companies in the survey, with one of the worst disclosure records and no evidence of any social and ethical policies.*

C & J Clark Limited

									Alert!
xx	?	?	**xx**	?	?	**x**	**y**	**n**	

Size: World: £636m	UK: £472m	UK employees: 22,825

Activities: Manufactures and retails footwear and retails clothing

- A privately owned company, retailing 24 million pairs of shoes per annum through 1,500 directly owned retail outlets worldwide.

- Clarks has a reputation for benevolence in its home town of Street, Somerset.

- The company stated that it did not wish to be included in any New Consumer publications. As a private company there is little publicly available information.

- Charitable donations were 0.13 per cent of pre-tax profit in 1988/89, below average for the UK. Clark's is a member of Business in the Community.

- Little information was available about the environmental impact of its shoe manufacturing operations.

- Material for shoes are sourced in Thailand and Taiwan, and some uppers for shoes are sourced from India.

- Clarks has two subsidiaries in South Africa, which the company stated are non-trading operations.

> *Although Clark's argued that its social policies were well known, its level of disclosure made it difficult to identify a comprehensive social responsibility policy.*

Coats Viyella Plc

SECRET ✔	♀ ?	⟨⟨ ✗	🏠 ✗✗	🌳 ?	🐰 ✔✔	👶 ✗	✈ Y	🔍 C	Alert! m

Size: World: £1,904m	UK: £996m	**UK employees:** 36,314

Activities: Textile and clothing manufacturer, clothing retailer

- Britain's largest textile and yarn company. It recently took over one of its rivals, Tootal.

- It produces a booklet, *Statement of Business Principles,* outlining the ethical principles underpinning its corporate behaviour.

- One of the main board of directors is a member of an ethnic minority community. No further equal opportunities information was available.

- Coats Viyella's charitable cash donations in 1990 amounted to 0.17% of pre-tax profit.

- Manufacturing subsidiaries have in the past been accused of discharging into waterways chemicals not specified in their consents. The company said it is improving its discharges.

- It has substantial involvement in third world countries, with a high proportion of its workforce based in the developing world.

- Coats has donated £7,500 annually for the last three years to the Conservative Party.

- South African operating subsidiaries employed 873 staff in 1989.

- The company has major military contracts supplying uniforms to the armed forces, including nuclear, biological and chemical anti-gas protection suits.

> *The company's average level of disclosure was disappointing, so it was not possible to substantiate many of the positive statements it made about corporate responsibility.*

Coca-Cola Great Britain

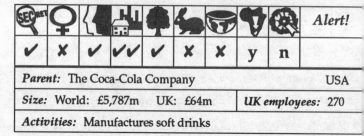

							Alert!
✔	✗	✔	✔✔	✔	✗	✗	y · n

Parent: The Coca-Cola Company		USA
Size: World: £5,787m UK: £64m		UK employees: 270
Activities: Manufactures soft drinks		

- The Coca-Cola Company, the US parent, is the world's largest soft drinks company.

- In the UK it has a bottling and distribution agreement with Cadbury Schweppes, in which Coca-Cola has a 49 per cent interest.

- Coca-Cola has equal opportunities monitoring in place both for women and ethnic minorities.

- Charitable giving in the UK is high at 1.3 per cent of pre-tax profit, though not as extensive as in the USA.

- Coca-Cola was a founding member of the European Recovery and Recycling Association (ERRA), and supports the multi-material kerbside collection aspect of 'Recycling City' in Sheffield. This is an initiative to try to maximise potential recycling of household waste by sorting it before collection.

- The parent company has extensive sales in the third world through indigenous bottling companies, to which the parent company sells concentrates and beverage bases.

- Its imaginative disinvestment in 1986 from South Africa was in favour of the black workforce. Coca-Cola established a major Equal Opportunities Foundation in South Africa, one of whose trustees is Archbishop Desmond Tutu.

> *An easy, though superficial, target for Coca-colonialism-type criticism. The US parent company has very strong programmes for ethnic minorities and a high level of awareness of social responsibility.*

Colgate-Palmolive Limited

									Alert!
✓✓	✗	✗	✗✗	✓	✗	✓	Y	n	

Parent: Colgate-Palmolive Company · USA

Size: World: £3,217m · UK: £91m · **UK employees:** 784

Activities: Manufactures personal care products, household products and pet foods

- Colgate is the world's best selling toothpaste, with over 40 per cent of the market.
- The company's *Code of Conduct* brochure outlines strong social and ethical policies.
- The company has well developed community action schemes in the USA, where giving exceeds one per cent of pre-tax profits. This size of giving and level of involvement are not mirrored in the UK.
- Carries out equal opportunities monitoring in the UK. It had eight women and one ethnic minority manager in the UK in 1990.
- It has a written environmental policy, and makes an environmental pledge in its *Code of Conduct* document.
- The company has operations in 30 third world countries. There has, in the past, been some controversy over its marketing policies in the developing world, which it has since revised.
- The US parent company has invested heavily in research into alternatives to animal tests. No animal testing is carried out in the UK on behalf of Colgate.
- It has a South African subsidiary which employed 631 staff in 1989.
- In the USA it has a policy of not advertising on TV programmes deemed anti-social or violent.

> *Like its parent company, Colgate-Palmolive appears to have a number of strong policies. In particular the parent company is a major proponent of the search for alternatives to animal testing.*

Conoco (U.K.) Ltd

SECRET	♀	⟨	🏠	🌳	🐇	👶	☠	⚙	Alert!
✔	?	?	XX	X	X	X	n	n	tm

Parent: E.I. du Pont de Nemours and Company	USA

Size: World: £22,638m UK: £353m	UK employees: 1,489

Activities: Oil, petroleum, chemicals, industrial products

- Conoco (a subsidiary of the US chemical company Du Pont) is one of the top six UK petrol suppliers UK through its JET stations.

- New Consumer questionnaires were referred to the parent company in the USA, indicating a high degree of corporate control.

- Conoco was unable to supply figures for women and ethnic minorities in management in the UK.

- In the UK community involvement contributions amounted to 0.3 per cent of pre-tax profit in 1988. In the USA community giving in the same year was one per cent of pre-tax profit.

- The parent company, whose activities have a potentially huge environmental impact, is noted in the USA for its high level of awareness of, and response to some high profile environmental issues.

- The parent company has major operations in developing countries involved in oil exploration, chemicals, and agrochemicals.

- In the USA it carries out some animal testing. Du Pont supports research into alternative testing methods.

- Military sales in the UK include fuel sales to the MoD worth £5-10 million in 1989.

> *Conoco's low level of disclosure was surprising for the subsidiary of a company with such a highly regarded reputation in many areas of corporate responsibility.*

Co-operative Movement

(SEC)RET	♀	👤	🏠	🌳	🐰	🧷	🐄	🏭	Alert!
✓✓	✓	✗	✓✓	✓	✓✓	✓	n	L	at

Size: World: £4,300m	UK: £4,300m	UK employees: 57,000

Activities: Department stores, retailing, agriculture, travel, opticians

Encompasses Britain's various retail co-operative societies, including the Co-operative Wholesale Society Ltd and Co-operative Retail Services Ltd, the two largest societies.

- There is one woman on the board of directors of both the CRS and CWS. An equal opportunities audit of the Co-op's head office was provided, and there was a notably high level of disclosure.

- The Movement has significant community programmes, mainly directed through the individual societies at the local community.

- As Britain's largest farmer, the CWS has a number of environmental initiatives, including an experimental organic farm.

- Environmental action by the Co-op in its retailing operations includes David Bellamy as its environmental consultant, a *Co-op Action Guide*, and an audit of its own and suppliers operations.

- Through the International Co-operative Alliance the movement is involved in trade with co-operatives worldwide.

- Own-label cosmetics, toiletries, household cleaning products and their ingredients have not been tested on animals.

- Donates to the Co-operative Party, which is aligned with the Labour Party.

- The CRS and CWS are the only large retailers with a ban on South African products.

Founded primarily for the benefit of its members, the movement's social policies are still in place and encompass many of the current social and ethical business issues.

Courage Limited

🔍SECRET	⚥	👤	🏠	🌳	🐰	👶	🌍	⚙	Alert!
✓✓	✗	✗	✓✓	✓	✓✓	?	n	n	Atg

Size: World: £6,826m	UK: £695m	UK employees: 9,649

Activities: Brewing and pubs

- The Australian parent company, formally Elders IXL, is now known as Foster's Brewing Group since its major restructure and disposal of all non-brewing interests.

- In November 1990 the MMC cleared the way for Courage to take over Grand Metropolitan's brewing operations, and some 8,000 pubs have been transferred to a joint venture, Inntrepreneur Estates.

- Courage is currently establishing an equal opportunities monitoring system, but so far no figures were available for the numbers of women and ethnic minorities in managerial positions.

- Charitable donations in the UK in 1988/89 amounted to a notable £1,328,667. Courage is a member of Business in the Community and of the Per Cent Club.

- Most donations were to alcohol abuse initiatives.

- Courage has an environmental policy, has reduced its packaging, encouraged recycling, reduced energy consumption, and screened ingredients for pesticides.

- Foster's has a number of subsidiaries in third world countries.

- Foster's is one of the world's leading brewers, and Courage is now the second largest brewer in the UK. It is notable as the UK brewer with the highest profile in terms of support for work combatting alcohol abuse.

Courage has shown that it is has taken a number of positive social and ethical initiatives, and it appears to be developing its weaker areas.

Courtaulds Textiles plc

🔍 SECRET	⚲	⟨	🏠	🌳	🐰	👶	🦃	⚙️	Alert!
✗	?	?	✗✗	✗	✓✓	✗	Y	n	

Size: World: £984m UK: £708m	UK employees: 29,600

Activities: Manufactures textiles and clothing and retails clothing

- Since its 1990 demerger from Courtaulds PLC, the chemicals company, it has concentrated on textile and garment manufacture and retail.

- It makes more underwear than any other company in Britain. It is a major supplier of own brand clothing including underwear to Marks & Spencer.

- As with other textile companies, it is in the process of restructuring which has involved substantial job losses.

- Although the company declined to supply any detailed information, its first annual report included detail of some social initiatives.

- These included active steps to encourage women to pursue careers in management.

- The only environmental initiative mentioned in its annual report was an audit to improve environmental compliance and water management.

- Courtaulds sources some garments and textiles from third world countries, particularly from South East Asia.

- It has three operating subsidiaries in South Africa.

A relatively new company in its own right that appears to have a number of social and ethical policies in place. However, lack of disclosure makes it difficult to make a full evaluation of its policies.

CPC United Kingdom Ltd

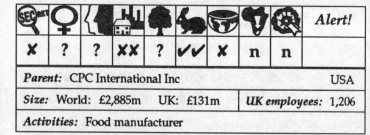

									Alert!
✗	?	?	✗✗	?	✔✔	✗	n	n	

Parent: CPC International Inc — USA

Size: World: £2,885m   UK: £131m | **UK employees:** 1,206

Activities: Food manufacturer

- It is owned by one of the largest and most geographically diversified US food companies, CPC International.

- It is better known by its international brands Knorr, Ambrosia, Hellmann's, and Napolina.

- CPC supplied some general company information, including a *Company Policy Manual* that deals with issues such as business ethics, community relations, employee relations and environmental protection, but declined to answer specific questions about its corporate social and ethical behaviour.

- Community donations in the UK were less than 0.2 per cent of pre-tax profit, below average by British standards. Donations in the USA are correspondingly low.

- The parent company has operations in Latin America, Africa and Asia which accounted for nearly 18 per cent of total turnover in 1989.

> *The lack of information makes it difficult to assess the extent to which CPC's corporate responsibility statements are implemented, particularly in its UK operations.*

James Thin,
53-59 South Bridge, Edinburgh
031-556 6743

James Thin, (Academic),
29 Buccleuch Street, Edinburgh
031-556 6743

James Thin (Scientific),
Kings Building's Campus, Edinburgh
031-667 0432

James Thin Penguin Bookshop,
Waverley Market, Edinburgh
031-557 1378

James Thin Edinburgh Bookshop,
57 George Street, Edinburgh
031-225 4495

James Thin,
18 Church Crescent, Dumfries
0387 54288

James Thin,
176 High Street, Perth
0738 35222

Melvens Bookshop,
Aviemore Centre, Aviemore
0479 810 797

Melvens Bookshop,
29 Union Street, Inverness
0463 233 500

James Thin, Student's Union,
St. Mary's Place, St. Andrews
0334 76367

James Thin,
- 7/8 High Street, Dundee
0382 23999

James Thin
Bookshops

Quality Bookshops
Serving the Local
Community

Dalgety PLC

SECRET	♀	⟨	🏠	🌳	🐇	👶	☠	🐱	*Alert!*
✓✓	✓	✗	✗✗	✓✓	✗✗	n	n	n	

Size: World: £4,634m	UK: £1,920m	*UK employees:* 15,221

Activities: Manufactures food and pet foods, agribusiness

- Originally an Australian business, the company moved its headquarters to the UK in the 1960s.

- Big own-brand and ingredient supplier to supermarkets and fast-food outlets.

- One of the more open food companies, providing additional material and completing some questionnaires.

- It has equal opportunities monitoring in operation, though its implementation varies within the organisation.

- Approximately ten per cent of senior managers are women or from ethnic minorities, but no information about separate numbers of women or members of ethnic minorities was provided.

- Community donations were below average, amounting to 0.12 per cent of pre-tax profits in 1989.

- A major agribusiness company in Europe supplying fertilizers, animal feed, seed and agrochemicals to farmers, although it is not directly involved in their manufacture.

- It is aware of the environmental problems associated with its activities, and has taken some steps to minimise their impact.

- Dalgety has significant involvement with animals in sensitive areas such as genetic 'improvements', factory farming, battery hens, lamb and bacon processing and pet food operations.

Dalgety's high level of disclosure indicates that the company may respond to consumer pressure on environmental and animal rights issues.

Dixons Group plc

SECRET	♀	👤	🏠	🌳	🐰	🍼	⚗	🔬	Alert!
✗	?	✗	✗	?	✓✓	✗	n	n	

Size:	World: £1,771m	UK: £1,071m	UK employees: 12,000

Activities: Retails consumer electronics goods

- A major high street electrical retailer. In 1990 over 75 per cent of its UK retail pre-tax profit was attributable to its financial services operations, such as the provision of consumer credit.

- Dixons declined to complete any questionnaires, but answered some specific questions.

- Three per cent of the senior managers listed in the latest annual report were women, but no details on overall managerial figures both for women and ethnic minorities were available.

- It has taken steps to improve opportunities for women in retailing through improved maternity benefits and career breaks.

- Has a small but emerging community involvement programme.

- Dixons is an active member of Business in the Community and of the Per Cent Club.

- Mastercare, its servicing warranty subsidiary, is negotiating with a third party to recover CFCs when conducting repairs to equipment. It already recovers CFCs on disposal of appliances.

- No further information about its environmental activities was available.

- It has no manufacturing operations in third world countries, but components and products are sourced from developing countries.

> **Some evidence of awareness and initiatives on social and ethical issues.**

Electrolux Ltd

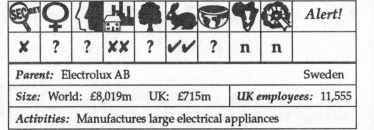

									Alert!
✗	?	?	✗✗	?	✓✓	?	n	n	

Parent: Electrolux AB		Sweden
Size: World: £8,019m UK: £715m		*UK employees:* 11,555
Activities: Manufactures large electrical appliances		

- The parent company is controlled by the Swedish Wallenberg family, noted for their extensive industrial interests in Sweden.

- There was little information available about employment conditions and equal opportunities in the UK.

- Its UK charitable donations amounted to less than 0.1 per cent of pre-tax profits in 1988. Electrolux Ltd is a member of Business in the Community.

- The parent company is involved in mining and manufacture of aluminium, operations with a potentially high environmental impact. No evidence was given of any steps to minimise this potential impact. It has taken steps to minimise the effects of CFCs in its domestic and commercial appliances, undertaking to replace them with alternatives as soon as they are available.

- Zanussi, an Italian subsidiary, has an imaginative appliance recycling scheme.

- In 1990 Electrolux won an order to build an 'ozone-friendly' plant for refrigeration manufacture near Moscow.

- It has substantial manufacturing and distribution operations in third world countries.

> *A parent company with some innovative environmental ideas and a willingness to share this knowledge with others. Evaluation of the UK company is impeded by poor disclosure.*

Esso UK plc

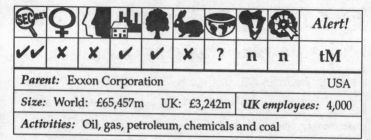

									Alert!
✓✓	✗	✗	✓	✓	✗	?	n	n	tM

Parent: Exxon Corporation	USA

Size: World: £65,457m	UK: £3,242m	**UK employees:** 4,000

Activities: Oil, gas, petroleum, chemicals and coal

- A subsidiary of the world's second largest oil refiner and producer. Operating in the UK since 1888 with considerable autonomy, yet the parent company's strong philosophy is evident.

- One of the more open companies.

- Staff pay and benefits are high, as is the case across this industry. Ninety per cent staff participation rate in company share schemes.

- Over half 1990's graduate recruits were women, which is notable as the majority of graduate recruits are engineering and science graduates, subject areas dominated by men, but did not provide any further equal opportunities figures.

- UK community involvement focuses on educational and sports sponsorship. Donations were 0.7 per cent of pre-tax profits.

- A number of international environmental incidents involving its parent company, including the *Exxon Valdez* incident in 1989, contrast with Esso's positive environmental record in the UK. Environmental action in the UK includes: the first national petrol chain to supply unleaded petrol; improving its underground storage facilities; and providing energy saving advice.

- Extensive oil exploration and production operations in third world countries, with evidence of some community initiatives.

- Major fuel supplier to the Ministry of Defence.

> *The* Exxon Valdez *disaster scarred its parent company's environmental image, obscuring what appears to be a responsibly-run subsidiary with well-established social and ethical policies.*

Ferguson Limited

🔍SECRET	♀	〈	🏭	🌲	🐇	👕	🍷	⚙	Alert!
✗✗	?	?	✗✗	?	✓✓	✗	n	n	**M**

Parent: Thomson S.A.	France

Size: World: £7,815m UK: £195m	**UK employees:** 3,003

Activities: Manufactures consumer electronics and defence systems

- The French state-owned parent company, Thomson SA, is Europe's largest defence contractor and one of the world's biggest consumer electronics companies.

- It has an extremely low level of disclosure — a common feature of the French-owned companies in the survey.

- No charitable donations were recorded in its latest annual report, nor was there was indication of any community involvement in its parent company's annual report.

- Thomson has had contracts to supply components for the nuclear power industries in Germany and France.

- No evidence of any environmental initiatives.

- Its involvement with developing countries includes the supply of aircraft to the Chinese Air Force, as well as non-military contracts. It has component manufacturing operations based in Malaysia and Mexico.

- Sales to the military sector in 1989 amounted to £3,346 million. In 1989 Thomson SA subsidiaries had contracts with the Ministry of Defence worth over £10 million.

An extremely poor level of disclosure which cannot entirely be attributed to the French national strategic interests of its parent company.

Fiat (U.K.) Limited

![SECRET]	![♀]	![tree/forest]	![factory]	![tree]	![rabbit]	![dish]	![spray]	![globe]	Alert!
✗	?	?	✗✗	✗	✓✓	?	y	n	**M**

Parent: Fiat S.P.A.	Italy

Size: World: £24,237m	UK: £265m	**UK employees:** 6,500

Activities: Manufactures cars and commercial vehicles

- Best known for its vehicles, Fiat is Italy's largest industrial group with activities from bioengineering to railway systems.
- Fiat (U.K.) Ltd is responsible for the distribution of cars and car parts in the UK. Fiat's other main operating subsidiary is a joint venture with Ford, Iveco Ford Truck Ltd.
- Its UK charitable donations in 1988 were modest. In Italy the parent company's community involvement is mainly through sponsorship of cultural activities.
- An Italian subsidiary is specifically involved in environmental protection; its main role appears to be to minimise the environmental problems arising from Fiat's other operations. Fiat was responsible for the world's first production electric car in June 1990.
- It has operations in a number of third world countries, where it has established strong community links. In 1988 Fiat employed nearly 20,000 workers in Central and Southern America.
- Fiat has a licensing agreement for the manufacture, sale and servicing of its products in South Africa, which is carried out by Nissan.
- It is a major military contractor, supplying aviation, naval and space technology as well as advanced munitions systems.

Fiat's corporate responsibility in the UK was hard to assess, but there is evidence that the parent company has a strong record on technology transfer in developing countries.

Ford Motor Company Limited

SECRET	♀	👤	🏠	🌳	🐰	🏺	🔪	⚙	Alert!
✗	✗	✓	✗✗	?	✓✓	✗	y	n	**M**

Parent: Ford Motor Company		USA
Size: World: £55,201m UK: £6,732m	**UK employees:**	46,100

Activities: Manufactures cars and commercial vehicles

- US parent company is the second largest vehicle manufacturer in the USA, but leads in the UK with around 25 per cent of sales.

- In 1989 it bought Jaguar, contributing to its first major losses in the UK in 25 years. Ford also owns 25 per cent of Mazda, and has a joint venture with Fiat in the UK — Iveco Ford Trucks Ltd.

- Ford UK's 'personal development' programme offers staff free education and health improvement courses, and has been taken up by more than 15,000 workers.

- Its equal opportunities initiatives include monitoring, local equal opportunities committees, and appointing a manager to Opportunities for the Disabled. No figures were available.

- In 1989 donations in the UK, including the contribution to the Ford of Britain Trust, were modest — less than 0.1 per cent of pre-tax profit. It is a member of Business in the Community.

- Environmental initiatives include research into alternative clean-fuel technology, and switching to alternatives to CFCs in its car air conditioning systems and in its manufacturing.

- The parent company has operations in third world countries, including a joint venture with Volkswagen in Latin America.

- In 1989 Ford had contracts worth £5-10 million with the Ministry of Defence.

Ford in the UK seems to emulate its parent company's progressive policies on equal opportunities and employee education with less evidence of action in other areas.

Forte PLC

⊕	♀	⟨	🏠	🌳	🐇	👖	🔻	⚙	*Alert!*
✗	?	?	✗✗	?	✓✓	?	n	C	**at**

Size: World: £2,641m	UK: £2,086m	*UK employees:* 73,600

Activities: Hotels, restaurants, fast food outlets and catering

- Britain's largest hotel and catering group. Has a joint venture with PepsiCo to run Kentucky Fried Chicken outlets in the UK.

- Until recently known as Trusthouse Forte. One of the company's original aims, which are maintained by a Council, is to promote 'the habits of temperance and furthering Public House Reform'.

- Declined to complete questionnaires, but has supplied additional information and comment.

- There is one woman, a Forte family member, on the board.

- Charitable donations, including those of the Council, amounted to only 0.25 per cent of pre-tax profits in 1989/90. Forte is a member of Business in the Community.

- Uses some organically-grown produce in its operations. Kentucky Fried Chicken conducted an anti-litter campaign.

- Has a number of subsidiaries in third world countries, and said that its 'philosophy is applied universally'.

- Regular annual political donations to the Conservative Party in excess of £50,000. One of the largest corporate donors.

- Substantial sales of alcohol and tobacco through the group.

> *Although providing information about some issues, Forte's overall corporate responsibility remains at the margins in many areas of its activities.*

Gallaher Limited

									Alert!
✗	?	?	✗✗	✗	✓✓	✗	y	n	AT

Parent: American Brands Incorporated		USA

Size: World: £7,790m UK: £4,685m	**UK employees:** 28,336

Activities: Tobacco, spirits, life insurance, leisure goods and office products

- Gallaher's tobacco sales accounted for almost half of its parent American Brands' total revenue in 1990.

- It is the leading tobacco producer in the UK, with a 45 per cent share of the market, including the top three selling cigarette brands: Benson & Hedges, Silk Cut, and Berkeleys Super Kings.

- It owns over 1,600 tobacco outlets in the UK through its Marshell and Forbuoys chains, and is the UK's largest vending machine business, selling cigarettes, drinks and snacks.

- Its UK charitable donations are low, less than 0.2 per cent of pre-tax profit in 1989, and include significant sums given to the tobacco-sponsored Health Promotion Research Trust.

- Gallaher provided an environmental statement outlining the company's position with regard to the potential impact of its tobacco operations.

- The parent company has operations in the third world, including tobacco retailing.

- American Brands has withdrawn its operations from South Africa, but still maintains a licensing agreement.

- In 1990 Gallaher acquired Whyte & MacKay, the whisky distiller, and Vladivar vodka, to strengthen its spirit interests.

> *The company makes no reference to the social implications of its main source of income, tobacco, and it appears to do little in the way of corporate social responsibility development.*

General Electric Company PLC

									Alert!
✓✓	✓	✓	✗	✓	✓✓	✗	Y	n	M

Size: World: £8,786m UK: £3,307m	*UK employees:* 74,653

Activities: Manufactures defence equipment, electrical goods and communications equipment

- A company with wide ranging interests in heavy and light industry, from consumer goods to weapons systems. Domestic appliances produced by a joint venture with US company, General Electric.

- Strong equal opportunities initiatives, including one woman executive director on the board.

- GEC carries out equal opportunities monitoring for both women and ethnic minorities, though only 11 per cent of managers are women and two per cent are from ethnic minority groups.

- For a company of this size, its UK charitable giving is low, less than 0.2 per cent of pre-tax profit in 1989/9. It is a member of both Business in the Community and the Per Cent Club.

- While it has no written environmental policy, it has taken a number of positive steps, such as using CFC alternatives where possible.

- GEC designs and produces nuclear power stations.

- It has extensive third world subsidiaries, plus very significant arms sales to developing countries, including China, Jordan, Saudi Arabia and Thailand.

- Its operations in South Africa employed over 4,000 in 1990.

- The company has strongly supported the Conservative Party, and also the Liberals, on anti-nationalisation grounds.

- Britain's second largest manufacturer of military equipment.

> *A high level of disclosure revealed a mixed policy on social issues — the company is not reticent about involvement in controversial areas.*

Gillette Industries Ltd

🔍SECRET	♀	⟨🏭	🏠🏭	🌳	🐰	👶	🌍	☢	Alert!
✗	?	?	✔	?	✗	?	Y	n	

Parent: The Gillette Company	USA

Size: World: £2,170m UK: £108m	*UK employees:* 1,413

Activities: Manufactures and distributes shaving products and toiletries

- Sells a wide range of goods from razors (both disposable and electric) to stationery.
- The company did not provide any information about its UK activities.
- No information was available about the numbers of women and ethnic minorities in managerial posts in the UK.
- Gillette's UK charitable donations in 1988 amounted to £50,000. It is member of Business in the Community and the Per Cent Club.
- Its parent company's environmental record has been noted by the US Environmental Protection Agency for its substantial improvement in recent years.
- Gillette operates in 28 developing countries, including China.
- In the USA Gillette contracts out its animal testing, though the parent company carries out its own research into alternative testing methods.
- It has two subsidiaries in South Africa, employing a total of 100 workers.
- Gillette in the US has an unusual post — Vice-President for Product Integrity — who has the power to stop production and review all advertising and labelling claims.

Lack of information from Gillette about its UK operations makes it difficult to assess its social and ethical performance in this country.

Granada Group PLC

										Alert!
✔	xx	✔	✘	?	✔✔	?	n	n		

Size: World: £1,392m	UK: £1,159m	*UK employees:* 22,340

Activities: Rental and retail of electrical goods, and involved in the media

- Granada is one of the UK's major leisure and entertainment groups. It produces the popular soap opera *Coronation Street* and other television series.

- It has completed a New Consumer questionnaire, and provided some specific social information.

- Of the top 100-200 senior managers in 1989, 15 were women and two were from ethnic minorities. It operates an ethnic monitoring scheme. There are no other supporting initiatives.

- From a low base, Granada is developing a reasonable community programme. In 1990 it sponsored the Granada Wheel Appeal.

- Little in the way of substantial environmental policies or examples of action were provided by the company.

- The company sold its bingo clubs to Bass in spring 1991.

> *A reasonably open company with evidence that it is aware of community involvement and equal opportunities issues, for which it has some established programmes.*

Grand Metropolitan PLC

SECRET	♀	⟨	🏠	🌳	🐰	👶	🐄	✿	Alert!
✓✓	✓	✗	✓	✓	✓✓	✗	Y	n	Atg

Size: World: £9,394m	UK: £3,685m	*UK employees:* 138,149

Activities: Manufactures and retails food, alcohol and soft drinks

- Claims to be world's second largest retailer, with a mix of outlets including pubs, fast food, and opticians.
- Innovative 'Corporate Governance' section in its annual report.
- Has a joint venture with Courage through the pub-owning 'Inntrepreneur' scheme, part of a complex pubs-for-breweries exchange allowed to proceed after a monopoly enquiry.
- Has a comparatively high level of charitable giving (0.5 per cent of pre-tax profit in 1990) and community involvement, but its US subsidiaries give over twice as much.
- Its US subsidiaries, Burger King and Pillsbury, had contrasting social responsibility records, though there is evidence that GrandMet has sought to push standards up to highest common denominator.
- It has some positive environmental initiatives and an active senior monitoring group.
- Does not conduct animal testing, but did not state whether a policy was in place for rearing conditions for meat-producing animals.
- GrandMet has extensive third world interests in food and alcoholic drinks.
- It has a number of active subsidiaries in South Africa.
- Thirty per cent of turnover is from alcoholic drinks, and it is the world leader in case sales of wines and spirits.

> *A diverse group in the process of consolidating both its product range and its social policies, the latter with some degree of serious application.*

William Grant & Sons Limited

SECRET	♀	👤	🏭	🌳	🐰	👶	🐑	✿	Alert!
✗	?	?	✗✗	?	✓✓	n	n	n	A

Size: World: £141m UK: £141m	UK employees: 923

Activities: Distils and markets malt whisky and spirits

- Its Glenfiddich distillery produces the world's most popular malt whisky.
- Grant's is a small, privately-owned family business.
- The company provided answers to some questions, but like most private companies is reticent about public disclosure.
- Grant's operates some initiatives for the disabled, but supplied no other information about equal opportunities.
- Community cash donations amounted to £1,145 in 1989 (0.005 per cent of pre-tax profit).
- No information was available about any environmental policies or initiatives.
- Grant's stated that it has an alcohol-help policy, and that it makes contributions to organisations working to alleviate the social costs of alcohol.

> *The extent of William Grant's corporate responsi-bility was difficult to assess because of lack of information.*

Great Universal Stores P.L.C.

SECRET	♀	👤	🏠	🌳	🐇	🍲	☮	🌐	Alert!
✗	?	?	✗✗	?	?	✗	Y	n	

Size: World: £2,693m	UK: £1,969m	*UK employees:* 30,686

Activities: Catalogue home shopping, finance, property and retailing

- The market leader in UK home shopping, with 25 million catalogues in production across 20 titles.
- The company's annual report provides only minimal information.
- Information on GUS is particularly sparse on social issues, and disclosure was poor.
- In 1989 it introduced both paternity leave and maternity leave for women adopting children.
- Though one of its largest stockholder is the wealthy Wolfson Foundation, the company itself has one of the poorest public records on charitable giving for a large company.
- GUS has been criticised for third world sourcing policies, but denies exploitation.
- Owns a major operating subsidiary, Lewis Stores (Pty) Ltd, in South Africa.

> *Surprisingly, a company linked with one of the UK's leading charitable foundations returns a poor record on disclosure, with evidence of a lack of serious consideration of corporate social responsibility policies.*

Guinness PLC

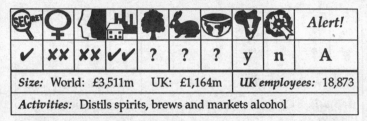

![SECRET]	⚥	👤	🏠	🌳	🐇	🥣	🍷	⚙️	Alert!
✔	✗✗	✗✗	✔✔	?	?	?	y	n	**A**

Size: World: £3,511m   UK: £1,164m   *UK employees:* 18,873

Activities: Distils spirits, brews and markets alcohol

- Its subsidiary, United Distillers, is the most profitable international spirits business in the world, and the brewing side is the world's fourth most profitable brewer.

- A name synonymous with stout and, during the late 1980s, with city scandal.

- Its ex-chief executive and associates were convicted in 1990 of massive illegal stockmarket dealings in its £2.7 billion takeover of Distillers Company.

- Corporate giving in the UK tops £1.4 million (0.9 per cent of pre-tax profit), a generous figure for the UK. It is a member of Business in the Community and of the Per Cent Club.

- No significant environmental initiatives were recorded in the *1990 Annual Report*.

- It has very widespread interests in brewing and spirits in the third world.

- One of world's leading alcoholic drinks companies. Some evidence of progressive policies on alcohol abuse initiatives, with an emphasis in the UK on moderate drinking.

Management is seeking to renew a tarnished reputation, and with some signs of more active social responsibility policies in selected areas.

Hanson PLC

![SECRET]	♀	🧑	🏠	🌳	🐰	🏺	📺	🔍	Alert!
✘	?	?	✘	?	?	✘	Y	C	Tm

Size: World: £7,153m	UK: £4,149m	UK employees: 28,000

Activities: Manufactures batteries, bricks, electrical goods and tobacco

- The creation over the last 27 years of Lord Hanson, expert in acquisitions, from bricks to batteries, clothing to cigarettes, word processors to windows.

- Huge cash reserves and previous record sustains a reputation as a corporate raider.

- Lord Hanson indulged his passion for horce-racing, using shareholders' funds via a loss-making subsidiary.

- Noted for 'rationalising' acquired companies. A notable case recently lost by Hanson involved access to a £200 million surplus in Imperial Tobacco's pension fund.

- Lord Hanson is one of Britain's highest paid executives: he was paid £1.45 million in 1990.

- Modest charitable giving and community involvement for a company of this size.

- The company has significant interests in extraction industries: gold, limestone, clay, gravel and coal. Owns SCM Chemicals, a major world producer of non-toxic white pigment used in paint.

- A strong supporter of the Conservative Party and free market philosophy.

- A wholly-owned subsidiary, Imperial Tobacco, has 35 per cent of the UK cigarette market.

A 'blue chip' reputation in management and earnings, not matched by the evidence on social responsibility policies in diverse subsidiaries.

H.J.Heinz Company Ltd

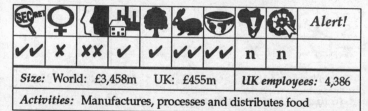

									Alert!
✓✓	X	XX	✓	✓	✓✓	✓✓	n	n	

Size: World: £3,458m   UK: £455m   **UK employees:** 4,386

Activities: Manufactures, processes and distributes food

- Heinz acquired its first UK company in 1905, already having a reputation for quality in USA; now it is Britain's largest manufacturer of canned and bottled foods.
- The parent company owns Weight Watchers International — over one million people attend weekly classes in 20 countries.
- A relatively high representation of women in management, but little in the way of initiatives.
- One of only four companies in the survey to disclose the number of registered disabled employees in the UK.
- UK charitable contributions in 1989 and 1990 amounted to around one per cent of pre-tax profit. A member of Business in the Community.
- Heinz won *The Grocer* magazine's 'Green Award' for wide-ranging environmental initiatives.
- Very positive record of creative joint ventures and technology transfer in the third world.
- '57 Varieties'; actually there are 4,500!
- The company has a written policy prohibiting political donations.

A company with strong policies and a willingness to respond to some key issues.

The Highland Distilleries Company plc

									Alert!
✗✗	?	?	✗	?	✓✓	n	n	C	A

Size: World: £148m	UK: £148m	UK employees: 347

Activities: Distils malt whisky

- With five distilleries and other related interests, the company controls a significant section of the scotch whisky market.
- Owns 'The Famous Grouse' scotch, market leader in Scotland.
- Minimal provision of information.
- Member of both Business in the Community and the Per Cent Club, though a low level of community involvement overall.
- No public information on environmental issues available.
- Modest but regular supporter of the Conservative Party

A relatively small company, with little evidence of a systematic policy approach to the issues surveyed.

179

Hillsdown Holdings PLC

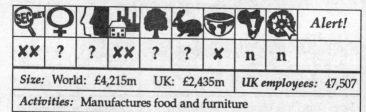

									Alert!
XX	?	?	XX	?	?	X	n	n	

Size: World: £4,215m	UK: £2,435m	UK employees: 47,507

Activities: Manufactures food and furniture

- One of UK's largest food manufacturers, both major brands and 'own label'.

- Hillsdown owns and produces chocolate biscuits and drinks under the Cadbury's label.

- Poor level of disclosure makes rating internal policies difficult.

- Relatively low level of giving or community involvement

- The company made no comment on environmental policies, or whether tropical timber is used by its furniture manufacturing subsidiaries (major suppliers to Marks & Spencer).

- Little direct third world involvement, but a significant user of tropical products as commodities and in foods.

- The company runs factory farms, abattoirs and breeding facilities. No comments were made about rearing conditions or animal welfare issues.

- In June 1989 a Hillsdown subsidiary, Daylay Eggs Ltd., was fined £800 plus £2,250 costs for causing unnecessary suffering and distress to battery hens in an incident in which 1,200 birds died.

A company with dramatic recent growth but little information to encourage a positive view of social responsibility.

Hitachi Consumer Products (UK) Ltd

SECRET	♀	🏠	🌳	🐰	👶	☢	🍬	Alert!
✗	?	?	✗✗	✗	✓✓	✓	n	n	m

Parent: Hitachi Limited	Japan

Size: World: £26,529m UK: £101m	**UK employees:** 960

Activities: Manufactures and markets electronic and electrical goods

- Hitachi's parent company is Japan's largest diversified manufacturer of electrical products, with over 20,000 lines in production.
- UK employee conditions and benefits appear above average. It stated that its employees reflect the ethnic composition of its locality, and that there are a number of women at team leader level, but it did not supply any specific figures for numbers in management or among graduate recruits.
- Although it gives no cash donations in the UK, Hitachi supports local activities and local education through secondments and in-kind giving.
- Hitachi provided no evidence of a written environmental policy, though it has taken a number of positive initiatives, including reduction of emissions, water conservation, and reduction in the use of CFC solvents.
- The parent company has involvement in nuclear power generation.
- Widespread, and growing, third world interests.

> *Hitachi appears to be aware of the social and ethical responsibility, though evidence to indicate concerted action in these areas is mixed.*

Hoover plc

									Alert!
✗	?	?	✗✗	?	✓✓	?	y	n	

Parent: Maytag Corporation		USA
Size: World: £1,755m UK: £264m		UK employees: 6,477
Activities: Manufactures, markets and services domestic appliances		

- Hoover is one of the most famous names in home appliance products, 'hoover' at one time being virtually synonymous with the term 'vacuum cleaner'.

- It is now owned by the American home appliance company Maytag Corporation.

- Maytag has a reputation in the United States as a conservative, paternalistic company, perhaps reflecting its rural base in Iowa.

- The Hoover PLC subsidiary is currently undergoing re-structuring, which has involved several hundred redundancies at its Scottish and Welsh plants.

- Maytag has disclosed limited information to American public interest research organisations in the past. Hoover disclosed only the statutory minimum about its activities.

- Maytag is a major manufacturer of refrigerators, but provided no indication of any steps taken to develop non-ozone-depleting refrigerants. This lack of response on such a high profile environmental issue is disappointing.

- The Hoover brand is licensed to a local company for use in South Africa under an 1987 agreement accompanying the sale of Hoover's interests there.

Hoover is a famous name in consumer products, with a reputation for quality and reliability which is not replicated in a policy of openness on corporate social responsibility issues.

House of Fraser Holdings plc

🔍 SECRET	♀	(	🏠	🌳	🐰	🏺	☤	⚙	Alert!
XX	?	?	✔	?	?	✗	n	n	

Size: World: £1,133m UK: £1,085m	**UK employees:** 21,675

Activities: Retailing through department stores

- Britain's biggest department store operator, with Harrod's as the flagship.

- Its owner, the Al Fayed brothers, in a DTI report on the Harrod's takeover, were said to have 'dishonestly misrepresented their wealth, their business interests and their resources'.

- The running of Harrods Bank was recently transferred to a trust corporation at the insistence of the Bank of England.

- A high level of charitable giving, but no information was made available as to recipients.

- Some limited environmental initiatives undertaken by the company.

- It stopped selling fur in 1990 on 'commercial and economic grounds only'.

- No reported policy on goods sourced from the third world.

A major retailer with a highly defensive attitude to the extensive criticism of the 'business practices' of its owners.

Iceland Frozen Food plc

									Alert!
✓✓	✗	✓	✓	✓✓	✓✓	n	n	n	a

Size: World: £725m UK: £725m	**UK employees:** 10,111

Activities: Retails frozen food, groceries and domestic appliances

- The largest frozen food retailer in the UK after it acquired Bejam.
- A company which has grown steadily in a single sector over the 21 years since opening its first store.
- One of the highest levels of disclosure and information provided in the survey.
- Three out of 30 senior managers are women and two are from ethnic minority groups.
- Strong and positive employee policies.
- Total community giving in 1990 amounted to 0.6 per cent of per-tax profits, a reasonable amount by UK standards.
- Well-constructed environmental policies are in place, and the company has been the winner of numerous environmental action awards.

> *A serious attempt by a growing company to treat most aspects of corporate responsibility in a positive way.*

Imperial Chemical Industries PLC

🔒	♀	👤	🏠	🌳	🐇	👶	🌍	⚙	Alert!
✓	✓	XX	✓✓	✓	X	X	Y	n	M

Size: World: £12,906m	UK: £6,126m	*UK employees:* 53,700

Activities: Manufactures chemicals, paint, explosives, fertilisers, pesticides and pharmaceuticals

- There is considerable existing public material available about ICI's social responsibility issues.
- It is one of the industry leaders in personnel and industrial relations policies.
- It has one female non-executive director; 3.5 per cent of senior managers and 12 per cent of managerial staff are women.
- In 1990 community giving amounted to £4.6 million, 1.5 per cent of UK pre-tax profit — a commendable sum.
- A company with potentially high environmental impact. Europe's largest producer of CFCs, its improvement and replacement policies are gathering pace but lagging behind some major competitors.
- Controversy continues around biotechnology and agrochemical research and production.
- Employs approaching 100,000 people in developing countries.
- One of UK's largest testers on animals (medical and crop chemicals), but has reduced the number used by 50 per cent since 1977.

Recent acceleration in environmental action policies and other areas indicate positive management commitment to social responsibility issues.

Isosceles plc

SECRET	♀	👤	🏠	🌳	🐇	🍯	☠	⚙	Alert!
✗	?	✗✗	✓	?	✓✓	✗	n	n	**at**

Size: World: £2,370m UK: £2,370m	*UK employees:* 61,839

Activities: Supermarkets

- Isosceles was specifically formed to acquire the Gateway Corporation (supermarket chain) in 1989.

- It provided information about some issues, in particular the environment, but its overall disclosure rate was low.

- The most senior woman in the company is the finance director. No further information about equal opportunities was provided.

- Isosceles continued to make charitable donations in spite of suffering a loss in 1989.

- In 1990 Gateway joined forces with the environmental consultancy Landbank in a 'green partnership' which included a commitment to a ten-point environmental policy. Results are awaited.

- No own-brand Gateway products have been directly tested on animals, and the ingredients have not been tested on animals in the last five years.

- Gateway stocks a number of South African products, which are clearly labelled, and believes that the decision to buy these products or to boycott rests with the consumer.

- No reported policy on goods sourced from the third world.

While the company, through Gateway, appears to be taking environmental issues very seriously, in other areas of social responsibility it apparently does little.

The Jacob's Bakery Limited

SECRET	♀	🗣	🏭	🌳	🐇	🍲	🐄	🔬	Alert!
✘	?	?	✔	?	?	✘	n	n	A

Parent: BSN Groupe S.A.	France

Size: World: £4,961m UK: £172m	**UK employees:** 3,570

Activities: Manufactures food and drinks

- Its French parent company, the BSN Groupe, also owns HP Foods Limited in the UK.

- Jacob's/HP provided minimal information about their operations.

- In France BSN is renowned for its progressive employment policies, and has a reputation for openness with trades unions.

- No information was available about equal opportunities initiatives.

- In 1989 Jacob's charitable donations were £340, an insignificant sum.

- No information is available about any environmental policies or initiatives.

- BSN, the parent company, has substantial operations in the third world.

- BSN is a major champagne producer, selling 13.6 million bottles worldwide in 1989. It also produces sparkling wine and low-alcohol beers as well as ordinary beers.

> *Although the parent company has a strong record on industrial relations in France, there is little evidence of any action in areas of social responsibility in its UK operations.*

187

John Lewis Partnership plc

SECRET	♀	(image)	🏠	🌳	🐰	(image)	🐄	(image)	Alert!
✗	?	✗✗	✓	?	✓✓	✗	n	n	

Size: World: £2,046m	UK: £2,046m	UK employees: 32,000

Activities: Department stores and supermarkets

- Unique arrangement whereby the ownership of this extensive department store and supermarket chain was placed in trust for its employees. This was established in 1929 by the son of the founder. Employees are known as 'partners'.

- Extensive published material about the company's unique structure, but little information about about other social policies.

- 'Partners'' annual bonus is profit-related, but can be very substantial, up to 25 per cent of earnings.

- Exceptional employee communications and consultation, with well-developed representation and policy contribution structures.

- Little information available concerning environmental policies.

- Policy of not advertising, and a continuing 'never knowingly undersold' commitment.

- No reported policy on goods sourced from the third world.

> *Indifferent ratings in most areas for this company which demonstrated an early commitment to 'stakeholder' principles by its visionary founders.*

Johnson Wax Ltd

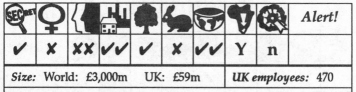

									Alert!
✔	✗	✗✗	✔✔	✔	✗	✔✔	Y	n	

Size: World: £3,000m UK: £59m	**UK employees:** 470

Activities: Manufactures personal care products, cleaning products and insecticides

- Since 1914 a branch of the long-established US family run and owned business, S C Johnson.

- Subsidiaries operate to well-defined and regularly-reviewed ethical and social policy statements which stand out as being amongst the earliest in corporate history.

- A strong reputation for good employee benefits, communication and training.

- The company records an exceptionally high UK figure for charitable donations and community support at 2.5 per cent of pre-tax profit, particularly unusual for a subsidiary owned by a foreign parent.

- UK subsidiary followed US parent by phasing out CFCs more than a decade before most UK competitors.

- In the USA S C Johnson has reduced the numbers of animals used in safety testing by around 50 per cent in the last three years. It is carrying out research into alternatives to animal testing.

- Well-formulated policies on its extensive operations in third world.

- Its parent has a subsidiary in South Africa, which in 1990 employed 150 staff.

> *A company with one of the clearest sets of statements and practices on corporate social responsibility.*

Kellogg Company of Great Britain Ltd

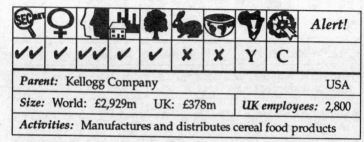

									Alert!
✓✓	✓	✓✓	✓	✓	✗	✗	Y	C	

Parent: Kellogg Company	USA

Size: World: £2,929m UK: £378m	**UK employees:** 2,800

Activities: Manufactures and distributes cereal food products

- Synonymous with breakfast cereals, where it takes nearly half the market.

- Notably good personnel, training and employee consultation structures.

- In 1990 six per cent of senior managers, ten per cent of managers and 50 per cent of graduate recruits were women, and one per cent of managers — good for the UK — were from ethnic minorities.

- High UK charitable giving and community support for a US subsidiary, at 0.9 per cent of pre-tax profit in 1990.

- It has a written environmental policy with wide-ranging initiatives in energy efficiency and recycling.

- Operates manufacturing plants in seven developing countries.

- Parent company has subsidiary in South Africa, and Kellogg's UK has made modest purchases of agricultural produce from South Africa.

- The only foreign-owned company in the survey to make political donations in the UK.

> *A company which is seriously committed to a comprehensive and positive approach to corporate citizenship.*

Kimberly-Clark Limited

SECRET	♀	🗣	🏠	🌳	🐰	🍲	🌶	⚙	Alert!
xx	?	?	**xx**	**x**	?	?	**Y**	**n**	

Parent: Kimberly-Clark Corporation	USA

Size: World: £3,258m UK: £212m	**UK employees:**	2,964

Activities: Manufactures and markets paper products

- A company probably better known by its Kleenex brand name.

- It has a very low level of disclosure with little publicly-available information.

- Its equal opportunities initiatives do not appear to match those of its US parent, which has three women and two ethnic minority directors on its main board.

- Community giving in the UK in 1988 amounted to £17,861, 0.15 per cent of pre-tax profit, below average for the UK.

- Kimberly-Clark claims that half of the fibre used in its products is recycled, and that the main sources of woodpulp used in the UK are Scandinavia and North America.

- For an operator in a high-profile environmental sector, it provides no substantial evidence of policies or action.

- It has a number of subsidiaries in third world countries.

- Owns investments in a South African affiliate company which in 1990 employed 1,721 workers.

The company's low level of disclosure make assessment of potentially positive environmental initiatives difficult.

Kingfisher plc

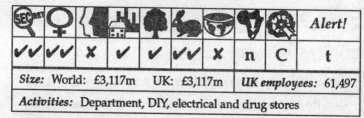

								Alert!
✓✓	✓✓	✗	✓	✓	✓✓	✗	n	C	t

Size: World: £3,117m	UK: £3,117m	*UK employees:* 61,497

Activities: Department, DIY, electrical and drug stores

- Owning outlets such as B&Q, Comet, Superdrug and Woolworths makes the company one of the UK's largest and most diverse retailers.

- B&Q is a major supporter of the campaign against Sunday trading restrictions.

- Extensive, active policies on advancement of women in management. Nine per cent of senior managers and 14 per cent of managers are women. There is one women, a non-executive director, on the board.

- B&Q operates a pioneering unit for the older worker, employing primarily over 50s.

- Active in community development programmes. Sponsored *Working in the Community*, a guide to corporate social responsibility.

- Sells several products which have given rise to environmental concerns, such as tropical timber, pesticides and peat.

- It has made annual donations of £25,000 to the Conservative Party in the last three years.

- It retails tobacco in selected Woolworths stores, sales in 1990 amounting to £1.1 milion.

A good level of disclosure with many initiatives reflecting social concern, though some inconsistency on environment and health.

Kraft General Foods Limited

SECRET	♀	〈	🏠	🌳	🐰	👶	🐄	🌹	Alert!
✗	?	?	✗✗	?	✗✗	✗	y	n	AT

Size: World: £25,431m	UK: £269m	*UK employees:* 2,015

Activities: Manufactures food, coffee and vending machines

- Kraft General Foods Limited is the amalgamation of General Foods' and Kraft Foods' UK following their takeover by Philip Morris. Separately, both were cited as good corporate citizens in the USA before their takeovers in 1985 and 1988 respectively.

- Philip Morris, the giant American alcohol-food-tobacco conglomerate, has a poor record of social disclosure in the USA. Kraft General Foods Limited appears to be closely controlled from its US base. It passed New Consumer's questionnaires onto Philip Morris, but no reply was received.

- Four women and three members of ethnic minorities are Philip Morris board members in the USA. Both groups are key growth markets for Philip Morris products, tobacco in particular. No evidence of a thoroughgoing equal opportunities policy available.

- There is little evidence that environmental concerns feature heavily in corporate planning.

- Philip Morris is vehemently opposed to restrictions on tobacco advertising, which it argues are intolerant and 'not consistent with free enterprise systems'.

- It states that it supports US legislation to restrict the sale of tobacco products to under-18s, but is actively committed to a corporate strategy of promoting tobacco consumption worldwide.

> *Philip Morris combines a reputation as a firm which manipulates social responsibility issues towards commercial gain with poor disclosure, and exerts tight control over its UK subsidiary.*

Kwik Save Group P.L.C.

🔍SECRET	♀	👤	🏠	🌳	🐰	👶	☠	⚛	Alert!
✗	?	✗✗	✗✗	✓	✓✓	✗	n	n	at

Size: World: £1,520m UK: £1,520m	**UK employees:** 11,640

Activities: Supermarkets

- Kwik Save has over 700 grocery outlets and is notable for its no-frills approach, selling national brands at low prices.

- A low level of disclosure, though the company does make some reference to social issues in its annual reports.

- No information was available about the numbers of women or ethnic minorities in managerial positions.

- In 1989/90 its charitable donations were £44,504, 0.05 per cent of pre-tax profit — a low figure.

- Kwik Save comments in its *1989/90 Annual Report* that it feels that 'our style of trading respects the environment more than the massive developments of our major competitors', referring to its policy of redeveloping old buildings.

- It has produced a *Special Report on Environmental Action* outlining its policy and environmental action, including recycling initiatives, use of alternative non-CFC refrigerants, avoiding use of tropical hardwoods, and conserving energy.

- It stocks South African products only when acceptable quality alternatives are not available.

- Kwik Save retails both alcohol and tobacco through its 615 units which trade under the Liquorsave fascia.

- No reported policy on goods sourced from the third world.

> *This 'no frills' retailer does not appear to have applied the same resources to corporate responsibility issues as have other comparable supermarket chains.*

Ladbroke Group Plc

									Alert!
✗	?	?	✗	✓	✓✓	✗	n	n	atG

Size: World: £3,801m	UK: £2,056m	UK employees: 52,039

Activities: Hotels, DIY retail, betting and property development

- This diversified company is best known for its Ladbroke chain of betting shops, Britain's largest. It also owns the Hilton International hotel chain and the Texas Homecare DIY chain.

- In overall terms Ladbroke's level of social disclosure is poor. However, its Texas DIY subsidiary did provide material on its sourcing of material in the third world which, while far from comprehensive, unlike most major companies at least demonstrates a willingness to discuss some of the key development issues.

- Texas provided details on a number of environmental initiatives but it was not clear if those extended to the rest of the group.

- There is no evidence of any significant equal opportunities initiatives.

- A significant supporter of the Alzheimers Disease Society but overall donations are however small for a company of its size. The Hon. Greville Janner MP (Labour) and the Right Hon. The Earl of Gowrie (Conservative), a former government Minister, are non-executive directors.

- No reported policy on goods sourced from the third world.

- It makes no reference in its annual report to any measures to counteract negative social problems associated with gambling.

> For a prominent national company, with parliamentarians from both major political parties on its board, which is involved in an industry (gambling) with negative social consequences Ladbroke displays a low overall level of awareness of corporate social responsibility issues.

LEC Refrigeration plc

🔒	♀	👤	🏠	🌳	🐰	🍯	🌍	⚙	Alert!
✘	?	?	✘✘	?	✔✔	?	n	n	

Size: World: £51m UK: £47m	UK employees: 1,680

Activities: Manufactures and markets refrigeration equipment

- This relatively small company focuses entirely on the manufacture and sale of refrigeration equipment.

- It provided specific information about its environmental initiatives, but no further information was available.

- No information was available on equal opportunities initiatives.

- In 1990 Lec's charitable contributions were £5,755, around 0.5 per cent of pre-tax profit, a reasonable figure.

- Lec has a joint arrangement with ICI for the collection and recycling of CFCs from domestic refrigerators. It has also developed a portable CFC recovery unit for service engineers.

- No other environmental information was available.

> *A small company in a very narrow market that has addressed the main environmental issue arising from its operations, but appears to have done little else in the way of corporate responsibility.*

The Littlewoods Organisation PLC

SECRET	♀	👤	🏠	🌳	🐇	🍼	🔫	⚙	Alert!
✗	?	✔	✗✗	?	?	✔	n	n	tG

Size: World: £2,248m	UK: £2,248m	*UK employees:* 27,515

Activities: Home shopping catalogues, department stores and football pools

- One of the UK's largest clothing retailers and catalogue companies with linked interests in football pools.
- Private company owned and controlled by members of the founding Moores family.
- Exceptional record on equal opportunities, and has pioneered many innovative policies in UK. It did not, however, supply any figures for the numbers of women and ethnic minorities in management.
- It has a target to employ ethnic minorities in direct proportion to their representation in local communities.
- Low level of charitable giving, at 0.14 per cent of pre-tax profit, for a company of this size.
- Progressive policy on the sourcing of garments from the third world.
- During the season eight million people participate in Littlewood's football pools.
- Stores incorporate franchised tobacco sales kiosks.

> *Privately owned but publicly accessible, though more disclosure would be welcomed. Apparently strong policies in personnel, equal opportunities and product sourcing.*

Lonhro Plc

SECRET	♀	👤	🏠	🌳	🐰	👶	💉	⚙️	*Alert!*
✗✗	?	?	✗✗	?	?	✗	Y	n	**AT**

Size: World: £5,476m	UK: £2,202m	*UK employees:* 14,790

Activities: Mining, agriculture, textiles, brewing, publishing and hotels

- A truly multinational conglomerate of almost 900 companies.
- Very little public information was available about the company's corporate social responsibility. The group is publisher of *The Observer* newspaper.
- No information was available about the company's equal opportunities policy and initiatives.
- Two of the directors of Lonhro are from third world countries: one from Zimbabwe and one from Mauritius.
- Charitable donations in the UK in 1990 amounted to £146,962, 0.27 per cent of UK pre-tax profit.
- As the company is extensively involved in mining its potential environmental impact is very high. Lonhro gave no indication that it had an environmental policy or had taken any positive initiatives.
- Lonhro has subsidiaries in 22 developing countries, with a range of activities from mining to hotels and wildlife reserves to management of tea, sugar cotton and tobacco plantations.
- Lonhro has five main subsidiaries in South Africa mainly involved in mining gold and platinum.
- Its African operations include brewing in Kenya and tobacco plantations in Malawi.

> *For such a huge multinational company, particularly in view of its intensive involvement in the third world, its lack of disclosure and evidence of any social policies is disappointing.*

Marks & Spencer p.l.c.

										Alert!
✗	✗	✗✗	✓	✓	✓✓	✗	n	C		a

Size: World: £5,775m	UK: £4,947m	**UK employees:** 61,565

Activities: Retails clothing, food, furnishing and toiletries

- Founded in 1894 by Russian refugee, Michael Marks, in partnership with Tom Spencer.

- It is widely recognised as offering the best pay and benefits package for a firm of its type.

- M&S provided some additional information but its overall disclosure on specific social issues was surprisingly below average.

  There is one woman non-executive director; eight per cent of executive level staff and 60 per cent of store management personnel are women. No similar figures were available for ethnic minorities.

- In 1990/91 M&S's community involvement amounted to £5.25 million, 0.9 per cent of pre-tax profits.

- It has an environmental policy which details those areas in which it is taking action, including recycling, pollution control, sponsorship of environmental projects, and energy conservation.

- Notably M&S stopped retailing organic produce at the end of 1990.

- Third world sourced goods feature proportionally less in the M&S range than in other major suppliers because of its 'Buy British' policy.

- A significant corporate supporter of the Conservative Party.

> *Marks & Spencer surpisingly did not entirely live up to its strong corporate image, particularly in relation to disclosure of information.*

Mars U.K. Limited

SECRET	♀	👤	🏠	🌳	🐰	🍼	🔺	⚙	Alert!
✔	✔	?	?	✔	✔✔	✘	n	n	

Parent: Mars Incorporated		USA
Size: World: £5,000m UK: £1,185m	UK employees: 7,036	

Activities: Manufactures food, confectionery and pet foods

- Mars U.K. is the holding company for a cluster of British subsidiaries of an American parent, wholly owned by the wealthy Mars family.

- Noted for a strong confectionery presence, but in fact much more dominant in the pet food market through Pedigree Petfoods.

- A reasonable level of disclosure within the UK, though this is not matched by its parent company.

- The company has developed a distinctive personnel culture where employees are described as 'associates', with excellent pay and benefits.

- Over 10 per cent of its UK managers are women, and two are board members of subsidiary companies. It has a comprehensive range of supporting equal opportunities benefits, but declined to provide information on the numbers of managers from ethnic minorities.

- Some evidence of extensive community work, though the company declined to put an exact figure on its involvement.

- Some clear environmental policies are in place, with distinctive emphasis on rail transport for distribution of the output from the Pedigree Petfoods subsidiary.

- Mars is a major buyer of third world commodities, and there is some evidence of company cooperation with third world governments in agro/technological developments.

> Decisively positive social policies in most areas characterise this foodstuffs manufacturing group.

McDonald's Restaurants Limited

									Alert!
XX	?	?	XX	?	✓✓	?	n	n	

Parent: McDonald's Corporation		USA
Size: World: £3,490m UK: £441m	**UK employees:**	25,412
Activities: Operates and franchises fast food outlets		

The world's largest fast food restaurant business, McDonald's 11,500 outlets in 52 countries serve over 22 million people daily.

The relative openness of its US parent company contrasts starkly with the UK subsidiary's minimum disclosure.

- McDonald's is admired by its competitors for its ability to extract a high degree of commitment and performance from staff, who are frequently young, part-time and short-stay.

- Like other fast food operators it is criticised by some commentators for its low wage levels, characteristic of the industry and sometimes described as exploitative.

McDonald's has a good equal opportunities record in the USA, but poor disclosure makes it impossible to assess the UK situation.

McDonald's extensive worldwide community involvement concentrates on programmes benefiting children. Charitable donations in the UK are minimal (£6,500 in 1990).

- In Spring 1991 McDonald's in the USA announced a major 'green' initiative aimed at reducing its waste production by 80 per cent.

- McDonald's in the UK provided no evidence of similar significant pro-environmental policies.

- McDonald's categorically refutes allegations that it has sourced beef from cattle raised on land cleared of rainforest.

McDonald's has frequently been the focus of generalised criticism of the fast food industry as a whole. Poor disclosure makes a clear evaluation of its UK operations difficult.

Merloni Domestic Appliances Limited

🔍	♀	🗣	🏠	🌳	🐇	👶	🐾	🌼	Alert!
XX	?	?	XX	?	✓✓	?	n	n	

Parent: Merloni Elettrodomestici S.p.A.		Italy
Size: World: £493m UK: £2m	UK employees: 550	

Activities: Manufactures domestic appliances

- The Italian parent company, Merloni Elettrodomestici SpA, is one of Europe's largest manufacturers of home appliances, making refrigerators, freezers, ovens, washing machines and dishwashers under the Ariston and Indesit brand names.

- The parent company is controlled by Vittorio Merloni, the son of its founder.

- Both the parent and UK subsidiary companies have extremely poor records on disclosure, providing virtually no published information about their social impact.

- There is one female director on the parent company board: Ester Merloni, a relative of the founder.

- Merloni is a major manufacturer of refrigerators, a major component of which are ozone-depleting CFCs. It offered no evidence of any pro-environmental initiatives designed to deal with CFC refrigerants, or of any other significant environmental policies.

- A parent company board member, Francesco Merloni, is chairman of the Fondazione Aristide Merloni, a foundation established to promote enterprise culture in Italy.

> For a company involved in the production of goods with a high negative environmental profile, its poor disclosure on 'green' and other social issues is notable.

MFI Furniture Group Limited

SECRET	♀	🗣	🏠	🌳	🐇	👶	🍇	🔍	Alert!
✗✗	?	?	✓	?	✓✓	✗	n	n	

Size: World: £595m UK: £595m	*UK employees:* 8,025

Activities: Manufactures and retails furniture

- MFI is one of Britain's leading furniture manufacturers and retailers.

- It pioneered the flatpack assemble-at-home furniture concept in the UK.

- It has been severely affected by the recession, making a small loss in 1989/90, which may account for the extremely low level of disclosure on social and environmental issues.

- MFI is notable in being one of the few UK companies to have an Employee Share Ownership Plan (ESOP), through which a trust owns five per cent of the company's shares on employees' behalf. The shares are free to employees, being bought out of company profits. The plan is considered generous, even extending to part-timers.

- It provided no indication of any significant equal opportunities initiatives.

- MFI's charitable donations in recent years have been modest. It is not a member of Business in the Community nor of the Per Cent Club.

- As a furniture manufacturer and retailer its activities involve a number of important environmental issues, which the company shows no indication of having publicly addressed.

- No reported policy on goods sourced from the third world.

Even allowing for its current financial difficulties MFI demonstrates little awareness of its social and environmental responsibilities.

Milk Marketing Board/ Dairy Crest

SECRET	♀	〈	🏠	🌳	🐰	💭	🍼	🔍	Alert!
XX	?	?	XX	?	XX	?	n	n	

Size: World: £1,254m	UK: £1,043m	UK employees: 12,755

Activities: Manufactures and markets processed milk and dairy produce

- The Milk Marketing Board (MMB) is a farmers' co-operative established by government statute, with monopoly powers to purchase all milk produced in the UK and to set the prices paid to farmer producers and by processors. The Board's powers have been criticised for allegedly inhibiting competition and impeding innovation.

- Dairy Crest, a wholly-owned subsidiary of the MMB, manufactures, transports and trades dairy products.

- The MMB and Dairy Crest have extremely poor records on social disclosure, contrasting unfavourably with other food companies in the survey.

- The MMB's eighteen member board has one female director, one of three ministerial appointments; the others are elected by the dairy farmers supplying the board. Neither the MMB or Dairy Crest offers evidence of significant equal opportunities initiatives.

- Apart from small donations of product no significant charitable contributions are made by either organisation.

- Evidence of any concerted pro-environmental initiatives by the MMB and Dairy Crest was scant.

- It is a big exporter of powdered milk to the third world.

> *The MMB's and Dairy Crest's protected position insulates them from direct consumer pressure, which may explain their reticence in providing a public account of their social impact.*

Mobil Oil Company Limited

🔍	♀	🏭	🌳	🐰	🍼	🔬			Alert!
✗	?	?	✔	✗	?	?	n	n	tM

Parent: Mobil Corporation		USA
Size: World: £31,925m UK: £914m	**UK employees:** 1,902	
Activities: Oil and petroleum products		

- Mobil Oil Company Limited, Britain's fourth largest petrol supplier, told New Consumer: 'we simply do not have the resources to research in detail and complete the questionnaire forms in the manner you require'.

- The huge Mobil parent company also has a record of reluctance in disclosing information to public interest research groups.

- No information is available about Mobil's UK equal opportunities initiatives, although its parent company's board includes two women and two members of ethnic minorities.

- Mobil has a reasonable UK charitable giving programme, and is a member of the Per Cent Club.

- American commentators have described Mobil's environmental record as mixed. It appears to lack a company-wide strategy for co-ordinating pro-environmental policies.

- US commentators have, in the past, commended Mobil for its work in identifying and utilising alternatives to animal testing.

- In 1989 Mobil, then the largest US company in South Africa and a consistent opponent of disinvestment, sold its South African interests to a local company. This was reputedly due to changes in US tax legislation which reduced the profitability of South African based subsidiaries.

Mobil has a mixed record on social responsibility issues in the USA, which it combines with an unwillingness to fully acknowledge the public's right to an account of its social impact.

Nestlé Holdings (U.K.) PLC

SECRET	♀	⚔	🏠	🌳	🐇	👶	☠	⚙	Alert!
✔	?	✗	✔✔	?	✗	✗	Y	n	a

Parent: Nestlé S.A.		Switzerland

Size: World: £18,292m	UK: £1,542m	**UK employees:** 21,820

Activities: Manufactures and markets food, coffee, chocolate, confectionery, pet foods and pharmaceuticals

- The Swiss-based Nestlé is the world's largest food company. It also owns approximately one third of the French cosmetics giant L'Oréal.

- It is renowned for its aggressive corporate culture, viewing social responsibility considerations as a poor second behind market advantage in setting business priorities.

- Nestlé in the UK has a good record on community involvement, with a programme valued at £1.3m in 1989.

- It has been slow to develop pro-environmental policies, although the appointment of senior staff to oversee environmental policy is an indication that this may change in the future.

- Nestlé has been the subject of a long-running boycott campaign over its aggressive marketing of baby and infant feeding formula in the third world. Critics argue that this discourages breast feeding, and that a combination of low literacy levels and contaminated water supplies can make the use of powdered feeds dangerous. Nestlé regard proposed restrictions on the marketing of what it sees as a nutritious product as unnecessarily restrictive.

- Nestlé subscribes to the information services of the Economic League, the right wing 'blacklisting' organisation now discredited due to its political bias and inaccurate records.

Nestlé's commitment to an aggressive corporate culture means that it is likely to be the focus of consumer action and boycotts for some time to come.

Next PLC

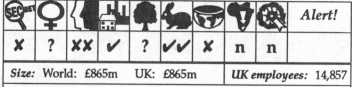

									Alert!
✗	?	✗✗	✓	?	✓✓	✗	n	n	

Size: World: £865m   UK: £865m   **UK employees:** 14,857

Activities: Catalogue home shopping, retails clothing and home furnishing products

- Next was one of the high street retail stars of the 1980s, led by the charismatic fashion guru George Davies. Davies was sacked at the end of 1988 when the company hit choppy financial waters due to over-expansion and depressed consumer spending.

- The Next board refused to disclose to shareholders the size of compensation payments to Mr Davies, as a result of which concerned shareholders voted unsuccessfully against the directors' re-election at the 1989 AGM in protest at its apparent lack of accountability.

- Like so many areas of corporate information disclosure, a board's obligation to disclose details of executive severance payments is a grey area.

- In 1990 Next stated that 33 per cent of its top 200 managers were women. It does not appear to carry out any significant designated equal opportunities initiatives.

- Next claims to be the first retailer to offer 'green' cotton, produced without harmful effluents.

- Next own brand cosmetics are 'cruelty free': they have not been tested on animals nor have their ingredients been tested on animals in the last five years.

- No reported policy on goods sourced from the third world.

> *The Next pattern of development — acquisitive growth and rapid expansion — has meant that social issues do not seem to have been a priority.*

Nissan Motor Manufacturing Co.

🔍	♀	👤	🏭	🌳	🐰	🧷	⚔	⚙	Alert
4	?	?	4	?	44	?	y	n	M

Parent: Nissan Motor Company Limited		Japan
Size: World: £18,035m	UK: £313m	**UK employees:** 2,100

Activities: Manufactures cars, aerospace and marine equipment, and textile machinery

- Nissan is Japan's second and the world's fifth largest car maker. It has a major manufacturing plant in Sunderland.

- High productivity has led to criticism that it pushes its employees too hard, criticism that Nissan is keen to refute. In a document entitled *Facts Against Fallacy*, Nissan comments: 'There are no exercise programmes at the start of each shift . . . no company songs . . . no salary deductions for lateness or absenteeism'.

- Of the top 2,600 senior officers in the Nissan parent company in 1990, only two were women. It is creditable that Nissan should disclose this information; Nissan in the UK did not disclose comparable local information.

- Nissan Motor Manufacturing Co. makes only minor charitable donations in the UK, but its parent has made significant donations in the past to Oxford University's Institute of Japanese Studies.

- Nissan provided some information about its pro-environmental initiatives, but not enough to make a realistic assessment of their commitment on 'green' issues.

- Nissan vehicles are manufactured under licence in South Africa by a locally owned company with technical assistance from Nissan.

Nissan's fierce commitment to maximum efficiency is not yet similarly reflected in the social responsibility sphere, although the parent company's openness bodes well for future developments.

Northern Foods plc

									Alert!
✔	?	✗	✗✗	✗✗	✔✔	?	n	n	

Size: World: £1,187m UK: £1,187m	UK employees: 22,924

Activities: Manufactures food: dairy, meat, grocery and convenience

- Northern Foods is one of the leading suppliers of own-label foods to Britain's major supermarket chains.

- The company expressed a willingness to provide information about its activities, but stated that because of the high degree of autonomy accorded to subsidiary operations 'we do not have central records covering many of the issues in your survey'.

- The company provided some information about equal opportunities, indicating that in 1990 14 of its 200 most senior managers were either women or from ethnic minorities.

- The firm has been slow to respond to growing public environmental concerns. It does, however, demonstrate a considerable awareness of the need to maintain the highest standards of hygiene and raw material quality in food manufacturing.

- The company's founder, and Honorary Life President, Alec Horsley, was one of the founders of the School of Peace Studies at Bradford University.

The company's strong position on food safety demonstrates a willingness to respond to consumer concerns, which may be translatable into action on wider social responsibility issues.

L'Oréal (U.K.) Limited

SECRET	♀	👥	🏠	🌳	🐰	🍼	🌹		Alert!
✔	✔	✗✗	✔	✔	✗	?	y	n	

Parent: L'Oréal S.A.		France
Size: World: £2,770m UK: £172m		UK employees: 2,043
Activities: Manufactures cosmetics and fragrances, publishing		

- The French-based parent company is one of the world's largest cosmetics firms. It also publishes *Marie Claire* magazine.

- Forty per cent of L'Oréal (U.K.) Limited's managerial staff are women, a high figure. In the last two years four out of seven graduate recruits have been women.

- While the representation of women is high, it did not receive a top rating due to lack of any supporting equal opportunities policies or benefits such as career breaks or monitoring procedures.

- Members of ethnic minorities are not represented in management, perhaps reflecting the weakness in supporting equal opportunities structures.

- L'Oréal demonstrated a very high level of disclosure on equal opportunities issues, which is encouraging as an indicator of possible future action.

- There is evidence of the development of a well-thought-out pro-environmental strategy for its activities.

- Although it has significantly reduced numbers of tests on animals and supports research into alternatives, L'Oréal remains, amongst other companies, the subject of a bitter boycott campaign. It believes that some testing is necessary to maintain its 'cast iron commitment to protect the consumer'.

While its policy on animal testing has been the subject of some controversy, L'Oréal's willingness to provide a public account of its position on several issues illustrates a positive awareness of the public's right to a social account of its activities.

Panasonic UK Limited

SECRET	♀	(	🏠	🌳	🐰	🍼	🎗	🍩	Alert!
✓✓	X	X	X	✓	✓✓	✓	y	n	

Parent: Matsushita Electric Industrial Co.		Japan
Size: World: £24,728m UK: £570m	**UK employees:** 2,200

Activities: Manufactures consumer electronic and electric equipment

- Panasonic's parent, Matsushita Electric Industries, is Japan's largest consumer electronics and electronic equipment manufacturer.

- Its 1990 $6 billion takeover of MCA, the Hollywood entertainment conglomerate, was the largest ever Japanese takeover of a US company.

- Its founder, the visionary Konosuke Matsushita, championed the principle that business has a constant mission to contribute to the well-being of society, but was also renowned for his acute business sense.

- In 1932, on the fourteenth anniversary of his firm's foundation, he announced a 250-year plan to his employees.

- Panasonic provided comprehensive information on the numbers of women and members of ethnic minorities in senior management. While it is clearly not an innovator in this area, such openness is encouraging as an indicator of possible future action.

- In contrast to other major industrial users of ozone-depleting CFCs Matsushita provided full details of phase-out programmes.

- Matsushita has a more progressive policy than most on technology transfer, such as an award from the Peruvian government for its training and educational activities.

> *The principles of its parent company's founder give it a strong philosophical base on social responsibility issues, which it appears to be building on in some areas.*

Paterson Zochonis

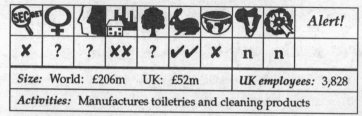

									Alert!
✗	?	?	✗✗	?	✓✓	✗	n	n	

Size: World: £206m UK: £52m	*UK employees:* 3,828

Activities: Manufactures toiletries and cleaning products

- Paterson Zochonis is best known for its Cussons and Imperial Leather soap brands.

- It was founded over a century ago as a general trader between West Africa and Europe. Around a third of its turnover still comes from its Nigerian operations.

- The Zochonis family have a controlling interest in the firm.

- The company provided too little information to make a realistic assessment in most categories.

- It has not carried out any animal testing since 1989, and states that it encourages research into alternative methods of testing.

- No reported policy on goods sourced from or operations in the third world.

A general reluctance to provide information prevents any positive assessment of the company's general policies.

PepsiCo

SECRET	♀	🗣	🏭	🌳	🐰	🏺	🥦	⚙	Alert!
✗	?	?	✗✗	✓	✗	✗	y	n	

Parent:	Pepsico Incorporated		USA
Size:	World: £10,064m	UK: £308m	UK employees: 5,147

Activities: Manufactures and markets soft drinks, snack foods and fast food

- PepsiCo is best known for its soft drinks, especially Pepsi Cola, which it markets in the UK through Britvic Soft Drinks. Britvic Soft Drinks is a collaborative venture with Allied-Lyons, Bass and Whitbread.

- Other joint ventures with UK operating partners include the restaurant businesses Pizza Hut (with Whitbread) and Kentucky Fried Chicken (with Forte Plc).

- With the acquisition of Smiths and Walkers crisps in 1989, PepsiCo is now the biggest crisp company in the UK. The charitable giving of these wholly-owned companies is negligible.

- PepsiCo has an extremely low level of social disclosure, providing no information on its UK activities.

- In the USA PepsiCo is recognised as a major supporter of ethnic minority business, and of equal opportunities for ethnic minorities generally. Ethnic minority communities represent a prime market for PepsiCo products.

- PepsiCo has licensing and franchising agreements in South Africa. It has sold its bottling interests and a number of Kentucky Fried Chicken outlets to former employees, stating that it did so to black employees where possible.

The US parent company demonstrates a number of positive initiatives, but evaluation of its UK activities is not possible due to poor disclosure.

213

Peugeot Talbot Motor Co. Limited

SECRET	♀	🗣	🏠	🌳	🐇	🍯	V	❀	Alert!
✗	?	?	✗✗	?	✓✓	?	n	n	

Parent: Peugeot S.A.	France

Size: World: £15,592m	UK: £1,596m	**UK employees:** 7,723

Activities: Car manufacture and mechanical engineering

- Best known for its Peugeot and Citroen cars, the Peugeot S.A. parent company also manufactures Peugeot bicycles.
- Poor disclosure makes it impossible to assess its equal opportunities and environmental initiatives in the UK.
- Peugeot S.A. was a long time opponent of EC proposals to tighten exhaust emission standards for small cars, stating that 'politicians have yielded to popular environmentalist arguments which sound worthwhile but which will in fact destroy jobs and have a negative impact on lower income groups'.
- Nevertheless, Peugeot S.A.'s publications do provide some evidence of intent to develop more pro-environmental technologies.
- Peugeot S.A. chief executive Jacques Calvet is a former Economics Ministry director in the 'conservative' government of Giscard d'Estaing.
- Renowned for his outspokenness on public affairs, he has commented that French business should concentrate more on attacking commercial challenges than 'good sentiments' such as the European Social Charter or boosting low wages.

> *Peugeot S.A.'s aggressive corporate culture is dictated from the top, and appears to offer only begrudging acknowledgement of the importance of social responsibility initiatives.*

Philips U.K. Limited

SECRET	♀	⟨	🏠	🌳	🐰	〰	♥	✿	Alert!
✗	?	?	✔	✔	✔✔	✗	Y	n	**M**

Parent: Philips' NV Gloeilampenfabrieken	The Netherlands

Size: World: £16,571m	UK: £1,336m	**UK employees:** 18,472

Activities: Manufactures electrical and electronic equipment

- The Dutch parent company, Philips Electronics, Europe's largest consumer electronics company and the world's biggest light bulb manufacturer, is currently in crisis as a result of a sudden plummet in sales and profits.

- A major restructuring programme involving widespread redundancies is currently under way, threatening its traditional reputation as a paternalistic cradle-to-grave employer.

- Its white goods products (cookers and fridges) are produced in a joint venture with the American Whirlpool Corporation.

- The poor level of disclosure by both the parent company and Philips U.K. Limited may be explained by the current organisational turmoil.

- Philips UK has a turnover of over £1 billion, but shows little evidence of a developed community involvement programme with donations in 1988 of only £29,000.

- There is some evidence of positive environmental stewardship, but the company does not appear to be one of industry's innovators.

- Philips Electronics is in the process of divesting itself of its military-related activities, which it feels are too small to compete in the longer term.

Philips good record on personnel policy and the development of innovative practices in other social responsibility issues is threatened by its current financial crisis.

Procter & Gamble Limited

									Alert!
✔✔	✔	✔✔	✗	✔	✗	✔	y	n	

Parent: The Procter & Gamble Company		USA
Size: World: £12,158m UK: £743m	**UK employees:** 3,335

Activities: Manufactures laundry and cleaning products, toiletries, food and OTC medicines

- A very open company, with both its US parent and main subsidiary providing substantial information.

- It has a woman executive director and an ethnic minority non-executive director on the UK company's main board. Twenty seven per cent of UK managers are women, and two per cent are from ethnic minorities.

- Over the last two years just over 50 percent of graduate recruits were women and four per cent were from ethnic minority groups.

- Charitable donations in the UK amounted to 0.15 per cent of pre-tax profit in 1990. A member of Business in the Community.

- Response to environmental issues includes refillable packaging, concentrated washing powder, labelling the contents of laundry and cleaning products, and research into the possibility of composting used disposable nappies.

- It has a number of subsidiaries in developing countries. A booklet entitled *Good Corporate Citizenship in a Host Country* outlines basic principles of social responsibility.

- P&G continues to reduce the number of animals used in testing its products, and funds research into alternative tests.

- The parent company has a licensing agreement in South Africa from the acquisition of Richardson-Vicks, an agreement which expires in 1995.

> *The parent company's high level of corporate responsibility in the USA appears to be developing in the UK.*

Quaker Oats Ltd.

![SECRET]	♀	🗣	🏭	🌳	🐰	🍼	🔬	⚙	Alert!
✗	?	?	✗✗	?	?	?	n	n	

Parent: The Quaker Oats Company		USA
Size: World: £2,844m UK: £159m	**UK employees:** 1,545	
Activities: Manufactures food and pet foods		

- The company is best known for its Quaker Oats and Sugar Puffs breakfast cereals.

- Quaker Oats Ltd has a poor level of disclosure in contrast to its US parent company, which has a fair record in this area. It has a Public Responsibility Committee made up of board members which sets policy on issues of corporate citizenship.

- The Quaker Oats parent company has a strong record on equal opportunities for all groups in the USA. For example, it explicitly forbids discrimination based on sexual orientation. The comprehensive nature of these policies do not appear to be replicated in the UK.

- An extensive US community involvement programme is not mirrored in the UK, where charitable donations are minimal.

- The company states it is in the process of developing pro-environmental initiatives, but did not provide details.

- In the USA the company has stated in the past that the only animal testing it carries out are feeding tests on cats and dogs 'to see if they like our products'. However, it has refused to elaborate on the specifics of what the tests entail.

> *Quaker Oats Limited, in stark contrast to its US parent, seems to have yet to have addressed the issue of policy development on most corporate social responsibility matters.*

Ranks Hovis McDougall PLC

SECRET	♀	👤	🏠	🌳	🐰	👶	🐂	⚙	Alert!
✗	?	?	✗	?	?	✗	n	C	

Size: World: £1,771m	UK: £1,369m	UK employees: 32,349

Activities: Manufactures food, bread and cakes

- RHM, a leading food manufacturer, is one of Britain's biggest bakers. Its brands include Hovis bread, Mr Kipling cakes and Bisto gravy.

- The firm provides more summary detail on its social policies in its annual report than most companies. However, its overall disclosure level is poor.

- RHM acknowledges the need to encourage more women to progress into higher management, but declined to provide details about how it intended to achieve this.

- A small but growing community involvement programme is in evidence, with an emphasis on secondment of staff to support local enterprise agencies around the country.

- RHM states that it recognises the need for industry to become more environmentally aware, but although it provided some examples of pro-environmental initiatives it is as yet unclear how significant a commitment it really has on this issue.

- The company is a major supporter of the Conservative Party, donating an average of £30,000 a year in the 1986-1990 period.

> *While it has acknowledged the need for business to act on most of the corporate social responsibility issues covered, RHM has yet to translate this recognition into action in the majority of cases.*

Reckitt and Colman plc

🔐	♀	👤	🏭	🌳	🐰	🏺	💊	🔬	*Alert!*
✗	?	✗	✗✗	?	✗	?	Y	C	

Size: World: £1,764m	UK: £364m	*UK employees:* 4,600

Activities: Manufactures home and personal care products, pharmaceuticals and food

- Reckitt & Colman has its origins in a flour mill established in 1819 by Isaac Reckitt.

- Reckitts commented that: 'We operate an ethnic monitor on locations where ethnic minorities form a significant part of the local labour market'. It declined to provide specific figures on their numbers in senior management.

- Reckitts acknowledges it has too few women in senior management. In response to this concern, between 1985 and 1989 the number of female graduate recruits was increased from 47 per cent of the total intake to 79 per cent. It declined to provide figures on the numbers of women in senior management or on additional equal opportunities initiatives.

- It provided limited information indicating awareness of the need for pro-environmental policies, but not enough to evaluate the degree this awareness is incorporated in business planning.

- It carries out limited animal testing for its pharmaceutical products only, has a stated commitment to keeping all testing to a minimum, and supports research into alternatives.

- Between 1987 and 1990 the company donated £130,000 to the Conservative Party via British United Industrialists.

- Extensive South African interests employ almost 2000 people.

> *Although it made only limited information disclosure, there is enough evidence to suggest a foundation exists for the development of strong social impact policies in the future.*

Renault UK Limited

SECRET	♀	〔	🏭	🌳	🐰	👶	☂	🔍	Alert!
✗✗	?	?	✗✗	?	✓✓	?	n	n	M

Parent: Regie Nationale des Usines Renault		France

Size: World: £17,786m	UK: £754m	**UK employees:** 803

Activities: Car and truck manufacturer

- Renault is 80 per cent owned by the French government and 20 per cent by Volvo, the Swedish motor manufacturer. Renault in turn owns a minority share of Volvo's car business.

- In addition to Renault UK Limited's distribution business, Renault also has a truck and van assembly plant in Britain.

- Until recently the French government subsidised Renault's substantial losses. The European Commission has demanded an end to these subsidies, which it sees as impeding competition, and the repayment of substantial amounts of the state aid.

- Traditionally Renault has had a good reputation as an employer in France, with well-developed consultative links with trades unions. It remains to be seen whether this culture will continue now that the company is being exposed to a more competitive environment.

- It disclosed little information relating to its social impact.

- Along with Peugeot, the other major French car manufacturer, Renault initially opposed the introduction of European Commission legislation setting tighter exhaust emission limits. While it has now accepted them, there are no indications that the development of pro-environmental initiatives are a priority for the company.

> *Poor information disclosure and exposure to more competitive forces make evaluation of current and future potential for development of social responsibility policies extremely difficult.*

Revlon Manufacturing (UK) Ltd

SECRET	♀	👤	🏠	🌳	🐰	👶	🐄	⚛	Alert!
XX	?	?	XX	?	✓✓	?	y	n	

Parent: MacAndrews & Forbes Holdings Inc.		USA
Size: World: £2,500m UK: £39m	UK employees: 408	

Activities: Manufactures toiletries and cosmetics

- Revlon Manufacturing (UK) Ltd is the British manufacturing and distribution arm of MacAndrews & Forbes Holdings Inc., best known for its Revlon cosmetics and toiletries products.

- MacAndrews & Forbes is owned by Roland Perelman, one of America's most aggressive corporate raiders in the 1980s.

- Mr Perelman is reputed to have started attending his father's company board meetings at the age of eleven.

- By 1991 Mr Perelman's $4 billion empire had become mired in debt, forcing him to sell his Max Factor cosmetics business to Procter & Gamble for $1.14 billion amid rumours that he might also have to sell the Revlon business.

- As a private company the MacAndrews & Forbes parent company is not required to publish an annual report, and both it and Revlon Manufacturing in the UK have poor social disclosure records.

- Nancy Reagan, wife of former US president Ronald Reagan, is a member of the MacAndrews & Forbes board.

- One notable aspect of Revlon Manufacturing is that in 1988 it indicated that 3.3 per cent of its workforce were registered disabled, an unusually high figure for a British company.

- In 1989 Revlon announced that it would no longer have any of its products tested on animals.

> *Apart from its animal testing position, little is known about the social policies of this secretive privately-owned conglomerate.*

Rothmans International p.l.c.

									Alert!
XX	?	?	XX	?	?	X	Y	C	T

Size: World: £1,549m	UK: £189m	UK employees: 13,906

Activities: Manufactures tobacco and luxury products

- Rothmans is one of the UK's four leading tobacco manufacturers.

- The company is also involved in luxury consumer goods through its interests in Dunhill and Cartier.

- It is ultimately controlled by the South African Rupert family.

- Rothmans approach to disclosure of social information in its annual reports could best be described as minimalist. It asked to be excluded from an earlier survey conducted by New Consumer.

- Its charitable donations are notably small for such a large company. In the 1987-90 period they were exceeded by donations to the Health Promotion Research Trust, a tobacco industry-sponsored body which examines the impact of smoking on health.

- The company is actively promoting its tobacco products in the third world, where there are fewer restrictions on marketing, to compensate for declining sales in the West.

- It actively opposes tobacco advertising restrictions: 'We believe in the consumer's right to free choice, and that all goods and services which are legally in the market place should enjoy the same freedom of commercial speech'.

- It chose not to comment on smoking's proven negative health effect.

- Between 1987 and 1989 cash donations of £4,600 were made to the 'free enterprise' pressure group Aims of Industry.

Rothmans appears to have adopted a policy of minimum disclosure on social issues. This is doubly disappointing given its involvement in a product with a proven adverse effect on health.

J Sainsbury plc

🔒	♀	👤	🏠	🌳	🐾	🧷	🐷	☢	Alert!
✓✓	✓✓	✓✓	✓	✓✓	✓✓	✗	n	n	at

Size: World: £8,201m	UK: £7,232m	*UK employees:* 70,848

Activities: Supermarkets, department stores and DIY retail

- Britain's biggest food retailer, Sainsbury also has a significant foothold in the DIY market through its Homebase chain.

- Sainsbury has an excellent record on social disclosure, evidently a company proud of its activities which accepts the public's right to a social account of its impact.

- In 1990, 30 per cent of UK managerial grade employees and 56 per cent of graduate recruits were women. Full supporting equal opportunities policies for non-managerial and managerial staff makes it one of the best companies for female employees in the survey.

- Despite having positive policies, representation of members of ethnic minorities is still low. However, Sainsbury's openness on this issue illustrates an awareness and willingness to act.

- It has a well-established community involvement programme.

- Sainsbury demonstrated a wide range of pro-environmental initiatives. Although environmentalists might argue that, like the rest of British industry, it still has a lot to do, it is clearly a company which treats environmental issues seriously.

- The company does not test its own-label products on animals.

- No reported policy on goods sourced from the third world.

- It carries South African goods, 'clearly and fully labelled as such; we leave the choice to the individual customer'.

Sainsbury has a reputation for high quality merchandise. This commitment to quality is reflected in the development of a range of constructive social responsibility policies.

223

Scottish & Newcastle Breweries plc

									Alert!
✗	?	?	✗	?	✓✓	?	n	C	Atg

Size: World: £1,240m	UK: £1,109m	UK employees: 30,812

Activities: Brewing and pubs

- S&N is the smallest of Britain's big six brewers. It also owns the Pontin's holiday group.

- It publishes some interesting snippets of social information in its annual reports, but its overall disclosure level is poor.

- In 1989/90 S&N shook off a takeover bid by what is now the Foster's Brewing Group, citing employee support as crucial to its success. Unusually, its annual report lists the number of working days lost to industrial disputes: only 87 in 1989/90, which would appear to confirm the view of a supportive workforce.

- In 1989/90 56 registered disabled people were employed. No further information about equal opportunities was forthcoming.

- An established but small community involvement programme.

- The company shows little evidence of having given serious consideration to the development of pro-environmental policies.

- One of the largest corporate contributors to the Conservative Party, it donated £130,000 in the three years to April 1990.

- While acknowledging alcohol abuse as a serious problem, S&N believes it unfair to penalise the majority of sensible drinkers because of the behaviour of a minority, believing it to be a symptom, not a cause, of social problems. It offers limited evidence of an ongoing commitment to combat alcohol abuse.

> *S&N obviously commands the respect of its work-force, but demonstrates no acknowledgement of the need to provide a social account to society as a whole.*

Scott Limited

![SECRET]	♀	👤	🏭	🌳	🐰	👶	✈	⚙	Alert!
✓	XX	XX	XX	✓	✓✓	?	n	n	

Parent: Scott Paper Company   USA

Size: World: £3,028m   UK: £306m   **UK employees:** 2,300

Activities: Manufactures paper products

- A company best known from its Andrex toilet paper advertisements. Its parent company is one of the world's leading paper manufacturers.

- It had a reasonable level of disclosure, providing information about its corporate responsibility.

- Unlike its US parent company, there are no women or ethnic minorities on the UK board, and no figures were available for the numbers in management.

- Charitable donations in the UK in 1988/89 amounted to 0.2 per cent of pre-tax profit.

- Scott has been cited in the USA in 1989 by the Environmental Protection Agency as a high-risk air polluter for its releases of chloroform. Other environmental criticisms levelled at Scott include its development of eucalyptus plantations, and the use of herbicides and pesticides in its softwood plantations.

- Scott stated that its 'forests are managed to provide a sustainable and ever-increasing resource'.

- The company has demonstrated that it has strong environmental policies, and has taken creative steps to address its environmental problems.

- Scott has operations in a number of third world countries.

The strong social record of its parent company is not fully reflected in its UK operations. The company's openness is an encouraging sign that other issues as well as the environment will be addressed.

225

Sears plc

![SECRET]	♀	![head]	![factory]	![tree]	![rabbit]	![nappy]	![bottle]	![globe]	Alert!
✗	?	?	✗✗	?	✓✓	✗	n	C	at

Size: World: £2,163m UK: £1,969m	UK employees: 51,114

Activities: Home shopping, clothing, footwear, retailing and department stores

- Britain's leading footwear retailer, and owner of Selfridges.

- The Al Fayed brothers (owners of House of Fraser) have an 11 per cent shareholding in Sears.

- The company provided some specific information, but generally had a low level of disclosure.

- There is one woman non-executive director, but no further information on equal opportunities was available.

- Sears maintained its charitable donations at £455,000 (£456,000 in 1990) in 1991 despite its falling profits, although this is a small amount for a company of this size.

- It does not appear to have an environmental policy, and has taken few positive initiatives in this area.

- Sears stated that its own label cosmetics and toiletries have not been tested on animals, and that the ingredients have not been tested in the last five years. Miss Selfridge own label cosmetics are included in BUAV's *Approved Product Guide* as 'cruelty-free'.

- The company sources footwear and shoe components from Brazil and the Far East, and clothing from many developing countries.

- It is a regular donor to the Conservative Party, and has made annual donations of £15,000 in the last three years.

Sears appears to have addressed some areas of social responsibility, including animal testing and community involvement, but it is not clear what other steps it has taken.

Sharp Electronics (UK) Limited

🔍SECRET	♀	〈	🏭	🌳	🐰	🍯	🗺️	⚙️	Alert!
✗	?	?	✗✗	?	✓✓	✗	n	n	

Parent: Sharp Corporation	Japan

Size: World: £4,643m UK: £264m	**UK employees:** 1,420

Activities: Manufactures and markets electrical and electronic equipment

- The seventh largest of the Japanese electronics giants. It produced the world's first desk top electronic calculator.

- It had a low level of disclosure, with little publicly social responsibility information available.

- No information about equal opportunities initiatives was available.

- No charitable donations are recorded in its UK annual report.

- Its parent company noted in its *1988/89 Annual Report* that 'by donating the 500,000th UK-produced microwave oven to a local hospital, Sharp enhanced its corporate image'.

- No information was available about any environmental policies or initiatives.

- In 1988 Sharp's three Malaysian factories accounted for 1.4 per cent of the country's Gross National Product. It also has subsidiaries in seven other developing countries.

- In its *1988/89 Annual Report* it refers to a strategy of transferring technology and manufacturing locally with reference to its operations in Thailand — a promising hint.

> *A company with a low level of disclosure and little evidence of any action in areas of social and ethical responsibility.*

The 'Shell' Transport and Trading Company p.l.c.

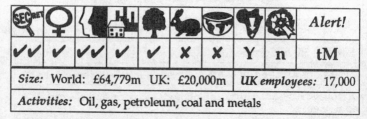

SECRET	♀	👥	🏠	🌳	🐰	🍯	☠	⚙	Alert!
✓✓	✓	✓✓	✓	✓	✗	✗	Y	n	tM

Size: World: £64,779m UK: £20,000m	*UK employees:* 17,000

Activities: Oil, gas, petroleum, coal and metals

- Shell comprises two parent companies, one British and the other Dutch.

- Shell in the UK completed the questionnaires and provided a large amount of detailed information about its operations.

- Four per cent of its senior managers are women and one per cent are from ethnic minorities. Of its recent graduate recruits, 20 per cent were women and two per cent from ethnic minorities.

- In 1989 community giving in the UK amounted to £5.8 million. Shell is a member of Business in the Community.

- The nature of Shell's business involves a high level of potential environmental impact, as illustrated by the oil spill into the River Mersey in 1989. Shell is fully aware of this responsibility and has taken steps to minimise its impact.

- Shell owns numerous companies in the third world, each of which is 'expected to maintain extremely high standards of practice'.

- Shell is involved in animal testing through its chemicals business, though the company is exploring alternative tests.

- In 1989 it had 8,455 employees in South Africa.

- Shell is a major supplier of fuel to the Ministry of Defence, with contracts worth £25-50 million in 1988/89.

> *Shell's high level of disclosure is reflected in its considered approach to policies with reference to areas of social responsibility.*

Smith & Nephew plc

									Alert!
✗	?	?	✗	✗	✓	✗	Y	n	

Size: World: £730m	UK: £243m	UK employees: 5,274

Activities: Manufactures and markets health care products and toiletries

- One of the largest healthcare consumer products business in the UK.

- A low level of disclosure, although the company did provide some limited information.

- An unusual absence of women on the board of this company, which has a significant share of the feminine personal hygiene market through Lil-lets and Dr. Whites brands.

- In 1990 Smith & Nephew gave £400,000 to charity, a high proportion of which was directed towards funding medical scholarships.

- The company has a seven-point environmental plan which covers steps to minimise the effects of its brands on the environment, but little evidence of positive action.

- It has a 33 per cent shareholding in a Swedish company, Cederroth, which manufactures aerosols containing CFCs.

- It has seven associate and five subsidiary companies in third world countries.

- Smith & Nephew carries out no animal testing with regard to cosmetics and toiletries, but in the development of new medical products it carries out some testing. It subscribes to FRAME.

- It has two subsidiaries in South Africa, which in 1989 employed 1,657 workers.

A company with little evidence of action in most social areas, especially the environment and equal opportunities.

229

W H Smith Group PLC

🔒SECRET	♀	👤	🏠	🌳	🐰	👶	☢	⚙	Alert!
✗	?	?	✔	?	✔✔	✗	n	n	

Size: World: £2,131m	UK: £2,087m	*UK employees:* 35,131

Activities: Retails books, stationery, newspapers, magazines, recorded music and DIY

- W H Smith is the largest bookseller and a leading retailer of greetings cards and stationery products in the UK.
- The company provided answers to some specific questions.
- An active supporter of the pro-Sunday trading lobby through its Do-It-All subsidiary, a joint venture with Boots.
- There is one woman non-executive director on the board. No other equal opportunities information was available.
- In 1989 its total community involvement in the UK amounted to 0.89 per cent of pre-tax profit, a high figure for the UK. It is a member of the Per Cent Club and of Business in the Community.
- W H Smith has a short corporate policy statement on 'green' issues, but provided no evidence of practical initiatives.
- It stated that its stationery products and hardwood DIY products are sourced from sustainably managed forestry sources. In the case of its hardwood products, the sources are Malaysia and Indonesia, countries not known for their sustainable forestry practices.
- Other environmental issues involving the sale of peat and pesticides were not commented on.

> *The company commented on selected items which indicated an awareness in some areas of corporate social responsibility, but the lack of information made it difficult to assess the extent of these initiatives.*

SmithKline Beecham plc

									Alert!
✗	?	?	✔	?	✔	?	Y	C	

Size: World: £4,501m UK: £801m	UK employees: 11,100

Activities: Manufactures human and animal pharmaceutical products, and OTC medicines

- An unusual example in 1989 of a friendly merger of US (SmithKline Beckman) and UK (Beecham) businesses, both strong in health products and pharmaceuticals.

- A low level of disclosure, with little publicly available information on social and ethical issues.

- There is one woman and one ethnic minority on the board of directors; both are non-executive members. No other figures for women and ethnic minorities in management were provided.

- In 1990 its worldwide charitable donations were £5 million, 0.58 per cent of pre-tax profit. It is a member of Business in the Community.

- Minimal information was available about the company's environmental initiatives, though a written policy is claimed.

- SmithKline Beecham markets products like Lucozade under the 'health/energy' banner, raising nutrition and food value queries.

- It carries out animal testing on its medical and pharmaceutical products, and funds research into alternatives.

- It has extensive third world production and marketing operations in pharmaceuticals and proprietary medicines

- It has three subsidiaries in South Africa.

- In the last four years it has donated annually £30,000 to the Conservative Party and £5,000 to the Centre for Policy Studies.

> *A company that appears to have some social policies with regard to community involvement, but does not appear to have addressed other social issues.*

231

Sony (U.K.) Limited

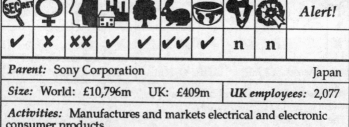

									Alert!
✔	✘	✘✘	✔	✔	✔✔	✔	n	n	

Parent: Sony Corporation — Japan

Size: World: £10,796m UK: £409m **UK employees:** 2,077

Activities: Manufactures and markets electrical and electronic consumer products

- One of world's leading brand names, not least through the 50 million plus Sony Walkmans sold. It operates in the entertainment field on a broad front, including CBS Records and Columbia Pictures.

- Completed the questionnaire and provided extra information.

- One of the few companies approached to provide labour turnover figures.

- In 1990, 32 managers in its sales companies were women. No overall figures were supplied for numbers of women and ethnic minorities in management.

- Sony stated that its community giving in the UK exceeded the requirements of the Per Cent Club (more than 0.5 per cent of pre-tax profit), of which it is a member. It is also a member of Business in the Community.

- Sony makes a brief environmental statement, and has taken some positive steps to improve its environmental performance.

- Sony switched much of its production to third world countries to obtain the benefit of lower labour costs.

- It states that it has a policy of 'global localisation'. By this it means hiring local nationals, providing training, and using local sources for parts.

> *A company with a reputation of being one of the more 'western' of the Japanese multinationals, with a fair level of disclosure.*

232

Storehouse PLC

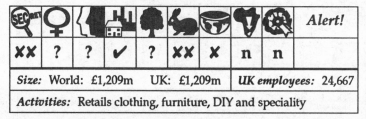

									Alert!
XX	?	?	✔	?	XX	X	n	n	

Size: World: £1,209m	UK: £1,209m	UK employees: 24,667

Activities: Retails clothing, furniture, DIY and speciality

- The creation of design guru and Habitat founder Sir Terence Conran, now no longer a director.

- One of Britain's major retailers, with over 600 UK stores under the BhS, Mothercare, Richards and Habitat names.

- Poor disclosure made it difficult to assess in detail policies in key areas.

- Exceptionally for a UK company it has two women on the main board, one of whom is a non-executive director. Unfortunately no further information was available about equal opportunities.

- Storehouse's community giving amounted to a notable 4.2 per cent of pre-tax profit. It has continued to maintain its charitable giving in spite of falling profits.

- The company retails some tropical hardwood furniture, though it claims it is from government-approved 'renewable sources'. No other information about its environmental activities was available.

- Its subsidiary Mothercare stated that whilst most of its products are made from tried and tested ingredients, and where possible alternative tests are used, some animal testing does take place.

- It had no policy on sourcing goods from the third world.

Lack of information made it difficult to assess what appear to be some interesting social policies, particularly in the areas of equal opportunities and community involvement.

Tambrands Limited

SECRET	♀	🗣	🏭	🌳	🐇	👶	🐂	✾	Alert!
XX	?	?	XX	?	?	?	n	n	

Parent: Tambrands Incorporated		USA
Size: World: £331m UK: £58m	**UK employees:** 849	
Activities: Manufactures sanitary protection products		

- Its main business is the sale of tampons, and the parent company has the avowed aim of becoming the world's leading supplier.

- Products from the UK factory are sold in 70 different countries and labelled in 19 different languages.

- It had a low level of disclosure, except to comment on adverse publicity.

- A high level of female representation on the main US board of directors does not appear to be mirrored in the UK. No information was available about other equal opportunity initiatives.

- Charitable donations in the UK amounted to 0.01 per cent of pre-tax profits in 1988. No mention is made of any community involvement in the parent company annual report.

- The company offers no evidence of any significant environmental initiatives.

- China, Brazil and Mexico are seen by the company as important consumer markets for its products.

- Toxic shock syndrome, a rare illness caused by toxin produced by a strain of bacteria, has been allegedly related to the use of internal sanitary protection, particularly high absorbency tampons. In the USA tampon packaging has carried health warnings about use of tampons for many years.

> *A very secretive company, with little evidence of any awareness of the need for corporate social responsibility policies.*

Tate & Lyle PLC

SECRET	♀	⟨	🏠	🌳	🐰	👶	☕	🔍	Alert!
✓✓	✗	✗✗	✗	✓	✗	✓	y	C	

Size: World: £3,432m	UK: £664m	UK employees: 4,300

Activities: Manufactures sugar, cereals, sweeteners and starches

- The leading refiner of cane sugar in the European Community.

- The company had a high level of disclosure.

- There is one woman non-executive director on the board, seven per cent of senior managers are women, and in 1990 43 per cent of its graduate recruits were women.

- No equal opportunities monitoring is carried out because 'we do not discriminate and therefore do not keep records of ethnic or any other type of background'.

- It is a member of the Per Cent Club, and gave over £1 million to charity in 1988/89.

- Booker Tate offers agricultural management advice in tropical countries. It sponsored the Programme for Belize, to acquire tropical forest as a wildlife conservation area.

- The sources of its main product are developing countries in Africa, the Caribbean and the Pacific. It is obliged by the Sugar Protocol to import a set amount of cane sugar at a guaranteed price, which benefits the producers and the company.

- Annual political donations to the Conservative Party have been around £25,000 per annum for the last three years.

- Has a subsidiary in South Africa trading in cane molasses, which employed 82 people in 1989.

> *The company's position as the main importer of cane sugar has gone hand in hand with its awareness of the issues surrounding its operations in the third world.*

Tesco PLC

🔒	♀	👥	🏠	🌳	🐰	🍼	☠	✊	Alert!
✓✓	X	XX	✓✓	✓✓	✓✓	X	n	n	at

Size: World: £6,346m UK: £6,346m	UK employees: 87,691

Activities: Supermarkets

- One of the UK's leading supermarket chains, with nearly 400 stores.
- There is one woman non-executive director, and ten per cent of senior managers are women.
- In 1989/90 it donated £4.6 million to charity (1.3 per cent of pre-tax profit, a notable sum), as well as providing additional community sponsorship.
- In its *1990/91 Annual Report* Tesco outlined its policy of 'Sustainable Development', including an audit on the environmental impact of its activities and the introduction of a new animal welfare code for its animal produce suppliers.
- It has a three-tier labelling system for its cosmetics, toiletries and household cleaning products to inform consumers about animal testing. Tesco is a FRAME sponsor.
- A limited number of fresh fruit and vegetables are sourced from South Africa 'when there are no alternative sources', and are clearly labelled as such, giving the consumer the opportunity to exercise their own choice.
- Tesco is a major alcohol retailer. It does not retail tobacco directly, but tobacco is freely available in its stores through the Marshell Group's concessions (owned by Gallaher Ltd).
- No policy on sourcing goods from the third world.

A retailer with a strong public image of a high level of awareness and action in many areas of corporate social responsibility.

Texaco Limited

🔒 SECRET	♀	👤	🏭	🌳	🐇	👶	☢	🔬	Alert!
✗	?	?	✗✗	✗✗	?	?	Y	n	**M**

Parent: Texaco Incorporated		USA
Size: World: £23,456m UK: £3,011m	***UK employees:*** 3,358	
Activities: Oil, gas and petroleum products		

- One of the top six petroleum suppliers in the UK.

- In 1989 the parent company established a Corporate Public Responsibility Committee to review the company's policies in this area.

- The UK subsidiary commented on specific issues, but did not complete any questionnaires.

- Direct charitable donations are very low, even by UK standards. It is a member of Business in the Community.

- In the USA Texaco's environmental record is considered to be poor, with a number of attributable incidents and fines. In the UK no specific or recent information was available about the company's operations.

- The parent company has a number of operations in third world countries, including China. There is some evidence that it is involved in the communities in which it works.

- It has a joint operation with Chevron, Caltex Petroleum Corporation, in South Africa, which in 1989 employed 2,056 staff.

- Texaco is a major fuel supplier to the Ministry of Defence. Its parent company supplies fuel to the military in a number of different countries.

> *Texaco Limited's poor response made a positive assessment of its UK activities difficult. Its US parent company's disclosure record is average.*

The Thomson Corporation PLC

🔲 SECRET	♀	👤	🏭	🌳	🐇	🍲	🎖️	🔬	Alert!
✗✗	?	?	✔	?	✔✔	✗	n	n	

Parent: The Thomson Corporation		Canada

Size: World: £3,032m UK: £1,530m	**UK employees:** 19,242

Activities: Publishing, leisure and tourism

- A subsidiary of the Canadian family-owned corporation, and an umbrella for the travel and publishing operations in the UK.

- Thomson Regional Newspapers is the UK's leading provincial newspaper publisher, with over 150 titles. The group owns 50 per cent of Thomson Directories.

- Thomson Travel Group leads the UK market in tour operating, travel retailing and charter airline operations. It owns Britannia Airways, the UK's leading holiday charter airline.

- Thomson's UK publishing operations have been involved in a number of protracted labour disputes over union recognition.

- No information was available about equal opportunities initiatives.

- No information was available about its charitable giving.

- The parent company has a few subsidiaries in third world countries, though it tends to operate in 'important, stable and developed economies'.

- The group has four subsidiaries in South Africa, including Thomson Publications SA (Pty) Ltd.

- Jane's Publishing Company, owned by Thomson, is the leading publisher of defence related magazines and books.

For a company with a high profile in the field of public communication the lack of any apparent corporate social responsibility initiatives and a low level of disclosure are notable.

THORN EMI plc

SECRET	♀	🏠	🌳	🐰	👝	🗺	⚙	Alert!
✓	✗	✓	✗	✓	✓✓	✗	Y	n	M

Size: World: £3,715m	UK: £1,790m	UK employees: 61,124

Activities: Recorded music, rental and retail of electronic and electrical goods

- Through its recording and music publishing companies it owns the rights to such popular favourites as 'Singing in the Rain' and 'Happy Birthday to You'.
- One of the main board directors is a member of an ethnic minority group. Around seven per cent of managers are women and one per cent are from ethnic minority groups.
- Has a developed community involvement programme which is, however, small for a company of its size. It is a member of Business in the Community and of the Per Cent Club.
- It owns an energy conservation and environmental control company, JEL Energy Conservation and Management.
- It has where possible switched from using CFCs.
- THORN carried out a comprehensive environmental audit of the whole company in 1989/90, and has a thought-out environmental policy. It appears to be addressing environmental issues.
- It has subsidiaries in 11 developing countries. Its two main subsidiaries in South Africa employed 1,029 staff in 1989, and recognise unions.
- It has been one of the UK's leading defence industry manufacturers and exporters. Since June 1989 the company has been trying, unsuccessfully, to dispose of these activities.

> THORN EMI *clearly takes its corporate responsibility very seriously, while still involved in some sensitive areas. An open company in contrast to some of its competitors.*

Time-Life International Limited

🔒	⚧	🚶	🏠	🌳	🐇	👶	☢	🔫	Alert!
✗✗	?	?	✗	?	?	?	y	n	

Parent: Time Warner Incorporated		USA
Size: World: £4,342m UK: £?m	UK employees: ?	
Activities: Media and entertainment		

- The parent company was formed from the merger of Time Inc. and Warner Communications Inc. in 1989.
- The Warner Music Group is the largest record company in the world, with artistes including Madonna and Paul Simon.
- The US parent company, Time Warner Inc., provided a copy of its *1990 Social Responsibility Report*.
- In the USA Time Inc. had a very strong record on social responsibility.
- It had a very poor level of disclosure in the UK, and little publicly available literature.
- No information was available about equal opportunities, charitable giving or environmental initiatives.
- Time has a branch office in South Africa employing 13 staff. Warner Communications maintains distribution agreements for records, films, music and videos in South Africa.

A poor level of disclosure in the UK made it impossible to assess the company's corporate responsibility.

Toshiba UK Limited

SECRET	♀	🗣	🏭	🌳	🐰	🍼	🦊	🎆	Alert!
✔	✘	✘	✔	✔	✔✔	✔	y	n	**M**

Parent: Toshiba Corporation		Japan

Size: World: £15,939m UK: £108m	**UK employees:** 1,445

Activities: Manufactures consumer electronics products

- The Japanese-owned parent company is one of the world's leading electronics manufacturing companies.
- Toshiba Corporation has six operating subsidiaries in the UK, all of whom provided some information.
- It provided figures for the numbers of women and of members of ethnic minorities in management and among its graduate recruits.
- Toshiba's community involvement in the UK amounted to £50,000 in 1990, and Toshiba International Europe Ltd. is a member of Business in the Community.
- In Japan Toshiba is the leading supplier of nuclear reactors. It holds 40 per cent of the Japanese thermal power market and 30 per cent of the hydroelectric plant market. It also claims to hold more than 50 per cent of the worldwide market in geothermal power.
- Toshiba has 23 subsidiary or associate companies in third world countries, mainly manufacturing electronic and electrical goods and components.
- Toshiba has an office in Johannesburg, South Africa, but no production facilities.
- One of Japan's top five defence contractors, with contracts worth £380 million in 1989.

> *Its reasonable level of disclosure and strengths in some personnel issues, are indicators of emerging social responsibility in a company involved in key energy and technology areas worldwide.*

Unigate PLC

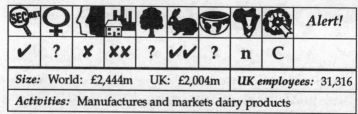

									Alert!
✔	?	✘	✘✘	?	✔✔	?	n	C	

Size: World: £2,444m UK: £2,004m	**UK employees:** 31,316

Activities: Manufactures and markets dairy products

- A major food manufacturer and distributor, known by its brand names St Ivel Fresh Foods and United Dairies.

- Provided some information, but overall had an average level of disclosure.

- Of the top 150 managers two were women and one was a member of an ethnic minority in 1989/90. It stated that it intended to implement a monitoring programme. No other equal opportunities information was available.

- Charitable donations amounted to less than 0.1 per cent of pre-tax profit in 1989/90, and Unigate stated that it makes no payment in kind for charitable purposes.

- Little information was provided about its environmental activities, particularly in the areas of food safety and hygiene.

- It states that it is the company's long-term aim 'to be the lowest cost producer of quality poultry products in the European market'. It made no comment on the issues of factory or intensive farming.

- In 1987/88, covering the election period, it made a £50,000 donation to the Conservative Party.

> *Unigate appears to be developing positive equal opportunities policies, but in other areas, particularly relating to environmental and animal welfare issues, there was little sign of action or awareness.*

Unilever PLC

🔒 SECRET	♀	👥	🏠	🌳	🐰	🍼	⚔	⚙	Alert!
✓✓	✓	✓✓	✓	✓	✗	✓✓	Y	n	AT

Size: World: £22,258m UK: £13,578m	*UK employees:* 30,000

Activities: Manufactures food, cleaning products and toiletries

- Two parent companies: Unilever PLC in Britain and Unilever NV in the Netherlands. Europe's largest non-oil multinational.

- A very open company that completed questionnaires and provided a great deal of background information on behalf of its widely diversified and independently-operated subsidiaries.

- There is one member of an ethnic minority group on the board of directors. Women make up 12 per cent of management in the UK. Around 40 per cent of recent graduate recruits were women and six per cent were members of ethnic minority groups.

- UK donations in the last two years were 0.3 per cent of pre-tax profit. A member of Business in the Community and of the Per Cent Club.

- With activities from palm oil plantations and aquaculture to cosmetics and chemical manufacture, it has a number of environmental initiatives and a written environmental policy.

- It employs around 130,000 in 34 developing countries, practises technology transfer, and has other well-developed social policies.

- Animal testing is used only for new materials to ensure their safety. Has carried out research in-house on alternatives. Subsidiaries Elida Gibbs, Rimmel and Lever Brothers all support FRAME.

- In 1989 Unilever employed 7,910 staff in South Africa.

- Unilever has a brewery operation in Nigeria, and has minor involvement in tobacco sales in West Africa.

A diversified company that worked hard to provide extensive information about its social and ethical corporate behaviour.

United Biscuits (Holdings) plc

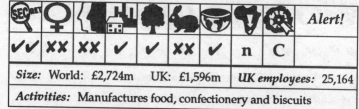

								Alert!
✓✓	✗✗	✗✗	✓	✓	✗✗	✓	n	C

Size: World: £2,724m UK: £1,596m	**UK employees:** 25,164

Activities: Manufactures food, confectionery and biscuits

- A major food manufacturer from biscuits to frozen food.

- It publishes a booklet entitled *Ethics And Operating Principles*, which spells out the company's behaviour towards its personnel, customers, suppliers and competitors.

- It has one woman non-executive director, but did not provide figures for the number of women or ethnic minorities in managerial positions.

- Charitable donations amount to around 0.6 per cent of pre-tax profit. United Biscuits is a member of both Business in the Community and of the Per Cent Club.

- It has a written environmental policy, and is taking some environmental initiatives. It is a member of INCPEN.

- Its involvement with the third world includes sourcing cocoa, fish and beef from developing countries. While it has a strong company ethos, it could do further work on the social issues arising from its operations in the third world.

- A major donor to the Conservative Party, with annual donations of over £100,000 in the last two financial years.

Has well-defined corporate ethics, particularly with respect to its community involvement and with its dealings with all its stakeholders, but is weaker in other areas such as equal opportunities.

Vauxhall Motors Limited

🔍 SECRET	♀	🏭	🌳	🐰	🏺	🔪	⚙	Alert!
✓✓	✗✗	✗✗	✗	✓	✗✗	✗	y	n	M

Parent: General Motors Corporation	USA

Size: World: £70,495m	UK: £2,620m	**UK employees:** 11,268

Activities: Car manufacturer, industrial products, defence equipment

- The US parent company, General Motors, is the world's largest industrial company. It also owns Lotus and 50 per cent of Saab.

- Since 1971 the parent company has produced a detailed *Public Interest Report*. It completed the New Consumer questionnaire, and provided additional information.

- Vauxhall did not supply any information about the numbers of women or ethic minorities making it impossible to contrast with the good record of its parent.

- Giving in the UK was less than 0.1 per cent of pre-tax profit, low by UK standards and much less than its parent's in the USA.

- General Motors and Vauxhall have detailed environmental brochures outlining the main issues relating to cars. Its environmental initiatives include reduction of emissions, recycling heat and water, use of water-based paint, use of alternative fuels, replacing CFCs, and waste management.

- Its parent has several manufacturing plants in the third world.

- General Motors cars are manufactured in South Africa under a licensing agreement with Delta, a South African company.

- In 1988/89 it had contracts worth between £5-£10 million with the Ministry of Defence. In the USA it is a major military contractor.

> *Some of the parent company's strong corporate responsibility is mirrored by Vauxhall, although in equal opportunities and community involvement it still has some way to go.*

The Virgin Organisation

SECRET	♀	〈	🏠	🌳	🐰	🍼	☤	⚙	Alert!
xx	?	?	x	?	✓✓	?	n	n	

Size: World: £602m UK: £?m	UK employees: 3,500

| Activities: Recorded music, travel, hotels | |

- It comprises five separate holding companies: Virgin Music Group, Virgin Retail Group, Virgin Communications, Virgin Group and the Voyager Group.

- Its charismatic founder Richard Branson holds the key to much of the group's philosophy and to its informal unbureaucratic structure.

- Has two women on the boards of the holding companies. In 1990 it claimed that out of 100 top senior managers 60 were women.

- Virgin provided the initial 'seedcorn' funding for Charity Projects, the group which organises Comic Relief events.

- Much of Virgin's community involvement, which has an annual budget of over £100,000, is through gifts in kind.

- It does not have a written environmental policy (the group has no written policies). It stated that its airline fleet is maintained with the most up-to-date technology to minimise fuel use. There is little evidence of concerted pro-environmental initiatives.

- Richard Branson has banned tobacco advertising from all Virgin operations, and the group is involved in the Parents' Against Tobacco campaign.

Virgin remains the creation and reflection of its founder Richard Branson, and it has been involved in some interesting initiatives. However, unwillingness to commit anything to paper makes assessment of the group difficult.

Volkswagen

SEC	♀	👤	🏭	🌳	🐰	🧷	🍷	🔍	Alert!
✗	?	?	?	?	✓✓	?	Y	n	

Parent: Volkswagen AG		West Germany
Size: World: £22,304m UK: £0m		**UK employees:** 0
Activities: Car manufacturer		

- It is the leading car manufacturer in Europe, formed in the mid-1930s to produce the 'people's car'.

- It has no operating subsidiary in the UK, and sells its cars through the VW/Audi franchise, VAG (United Kingdom), owned by Lonhro.

- It has a department to promote women within the group.

- As it has no operations in the UK there are no figures for community involvement in the UK. No figures were available for worldwide charitable giving.

- In its *1989 Annual Report* Volkswagen devoted twelve pages to its response to environmental issues, including catalytic converters, alcohol (methanol) engines, more recyclable plastic components, and high standards of water management.

- Volkswagen manufactures 14 per cent of its vehicles cars in third world countries. The majority of these are made in Brazil through its joint venture with Ford, Autolatina.

- There is some evidence that Volkswagen has some enlightened policies in its operations in the developing world, though this needs further substantiation.

- It has manufacturing operations in South Africa that employed 8,523 workers and produced 58,766 vehicles, in 1989.

> *A company which markets its products in the UK but has no direct operations, with evidence of some progressive social and ethical policies in its operations elsewhere.*

Volvo Trucks
(Great Britain) Limited

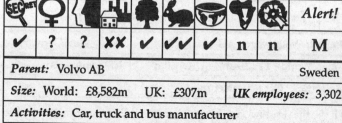

									Alert!
✔	?	?	✗✗	✔	✔✔	✔	n	n	**M**

Parent: Volvo AB		Sweden

Size: World: £8,582m	UK: £307m	**UK employees:** 3,302

Activities: Car, truck and bus manufacturer

- The Swedish parent company is the largest industrial group in th Nordic countries, and has 43 per cent of the equity of Procordi AB, Sweden's largest pharmaceutical and food group. It own UK's largest garden seed merchant, Suttons.

- A written code of conduct is applied throughout its operations.

- Charitable donations in the UK in 1988 amounted to 0.005 per cen of pre-tax profit, a very low figure for the UK.

- Volvo has had a written environmental policy since the early 1970 which is regularly reviewed and updated. Volvo conducted it first environmental audits in 1990. Volvo, in collaboration wit Bosch of Germany, developed the three-way catalytic converte first launched in the USA in 1977. In 1990 catalytic converters wer available on the UK model range as an option at no extra cost.

- The group has operations in Argentina, Brazil, Hong Kong, India Malaysia, Panama, Peru, Philippines, Singapore and Thailand Volvo stated that 'with few exceptions subsidiaries in developin countries have national management teams'.

- Policy that it 'shall observe party-political neutrality'.

- Volvo supplies aircraft engines to the Swedish Air Force. It has no exported any military equipment in the last three years.

The company has a strong record on safety and the environmental impact of its operations. A lack of specific information about its UK operations made it difficult to assess other areas.

Weetabix Limited

SECRET	♀	👤	🏠	🌳	🐰	🍼	☣	🐑	Alert!
xx	?	?	xx	?	?	?	n	n	

Size: World: £139m UK: £96m	*UK employees:* 2,299

Activities: Manufactures cereals

- Weetabix is a private company owned by the George family of Northamptonshire. Its breakfast cereal of the same name is the second leading brand in the UK.

- Little public information was available about the company, and it declined to respond to requests for information.

- Weetabix is reputed to be a good employer.

- It has been reported that 'Weetabix runs language courses for its many ethnic minority employees'.

- No evidence of any environmental initiatives

- Charitable donations in 1989 amounted to 0.07 per cent of pre-tax profit, a notably low figure.

A company that appears to have strong personnel policies, which it was not possible to confirm because of its secretive nature.

Whitbread PLC

![SECRET]	⚲	👤	🏠	🌳	🐰	👶	🌍	⚙	Alert!
✗	?	?	✗	?	✓✓	?	n	C	Atg

Size:	World: £2,488m	UK: £1,775m	UK employees: 62,604

Activities: Brewing, hotels, pubs, off-licenses and restaurants

- 'The Beer, Food and Leisure Group' runs Pizza Hut (UK) Ltd as a joint venture with PepsiCo, and owns 25 per cent of Britannia Soft Drinks Ltd which in turn owns the soft drinks company Britvic.

- The company stated that there were women in senior management, particularly in the non-beer areas, but did not supply any figures. Three of the six board members of Pizza Hut are women.

- Charitable cash donations amounted to 0.3 per cent of pre-tax profit in 1989/90, above average for the UK. Whitbread appointed five regional Community Affairs Directors in 1989/90. There is a specialist director of community affairs, and it publishes an annual review of its community work.

- Whitbread provided a copy of its interim environment statement and said that its policy was in preparation.

- Whitbread has made donations over the last three years to the Conservative Party, ranging from £76,500 in 1987/88 to £15,000 in 1989/90.

- One of the 'big six' brewers in the UK. It produces a credit-card size information pack aimed at encouraging a sensible approach to alcohol consumption.

- It owns JPM Holdings, a leading manufacturer of gaming and amusement machines.

> *The company appears to be in the process of developing a number of corporate responsibility policies.*

Williams Holdings PLC

SECRET	♀		🏠	🌳	🐰	👶	☠	🔍	Alert!
XX	?	?	XX	?	✔✔	?	Y	C	M

Size: World: £1,134m	UK: £636m	*UK employees:* 17,263

Activities: Manufactures and markets industrial, military, consumer DIY and building products

- Williams describes itself as an industrial management company which endeavours to act as a catalyst for change, through acquiring, reorganising, promoting, encouraging and investing in businesses which have the potential for above average growth.

- Charitable donations amounted to 0.08 per cent of pre-tax profits in 1989. From 1989 its charitable donations have been concentrated into a single donation. It agreed to give the Prince's Youth Business Trust a total of £500,000 over five years.

- One of its subsidiary companies is registered for its production of di-isocyanates, highly toxic chemicals, discharges of which must be carefully monitored.

- No evidence of any environmental policy or initiatives was available.

- Williams Fairey Design and Projects is involved in the nuclear power generation market.

- Annual donations to the Conservative Party have amounted to £25,000 in the last two years, and £50,000 in 1987.

- It has a subsidiary in South Africa, but no information was available about its operations.

- In 1989 Williams recorded a £355 million turnover from its industrial and military products section.

A diverse company that provided no evidence to suggest that it has taken any significant corporate responsibility measures.

About the Research

The preparation of this guide has drawn on a detailed research programme that has been running for over two years. The products included in *Shopping for a Better World* are made by companies who dominate manufacturing and retailing in the UK. Over 30 per cent of our spending will be through the 125 companies who make the 2,500 brands listed. Some markets are very fragmented with lots of very small producers — clothing and DIY are examples — and the only way to offer some guidance is to look at the retailers, which we have done. Markets which were small, specialised, or where there was no effective consumer choice were also excluded. Neither have we covered the public sector, financial services or media-related products in this edition.

We have gathered information in a number of different ways: firstly through detailed questionnaires to companies followed up by telephone or direct discussions; secondly through the public literature of companies and through material which they made available to us; thirdly though our own analysis of press and trade publications, business information services, and corporate databases; fourthly, though the advice of specialist organisations, both trade associations and campaigning groups.

This material was used to determine objective answers to several questions under each category. From these answers a scored rating was derived which in turn was translated into a symbol used in the chart. The ratings have been reviewed by our advisory panel and Council, who have particular experience in different areas.

The commercial world is constantly changing, and our research keeps abreast of the latest developments. In November 1992 we will be publishing the 1993 edition of *Shopping for a Better World*, fully revised, but there is a way to keep in touch with the latest on the issues in the meantime. New Consumer publishes a quarterly magazine which gives current information as well as help and advice on sustainable living. See page 287 for further details.

Co-operation from a company enables a clearer picture of its activities to be built up. More than 60 per cent of the companies approached did provide such co-operation. We believe that the effort and expense incurred by firms prepared to make responses on these issues will be justified through the reaction of consumers and investors. The accuracy of material provided by companies is checked wherever possible, the final test being in exposure to competitors and the general public in this publication. We are always eager to receive comments which supplement, correct or cause us to review any rating.

New Consumer would like to thank the many companies which have co-operated with the research programme when some of their peers chose not to do so.

Shopping for a Better World: Advisory Panel

New Consumer Charitable Trust

New Consumer has been supported by thousands of individual donations from the public and also with generous grant funding from the Allen Lane Foundation, the Baring Foundation, the Calouste Gulbenkian Foundation, CAFOD, Christian Aid, the Elm-grant Trust, the Forbes Trust, the Hadrian Trust, the Joseph Rowntree Charitable Trust, the Lyndhurst Settlement, Oxfam, the Scott Bader Commonwealth, the Traidcraft Exchange and the Twenty First Century Trust. Thanks also to individual sponsors Adrian Mann, George Goyder, J.T. Hodgson, Dr. M.P. Thorne and David and Mollie Somerville.

The Next Step

Buying and using this book is one very effective way of making your voice heard in the boardrooms of our largest companies. Here are some other things you can do to let companies know that you care about their social and environmental policies.

Letters to companies

Our research shows that, where a company has a well-developed set of social responsibility policies, they are often originate at the highest levels in companies management. Why not write to the managing director explaining what you like — or don't like — about their policies, practices or products. If you've changed brands then tell both companies. We can assure you that they will listen.

To help you do this we have included the addresses of all the companies listed in *Shopping for a Better World*, beginning on page 259. Here are two sample letters, written by a member of New Consumer after reading our detailed research book, *Changing Corporate Values*. When you write you'll be able to quote *Shopping for a Better World*; we'd be very grateful for copies of your letters.

Letter to United Biscuits

As a 'shopper with a conscience', I was very pleased, when I read the profile of United Biscuits in the book Changing Corporate Values, *to see that your company holds such enlightened views.*

Though — let me mention it briefly — I don't agree with your policy on political donations, your interest in community involvement, your gifts to charity, your adherence to the principles of equal opportunities impress me.

I will naturally continue to buy United Biscuits products. Also, when feasible, I now select your products rather than those of Hillsdown Holdings plc, whose profile — in most instances — compares unfavourably with yours. (I have for example, replaced Hillsdown Holdings' Cadbury's and Allinson Cookies with your Abbey Crunch and Hob Nobs).

I have been talking to many of my friends about my new shopping habits, and they, as well as my family, are beginning to follow suit. I am heartened by their interest, and I thought you would like to know about it.

Letter to Hillsdown Holdings

It is with regret that I noticed — as I read the profile of your company in the book Changing Corporate Values *— your firm's lack of information on a number of important social issues.*

I am troubled that you should have disclosed no information on your policies concerning such issues as environment, factory farming and sourcing of products from the third world. It surprises me that, being approached on several occasions by New Consumer for information, you didn't respond.

In view of this lack of disclosures, I have felt compelled to make changes in my shopping: I now endeavour to avoid purchasing products made by companies owned by Hillsdown Holdings. I have instead switched to brands from United Biscuits, Unilever and Northern Foods, whose records are so much more positive. It has meant giving up, amongst other things, old favourites such as Cadbury's Chocolate Break, Allinson Cookies and Harvest Cereal.

It does complicate my shopping, but I am quite determined to stick to this new discipline until your position has changed for the better.

I have been talking to many of my friends about my new shopping habits, and they, as well as my family, are beginning to follow suit. I think it is important that you should know about our feelings on the matter.

Letters to the Editor

Why not let the people in your area know about consumer-power by writing a letter to your local newspaper? Tell them how you have changed your shopping patterns and the ways in which you became aware of just how much influence you could exert. One word of warning: many newspapers are cautious about printing critical comments about companies because of libel, but the letter is likely to be thought an attempt to get free advertising if you just say positive things about a company! So mention that the information came from national research published in *Shopping for a Better World* and include both critical *and* positive comments.

You can also use our research to talk about national policy issues which seldom get covered in the local press. One way of doing this is to see which of the companies covered in this book have a factory or outlet in your area. For example, you might find that British Aerospace or one of its subsidiaries like Rover has a local base. This could provide an opportunity to discuss whether firms that make military equipment sell it in a responsible way. British Aerospace was trying to sell £300 million of equipment to Saddam Hussein in 1989, the same year that it introduced an environmentally friendly, non-toxic shotgun cartridge for the 'green' sportsperson. We report regularly on such matters in our quarterly members magazine.

Consider Social Investment

Financial planning has always been worth doing, whatever your resources. Thoughtful financial planning can also benefit society and as concerned consumers we are realising that by choosing carefully where our money goes we can express our concerns for peace, human rights, the environment, economic development and working conditions.

Few people invest in shares directly, but many more have pensions, life insurance or units in unit trusts, all of which usually have some stake in the shares of companies. In Britain there is now more than £300 million invested in socially 'screened' companies where investment managers exclude certain companies, like those who make or sell cigarettes, or only include companies for positive reasons, like a good record on the environment. You can write to your pension group, insurance company or unit trust and ask them if they have such an investment policy. You can also use this book to draw up your own list of companies that you would invest in on social grounds.

If you join New Consumer you will, in addition, receive details about our free financial advisory service for ethical savings and investment. It is certainly helpful to put your own financial situation on paper and set out the social values and concerns you wish to support or avoid in your savings or other investments.

Company Addresses

Where a company is a subsidiary of a foreign owned parent we have provided the corporate headquarters address (in *italics*) as well as an address for a main subsidiary in the UK.

Alberto-Culver Company
2525 Armitage Avenue
Melrose Park
Illinois 60160
USA

Alberto-Culver Co (UK)
Limited
Telford Road
Houndsmill Industrial Estate
Basingstoke
Hampshire
RG21 2YZ

Allied-Lyons PLC
Allied House
24 Portland Place
London
W1N 4BB

Amstrad plc
Brentwood House
169 King's Road
Brentwood
Essex
CM14 4EF

The New Zealand Dairy Board
PO Box 417
25 The Terrace
Wellington
New Zealand

Anchor Foods Limited
P O Box 82
Frankland Road
Swindon
Wiltshire
SN5 8YZ

Argos plc
489-499 Avebury Boulevard
Saxon Gate West
Central Milton Keynes
MK9 2NW

Argyll Group PLC
Safeway House
Millington Road
Hayes
Middlesex
UB3 4AY

Asda Group plc
Asda House
South Bank
Great Wilson Street
Leeds
LS11 5AD

Sara Lee Corporation
Three First National Plaza
Chicago
Illinois
IL 60602-4260
USA

Aspro Nicholas plc
225 Bath Road
Slough
Berkshire
SL1 4AU

Associated British Foods plc
Weston Centre
Bowater House
68 Knightsbridge
London
SW1X 7LR

Avon Products Incorporated
9 West 57th Street
New York
NY 10019
USA

Avon Cosmetics Limited
Public Relations Officer
Nunn Mills Road
Northampton
NN1 5PA

Bass PLC
66 Chiltern Street
London
W1M 1PR

Blue Circle Industries PLC
84 Eccleston Square
London
SW1V 1PX

The Body Shop International
PLC
Hawthorn Road
Wick
Littlehampton
West Sussex
BN17 7LR

Booker plc
Portland House
Stag Place
London
SW1E 5AY

The Boots Co PLC
Head Office
Nottingham
NG2 3AA

Brent Walker Group PLC
Brent Walker House
19 Rupert Street
London
W1V 7FS

The British Petroleum
Company p.l.c.
Britannic House
1 Finsbury Circus
London
EC2M 7BA

British Aerospace PLC
11 Strand
London
WC2N 5JT

British Airways Plc
Speedbird House
P O Box 10
Heathrow Airport
Hounslow
TW6 2JA

British Gas plc
Rivermill House
152 Grosvenor Road
London
SW1V 3JL

The Burton Group plc
214 Oxford Street
London
W1N 9DF

C & A
64 North Row
London
W1A 2AX

Cadbury Schweppes p.l.c.
1-4 Connaught Place
London
W2 2EX

Campbell Soup Company
Campbell Place
Camden
New Jersey
NJ 08103-17799
USA

Campbell's UK Limited
Crayfield House
Main Road
St Paul's Cray
Orpington
Kent
BR5 3HP

City Centre Restaurants plc
122 Victoria Street
London
SW1E 5LG

C & J Clark Limited
40 High Street
Street
Somerset
BA16 0YA

Coats Viyella Plc
Bank House
Charlotte Street
Manchester
M1 4ET

The Coca-Cola Company
One Coca-Cola Plaza
N.W. Atlanta
Georgia
GA 30301
USA

Coca-Cola Great Britain
Pemberton House
Wrights Lane
London
W8 5SN

Colgate-Palmolive Company
300 Park Avenue
New York
NY 10022-7499
USA

Colgate-Palmolive Limited
Guildford Business Park
Middleton Road
Guildford
Surrey
GU2 5LZ

E.I. du Pont de Nemours and Company
1007 Market Street
Wilmington
Delaware
DE 19898
USA

Conoco (U.K.) Ltd
Park House
116 Park Street
London
W1Y 4NN

Co-operative Movement
PO Box 53
New Century House
Manchester
M60 4ES

Foster's Brewing Group
One Garden Street
South Yarra
Victoria
Australia 3141

Courage Limited
Ashby House
1 Bridge Street
Staines
Middlesex
TW18 4TP

Courtaulds Textiles plc
13-14 Margaret Street
London
W1A 3DA

CPC International Inc
International Plaza
Englewood Cliffs
New Jersey
NJ 07632
USA

CPC (United Kingdom) Limited
Claygate House
Littleworth Road
Esher
Surrey
KT10 9PN

Dalgety PLC
19 Hanover Square
London
W1R 9DA

Dixons Group plc
29 Farm Street
London
W1X 7RD

Electrolux AB
Luxbacken 1
S-105 45 Stockholm
Sweden

Electrolux Limited
Oakley Road
Luton
Bedfordshire
LU4 9QQ

Exxon Corporation
1251 Avenue of the Americas
New York
NY 10020-1198
USA

Esso UK plc
Esso House
Victoria Street
London
SW1E 5JW

Thomson S.A.
Corporate Headquarters
51 Esplanade du Général de
Gaulle
Paris La Defénse 10
France

Ferguson Limited
Cambridge House
270 Great Cambridge Road
Enfield
Middlesex
EN1 1ND

Fiat S.P.A.
Corso Marconi 10
Turin
Italy

Fiat U.K. Limited
Berkeley Square House
Berkeley Square
London
W1X 6AL

Ford Motor Company
The American Road
PO Box 1899
Dearborn
Michigan
MI 48121-1899
USA

Ford Motor Company Limited
Eagle Way
Brentwood
Essex
CM13 3BW

Forte PLC
166 High Holborn
London
WC1V 6TT

American Brands Incorporated
1700 East Putnam Avenue
P.O.Box 819
Old Greenwich
Connecticut
CT 06870
USA

Gallaher Limited
Members Hill
Brooklands Road
Weybridge
Surrey
KT13 0QU

The General Electric Company
p.l.c.
1 Stanhope Gate
London
W1A 1EH

The Gillette Company
Prudential Tower Building
Boston
Massachusetts
MA 02199
USA

Gillette Industries Limited
Great West Road
Isleworth
Middlesex
TW7 5NG

Granada Group PLC
36 Golden Square
London
W1R 4AH

Grand Metropolitan PLC
11-12 Hanover Square
London
W1A 1DP

William Grant & Sons Limited
206 West George Street
Glasgow
G2 2PE

Great Universal Stores P.L.C.
Universal House
Devonshire Street North
Ardwick
Manchester
M60 6EL

Guinness PLC
39 Portman Square
London
W1H 9HB

Hanson PLC
1 Grosvenor Place
London
SW1X 7JH

H. J. Heinz Company
PO Box 57
Pittsburgh
Pennsylvania
PA 15230
USA

H. J. Heinz Company Limited
Hayes Park
Hayes
Middlesex
UB4 8AL

Highland Distilleries Company
plc
106 West Nile Street
Glasgow
G1 2QY

Hillsdown Holdings plc
Hillsdown House
32 Hampstead High Street
London
NW3 1QD

Hitachi Limited
6 Kanda Surugadai 4-chome
Chiyoda-ku
Tokyo 101
Japan

Hitachi Consumer Products
(UK) Ltd
Hirwaun Industrial Estate
Aberdare
Mid Glamorgan
CF44 9UP

Maytag Corporation
403 West Fourth Street North
Newton
Iowa
IO 50208
USA

Hoover PLC
Dragon Park
Merthyr Tydfil
Mid Glamorgan
CF48 1PQ

House of Fraser Holdings plc
1 Howick Place
London
SW1P 1BH

Iceland Frozen Foods
Holdings plc
Second Avenue
Deeside Industrial Park
Deeside
Clwyd
CH5 2NW

Imperial Chemical Industries
PLC (ICI)
Millbank
London
SW1P 3JF

Isosceles PLC
11 Walker Street
Edinburgh
EH3 7NE

BSN Groupe S.A.
7 Rue de Teheran
75381 Paris
France

The Jacob's Bakery Limited
121 Kings Road
Reading
Berkshire
RG1 3EF

John Lewis Partnership plc
171 Victoria Street
London
SW1E 5NN

S. C. Johnson & Son Incorporated
1525 Howe Street
Racine
WI 54303-5011
USA

Johnson Wax Limited
Frimley Green
Camberley
Surrey
GU16 5AS

Kellogg Company
Battle Creek
Michigan
MI 49016-3599
USA

Kellogg Company of Great
Britain Limited
The Kellogg Building
Talbot Road
Manchester
M16 0PU

Kimberly-Clark Corporation
P.O.Box 619100
Dallas
Texas
TX 75261
USA

Kimberly-Clark Limited
Larkfield
Maidstone
Kent
ME20 7PS

Kingfisher plc
North West House
119 Marylebone Road
London
NW1 5PX

Philip Morris Companies Inc.
120 Park Avenue
New York
NY 10017
USA

Kraft General Foods Limited
St Georges House
Bayshill Road
Cheltenham
Gloucestershire
GL50 3AE

Kwik Save Group P.L.C.
Warren Drive
Prestatyn
Clwyd
LL19 7HU

Ladbroke Group PLC
10 Cavendish Place
London
W1M 9DJ

LEC Refrigeration plc
Shripney Works
Bognor Regis
West Sussex
PO22 9NQ

The Littlewoods Organisation PLC
J M Centre
Old Hall Street
Liverpool
L70 1AB

Lonhro Plc
Cheapside House
138 Cheapside
London
EC2V 6BL

L'Oréal S.A.
Centre Eugene Schueller
41 Rue Matre
92117 Clichy
France

L'Oréal (U.K.) Limited
30 Kensington Church Street
London
W8 4HA

Marks & Spencer p.l.c.
Michael House
Baker Street
London
W1A 1DN

Mars Incorporated
6885 Elm Street
McLean
Virginia
VA 22101-3883
USA

Mars G.B. Limited
3D Dundee Road
Slough
Berks
SL1 4LG

McDonald's Corporation
McDonald's Plaza
Oak Brook
Illinois
IL 60521
USA

McDonald's Restaurants
Limited
11-59 High Road
East Finchley
London
N2 8AW

Merloni Elettrodomestici S.p.A.
Viale Aristide Merloni 45
60044 Fabriano (AN)
Italy

Merloni Domestic
Appliances Limited
20 Kennet Road
Crayford
Kent
DA1 4GN

MFI Furniture Group Limited
Southon House
333 The Hyde
Edgware Road
London
NW9 6TD

Milk Marketing Board/Dairy
Crest Limited
Dairy Crest House
Portsmouth Road
Surbiton
Surrey
KT6 5QL

Mobil Corporation
150 East 42nd Street
New York
NY 10017-5666
USA

Mobil Oil Company Limited
Mobil House
54/60 Victoria Street
London
SW1E 6QB

Nestlé S.A.
Avenue Nestle 55
CH-1800 Vevey
Switzerland

Nestlé Holdings (U.K.) PLC
St George's House
Croydon
Surrey
CR9 1NR

Next PLC
Desford Road
Enderby
Leicester
LE9 5AT

Nissan Motor Company Limited
6-17-1, Ginza 6-chome
Chuo-Ku
Tokyo-104-23
Japan

Nissan Motor
Manufacturing Co.
Washington Road
Sunderland
Tyne & Wear
SR5 3NS

Northern Foods plc
Beverley House
St Stephen's Square
Hull
East Yorkshire
HU1 3XG

*Matsushita Electric Industrial
Co. Limited*
1006 Kadama
Osaka
Japan

Panasonic UK Limited
Panasonic House
Willoughby Road
Bracknell
Berkshire
RG12 4FP

Paterson Zochonis plc
Bridgewater House
60 Whitworth St
Manchester
M1 6LU

Pepsico Incorporated
Anderson Hill Road
Purchase
New York
NY 10577
USA

Pepsico
Eurafme House
2 Woodgrange Avenue
Kenton
Middlesex
HA3 0XD

Peugeot S.A.
75 Avenue de la Grande Armée
75116 Paris
France

Peugeot Talbot Motor Co.
Limited
International House
PO Box 712
Bickenhill Lane
Marston Green
Birmingham
West Midlands
B37 7HZ

Philips' Electronics
Groenewoundseweg
5621 BA Eindhoven
The Netherlands

Philips U.K. Limited
Philips House
188 Tottenham Court Road
London
W1P 9LE

The Procter & Gamble Company
One Procter & Gamble Plaza
Cincinnati
Ohio
OH 45202
USA

Procter & Gamble Limited
PO Box 1EL
New Sandgate House
City Road
Newcastle upon Tyne
NE99 1EL

The Quaker Oats Company
321 North Clark Street
Chicago
Illinois
IL 60610
USA

Quaker Oats Limited
P O Box 24
Bridge Road
Southall
Middlesex
UB2 4AG

Ranks Hovis McDougall PLC
RHM Centre
P O Box 178
Alma Road
Windsor
Berkshire
SL4 3ST

Reckitt & Colman plc
One Burlington Lane
Chiswick
London
W4 2RW

Regie Nationale des
Usines Renault
34 Quai du Pont du Jour
92109 Boulogne-Billancourt
France

Renault UK Limited
Western Avenue
London
W3 0RZ

MacAndrews & Forbes
Holdings Inc.
36 East 63rd Street
New York
NY 10021
USA

Revlon Manufacturing
(UK) Limited
86 Brook Street
London
W1Y 2BA

Rothmans International p.l.c.
15 Hill Street
London
W1X 7FB

J Sainsbury plc
Stamford House
Stamford Street
London
SE1 9LL

Scottish & Newcastle
Breweries plc
Abbey Brewery
111 Holyrood Road
Edinburgh
EH8 8YS

Scott Paper Company
Scott Plaza
Philadelphia
Pennsylvania
PY 19113
USA

Scott Limited
Scott House
East Grinstead
West Sussex
RH19 1UR

Sears plc
40 Duke St
London
W1A 2HP

Sharp Corporation
22-22 Nagaike-cho
Abeno-ku
Osaka-545
Japan

Sharp Electronics (UK) Limited
Sharp House
Thorp Road
Manchester
M10 9BE

The Royal Dutch/Shell Group
Shell Centre
London
SE1 7NA

SmithKline Beecham plc
SB House
Great West Road
Brentford
Middlesex
TW8 9BD

Smith & Nephew plc
2 Temple Place
Victoria Embankment
London
WC2R 3BP

W H Smith Group PLC
Strand House
7 Holbein Place
London
SW1W 8NR

Sony Corporation
7-35 Kitashinagawa 6-chome
Shinagawa-ku
Tokyo-141
Japan

Sony (U.K.) Limited
Sony House
South Street
Staines
Middlesex
TW18 4PF

Storehouse PLC
The Heal's Building
196 Tottenham Court Road
London
W1P 9LD

Tambrands Incorporated
One Marcus Avenue
Lake Success
New York
NY 11042
USA

Tambrands Limited
Dunsbury Way
Havant
Hampshire
PO9 5DQ

Tate & Lyle PLC
Sugar Quay
Lower Thames Street
London
EC3R 6DQ

Tesco PLC
PO Box 18
Tesco House
Delamare Road
Cheshunt
Waltham Cross
Hertfordshire
EN8 9SL

Texaco Incorporated
2000 Westchester Avenue
White Plains
New York
NY 10650
USA

Texaco Limited
1 Knightsbridge Green
London
SW1X 7QJ

The Thomson Corporation
Toronto Dominion Bank Tower
PO Box 24
Toronto Dominion Centre
Toronto
Ontario
Ont. M5K 1A1
Canada

The Thomson Corporation PLC
1st Floor
The Quadrangle
180 Wardour Street
London
W1A 4YG

THORN EMI plc
4 Tenterden Street
Hanover Square
London
W1A 2AY

Time Warner Incorporated
1271 Avenue of the Americas
New York
NY 10020
USA

Time-Life International Limited
Time & Life Building
New Bond Street
London
W1Y 0AA

Toshiba Corporation
1-1-1 Shibaura
Minato-ku
Tokyo 105
Japan

Toshiba UK Limited
Europe Office
Audrey House
Ely Place
London
EC1N 6SN

Unigate PLC
Unigate House
Western Avenue
London
W3 0SH

Unilever
Unilever House
Blackfriars
London
EC4P 4BQ

United Biscuits (Holdings) plc
Grant House
PO Box 40
Syon Lane
Isleworth
Middlesex
TW7 5NN

General Motors Corporation
General Motors Building
3044 West Grand Boulevard
Detroit
Michigan
MI 48202
USA

Vauxhall Motors
PO Box 3
Luton
LU2 0SY

The Virgin Organisation
120 Campden Hill Road
London
W8 7AR

Volkswagen AG
D-3180 Wolfsburg 1
Germany

VAG (UK) Ltd
Yeomans Drive
Blakelands
Milton Keynes
MK14 5AN

(The Volkswagen-Audi Group in
the UK is a distributorship owned
by Lonhro plc.)

Volvo AB
S-405 08 Gotenborg
Sweden

Volvo Trucks
(Great Britain) Limited
Wedgenock Lane
Warwick
CV34 5YA

Weetabix Limited
Weetabix Mills
Burton Latimer
Kettering
Northamptonshire
NN15 5JR

Whitbread PLC
Brewery
Chiswell Street
London
EC1Y 4SD
SW1W 8NR

Williams Holdings PLC
Pentagon House
Sir Frank Whittle Road
Derby
DE2 4XA

Company Abbreviations

ABF	Associated British Foods plc
AGY	Argyll Group PLC
ALB	Alberto-Culver Co (UK) Limited
ALL	Allied-Lyons PLC
AMB	Gallaher Limited
AMS	Amstrad plc
ARG	Argos plc
ASD	Asda Group plc
AVN	Avon Cosmetics Limited
BAE	British Aerospace PLC
BAS	Bass PLC
BAW	British Airways Plc
BCI	Blue Circle Industries PLC
BOD	The Body Shop International PLC
BOK	Booker plc
BOO	The Boots Co PLC
BRG	British Gas plc
BRP	The British Petroleum Company p.l.c.
BSN	The Jacob's Bakery Limited
BUR	The Burton Group plc
BWG	Brent Walker Group PLC
CAA	C & A
CAD	Cadbury Schweppes p.l.c.
CAM	Campbell's UK Limited
CCR	City Centre Restaurants plc
CJC	C & J Clark Limited
COC	Coca-Cola Great Britain
COP	Colgate-Palmolive Limited
COT	Courtaulds Textiles plc
CPC	CPC (United Kingdom) Limited
CVI	Coats Viyella Plc
CWS	Co-operative Movement
DAL	Dalgety PLC
DIX	Dixons Group plc
DUP	Conoco (U.K.) Ltd
ELE	Electrolux Limited
EXX	Esso UK plc
FIA	Fiat U.K. Limited
FOR	Ford Motor Company Limited
FOS	Courage Limited
GEC	The General Electric Company p.l.c.
GEM	Vauxhall Motors
GIL	Gillette Industries Limited

GRA	Granada Group PLC
GRM	Grand Metropolitan PLC
GUI	Guinness PLC
GUS	Great Universal Stores P.L.C.
HAN	Hanson PLC
HEN	H. J. Heinz Company Limited
HIG	Highland Distilleries Company plc
HIL	Hillsdown Holdings plc
HIT	Hitachi Consumer Products (UK) Ltd
HOU	House of Fraser plc
ICE	Iceland Frozen Foods Holdings plc
ICI	Imperial Chemical Industries PLC (ICI)
ISO	Isosceles PLC
JLP	John Lewis Partnership plc
JSA	J Sainsbury plc
KEL	Kellogg Company of Great Britain Limited
KIN	Kingfisher plc
KMB	Kimberly-Clark Limited
KWK	Kwik Save Group P.L.C.
LAD	Ladbroke Group PLC
LEC	LEC Refrigeration plc
LIT	The Littlewoods Organisation PLC
LON	Lonrho Plc
LOR	L'Oréal (U.K.) Limited
MAR	Mars G.B. Limited
MAT	Panasonic UK Limited
MAY	Hoover PLC
MCD	McDonald's Restaurants Limited
MCF	Revlon Manufacturing (UK) Limited
MFI	MFI Furniture Group Limited
MKS	Marks & Spencer p.l.c.
MMB	Milk Marketing Board/Dairy Crest Limited
MOB	Mobil Oil Company Limited
MRL	Merloni Domestic Appliances Limited
NES	Nestlé Holdings (U.K.) PLC
NEX	Next PLC
NIS	Nissan Motor Manufacturing Co.
NOR	Northern Foods plc
NZD	Anchor Foods Limited
PAG	Procter & Gamble Limited
PEP	Pepsico
PEU	Peugeot Talbot Motor Co. Limited
PHI	Philips U.K. Limited
PHM	Kraft General Foods Limited
PZO	Paterson Zochonis plc
QOC	Quaker Oats Limited
REC	Reckitt & Colman plc

REN	Renault UK Limited
RHM	Ranks Hovis McDougall PLC
RTH	Rothmans International p.l.c.
SAL	Aspro Nicholas plc
SCJ	Johnson Wax Limited
SCN	Scottish & Newcastle Breweries plc
SCT	Scott Limited
SEA	Sears plc
SHL	The Shell Transport and Trading Company
SHP	Sharp Electronics (UK) Limited
SKB	SmithKline Beecham plc
SMN	Smith & Nephew plc
SON	Sony (U.K.) Limited
STH	Storehouse PLC
TAL	Tate & Lyle PLC
TAM	Tambrands Limited
TEM	THORN EMI plc
TES	Tesco PLC
TEX	Texaco Limited
THF	Forte PLC
TIW	Time-Life International Limited
TOC	The Thomson Corporation PLC
TOS	Toshiba UK Limited
TSA	Ferguson Limited
UGT	Unigate PLC
UNB	United Biscuits (Holdings) plc
UNL	Unilever PLC
VIR	The Virgin Organisation
VOL	Volvo Trucks (Great Britain) Limited
VWG	Volkswagen
WBR	Whitbread PLC
WGT	William Grant & Sons Limited
WHS	W H Smith Group PLC
WIH	Williams Holdings PLC
WTB	Weetabix Limited

Product Category Index

Cake Mixes	*see* Baking Aids, Cake Mixes and Flour
Cane Sugar	*see* Sugar and Sweeteners
Canned Fish	*see* Fish (Canned and Smoked)
Carpet Cleaners	*see* Household Cleaners
Carpet Fresheners	*see* Household Cleaners
Carpets	*see* Floor Coverings
Casserole Mixes	*see* Condiments, Pickles and Sauces
Cat Food	*see* Pet Products
CD Players	*see* Audio and Video Equipment
CDs	*see* Recorded Music
Cereal Bars	*see* Biscuits
Cereal	*see* Rice and Pasta
Cereals, Breakfast	*see* Breakfast Cereals
Champagne	*see* Wine
Cheese	*see* Dairy Products
Chicken	*see* Poultry
Chilli, Canned	*see* Prepared Food
Chocolate	*see* Confectionery
Chocolate, Drink	*see* Food Drinks
Chutney	*see* Condiments, Pickles and Sauces
Cider	*see* Beer
Cigarettes	*see* Tobacco
Cigars	*see* Tobacco
Cinema	*see* Entertainment
Cleaners and Cleaning Fluids	*see* Household Cleaners
Clothing Shops	*see* Clothing Retailers
Coats	*see* Clothing
Cocoa	*see* Food Drinks
Coffee Creamers	*see* Milk (Canned and Powdered)
Cola	*see* Soft Drinks and Mixers
Cologne	*see* Deodorants and Fragrances
Colouring, Hair	*see* Hair Care
Condensed Milk	*see* Milk (Canned and Powdered)
Conditioner, Hair	*see* Hair Care
Consommé	*see* Soups
Convenience Desserts	*see* Desserts
Cookers	*see* Cooking Appliances
Cookies	*see* Biscuits
Cooking Sauces	*see* Condiments, Pickles and Sauces
Cordial	*see* Soft Drinks and Mixers
Cornflour	*see* Baking Aids, Cake Mixes and Flour
Cosmetics and Skin Care Products	*see* Toiletries
Cosmetics	*see* Cosmetics and Skin Care
Cottage Cheese	*see* Dairy Products
Cough Remedies	*see* Proprietary Medicines Crackers
Crackers	*see* Biscuits
Cream, Hand and Body	*see* Cosmetics and Skin Care

Fromage Frais	*see* Dairy Products
Frozen Dinners	*see* Frozen Prepared Food
Frozen Fish	*see* Fish (Frozen)
Frozen Meals, Ready-Prepared	*see* Frozen Prepared Food
Fruit Spread	*see* Preserves and Spreads
Fruit, Canned	*see* Fruit and Vegetables (Canned)
Fruit Juice	*see* Soft Drinks and Mixers
Furnishings, Soft	*see* Soft Furnishings and Textiles
Furniture Polish	*see* Polishes
Furniture Shops	*see* Furniture Retailers
Gâteaux	*see* Cakes
Gel, Hair	*see* Hair Care
Gin	*see* Spirits
Gravy Browning	*see* Extracts, Gravy and Stock
Gravy Powder	*see* Extracts, Gravy and Stock
Hair Care Products	*see* Hair Care
Hair Remover	*see* Cosmetics and Skin Care
Hand Cream	*see* Cosmetics and Skin Care
Hand Mixers	*see* Small Electrical Appliances
Health Drinks	*see* Food Drinks
Health Food Shops	*see* Health Food retailers
Heaters, Electric	*see* Heating Appliances and Systems
Herbal Remedies	*see* Proprietary Medicines
Home Perm Kits	*see* Hair Care
Home Shopping	*see* Catalogues
Honey	*see* Preserves and Spreads
Icing Sugar	*see* Baking Aids, Cake Mixes and Flour
Instant Tea Mix	*see* Tea
Instant Potato	*see* Prepared Food
Jam	*see* Preserves and Spreads
Jellies	*see* Desserts
Juice	*see* Soft Drinks and Mixers
Jumpers	*see* Clothing
Ketchup	*see* Condiments, Pickles and Sauces
Kettles	*see* Small Electrical Appliances
Kitchen Roll	*see* Paper Products
Knives, Electric	*see* Small Electrical Appliances
Lager	*see* Beer
Lamb	*see* Meat
Lawn Mowers	*see* DIY and Gardening Products
Laxatives	*see* Proprietary Medicines
Lemonade	*see* Soft Drinks and Mixers
Lemon Juice	*see* Baking Aids, Cake Mixes and Flour
Lino	*see* Floor Coverings
Lip Care Products	*see* Cosmetics and Skin Care
Lotions, Hand and Body	*see* Cosmetics and Skin Care
Luncheon Meat	*see* Meat

Shaving Foam	*see* Shaving Products
Shaving Products	*see* Toiletries
Sherry	*see* Wine
Shirts	*see* Clothing
Shoe Shops	*see* Footwear Retailers
Shoe Polish	*see* Polishes
Shoes	*see* Footwear
Shortening	*see* Fats and Oils
Shower Gel	*see* Toiletries
Shower Fittings	*see* Bathroom Products
Skin Care Aids	*see* Cosmetics and Skin Care
Skirts	*see* Clothing
Sleeping Aids	*see* Proprietary Medicines
Slow Cookers	*see* Small Electrical Appliances
Soap Powder and Liquid	*see* Laundry Products
Soap	*see* Toiletries
Soda	*see* Soft Drinks and Mixers
Softeners, Fabric	*see* Laundry Products
Soup, Dehydrated	*see* Soups
Soup, Canned	*see* Soups
Soy Sauce	*see* Condiments, Pickles and Sauces
Spaghetti	*see* Rice and Pasta
Sparkling Wine	*see* Wine
Sports Wear	*see* Clothing
Spray, Hair	*see* Hair Care
Spreads, Sandwich	*see* Preserves and Spreads
Stain Removers	*see* Laundry Products
Starch	*see* Laundry Products
Stew, Canned	*see* Meat
Sticking Plaster	*see* Proprietary Medicines
Stock Cubes	*see* Extracts, Gravy and Stock
Stuffings	*see* Condiments, Pickles and Sauces
Suet	*see* Fats and Oils
Sun Tan Lotion and Oil	*see* Cosmetics and Skin Care
Sweets	*see* Confectionery
Syrup	*see* Sugar and Sweeteners
Take-aways	*see* Fast Food
Talcum Powder	*see* Toiletries
Tampons	*see* Feminine Hygiene
Tapes	*see* Recorded Music
Tape/Cassette Recorders	*see* Audio and Video Equipment
Tapioca	*see* Desserts
Tartar Sauce	*see* Condiments, Pickles and Sauces
Tea, Leaf	*see* Tea
Tea, Bags	*see* Tea
Televisions	*see* Audio and Video Equipment
Toasters	*see* Small Electrical Appliances

Survey

Now that you've had the chance to review *Shopping for a Better World*, we would like to know how you feel about it; whether you've used it, found it helpful, or have any ideas or suggestions for changes that would make future editions better.

Please take a moment to answer these questions, cut them out along the dotted line, and send them to New Consumer, 52, Elswick Road, Newcastle upon Tyne, NE4 6JH.

1. What companies, products or brands not listed in *Shopping for a Better World* would you like to see listed in future editions? (Please be specific)

....

....

....

2. Which would you prefer? (tick one)

❑ Brands listed within their product categories (they way they are in this book).

❑ All brands listed alphabetically in one long list.

3. Which three of the ten categories under which New Consumer analyses the companies do you think are the most important? (Please be specific)

....

....

4. What other social categories, if any, would you like to see companies rated on in the next edition of *Shopping for a Better World*?

....

....

5. Has *Shopping for a Better World* changed any of your shopping decisions?

❑ Yes

❑ No

(If yes, please give a specific example)

....

....

....

6. How do you use *Shopping for a Better World*?

☐ Take it for reference when I go shopping

☐ Check first at home before buying products

☐ Read it occasionally and remember my preferences

Other

....

....

7. How often do the ratings in *Shopping for a Better World* influence your shopping decisions?

☐ All the time

☐ Frequently

☐ Seldom

☐ Never

8. Have you written to a company, financial institution, newspaper or MP as a result of this guide?

☐ Yes

☐ No

If yes, can you give us some details?

....

....

....

....

9. What other comments would you like to make about *Shopping for a Better World*?

....

....

....

Become part of the new consumer movement today!

Since 1961 our standard of living in Britain has more than doubled in real terms. But as consumer spending has boomed so the number of companies which supply the goods we buy regularly has declined. We have seen high streets all over the country fill up with the same shopfronts. Smaller manufacturers and retailers have gone out of business or been taken over so that now over a third of what we spend goes to just 100 companies. This gives them immense commercial and social power.

Often the consumer is blamed for encouraging this trend, for being socially irresponsible. But *Shopping for a Better World* shows how the everyday shopper needn't be a 'problem' but can be part of the *solution*. The next step is to join our individual actions to create a movement with national impact.

Members receive a quarterly, fact-filled magazine and updates to this shopping guide. There's a free advisory service for ethical savings and investment and every member receives future copies of the next, updated, full edition of *Shopping for a Better World* at 30 per cent discount. There is also a special display pack containing 15 copies of *Shopping for a Better World* available. Join with the card in this book, or by filling in the form below.

....

Regular Membership £15 ...../Special Membership £55 .....*/Send me ..... copy(ies) of *Shopping for a Better World* @ £3.50 £......./Send me ..... display packs @ £50 (saving £24.85) £......./Please send me ..... copies of *The Global Consumer* @ £5.99   Total cost £..............

* Receives a free copy of *Changing Corporate Values* (value £48)

Name ....

Address ....

.... Postcode ....

Visa/Access No. .... Expiry ....

Card Holder's Name .... Signature ....
or enclose a cheque payable to New Consumer

Please return with payment to New Consumer, 52 Elswick Road, Newcastle upon Tyne NE4 6JH.